50 WISCONSIN CRiMeS OF THE CENTURY

D1602421

MARV BALOUSEK

Badger Books Inc.
P.O. Box 192
Oregon, WI 53575

© Copyright 1997, 1993, 1989 by Marv Balousek

Published by Badger Books Inc. of Oregon, Wis.

Edited by J. Allen Kirsch

ISBN 1-878569-47-3

Printed by BookCrafters of Chelsea, Michigan

All photos used by permission.

For Barbara and my colleagues, Richard Jaeger and George Hesselberg, who covered or suggeseted many of these cases.

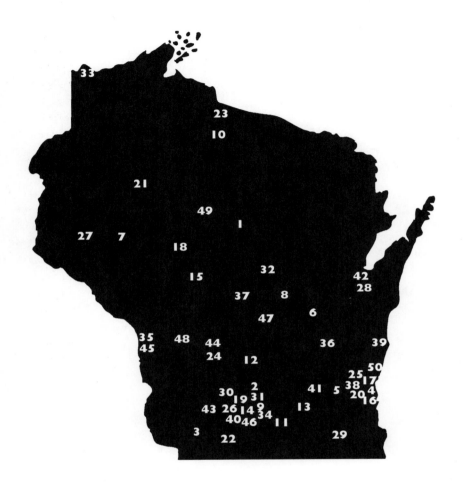

Crimes of the Century locations

Map numbers are placed at the location of the crime and refer to
the chapter number.

Contents

<u>Crimes of Politics</u>

Crimes of Greed

Crimes Involving Children

Multiple Murders

Introduction

During the last century, Wisconsin has become known for its bizarre crimes and criminals. New York City, Chicago and Los Angeles have far more murders but our state certainly is well-represented when it comes to notorious criminals. Edward Gein and Jeffrey Dahmer are in the same class with New York City's Son of Sam, Chicago's John Wayne Gacy and Los Angeles' Charles Manson.

It's a dubious honor, of course, but a study of crime serves more than a sensationalistic purpose. From these fifty cases, I believe we can learn a lot about the criminal motives and the efforts of Wisconsin legal system to reduce crime.

Throughout the century, the theories of Sigmund Freud and Charles Darwin were influential in much of our social policy. Freud's theories about the impact of childhood experiences on sexuality spawned theories that crime grew from childhood deprivation and trauma. Roger Lange, who brutally murdered young Paula McCormick in 1982, would substantiate this idea. We've recently seen many people claiming that forgotten memories of sexual assault as children ruined their adult lives.

Darwin's theories, when applied to criminology, seemed to indicate that crime was a genetic trait, inherited from criminal parents. This view of crime is illustrated by *The Bad Seed,* an excellent 1950s movie with an Oscar-winning performance by Patty McCormack as a young girl who becomes a serial killer.

The problem with both of these approaches to crime, however, is that it gives the criminal an excuse for his or her behavior. During the past two decades, personal responsibility has received more emphasis.

Inside the Criminal Mind, a 1984 book by Stanton E. Samenow, tosses aside both the Freudian and Darwinian approaches to crime and argues that the perpetrator bears sole responsibility. What else would explain why Jeffrey Dahmer's brother hasn't become a serial killer?

I have divided the fifty cases here into five sections that include "Crimes of Passion," "Crimes of Politics," "Crimes of Greed," "Crimes Involving Children" and "Multiple Murders." Thirty-nine of these cases were profiled in my two previous books, *Wisconsin Crimes of the Century* and *More Wisconsin Crimes of the Century.* All cases with recent developments have been fully updated for this volume. For example, Richard Nickl, one of three men convicted of killing a Lake Delton police officer was captured shortly after my first book profiling that case was released.

Selection of new cases for this book was difficult as usual. Many people suggested cases for inclusion and I tried to include crimes that outraged the community or had an impact on Wisconsin criminal law. Worthy cases inevitably have been left out.

The eleven new cases include some that I covered personally as a police and courts reporter at the *Wisconsin State Journal.* Most notable among these are the 1982 murder of Paula McCormick, the 1988 murder of Eleanor Townsend and Clyde "Bud" Chamberlain and the 1987 murders of Angela Hackl, Barbara Blackstone and Linda Nachreiner. Other new cases include several covered by my *Wisconsin State Journal* colleagues, Richard Jaeger and George Hesselberg. These are the Fort Atkinson murder of Ruben Borchardt, the Barbara Hoffman case, the murders of Cora Jones and Ronelle Eichstedt, the Onalaska murders by Bryan Stanley and the Jefferson County murders of Kelly Drew and Timothy Hack.

I also have included the 1917 bomb explosion in a Milwaukee police station that killed eleven people, the 1992 murder of Thomas Monfils in a paper pulp vat and an unusual 1990 Oshkosh sexual assault case involving a woman with multiple personality disorder.

Besides Jaeger and Hesselberg, I also want to thank Ronald Larson, the newsroom librarian at Madison Newspapers Inc., for giving permission to use photos from his files.

— *Marv Balousek*
September 1997

Crimes of Passion

1

Fatal Attraction for
a Dairy Princess

Wausau, 1989

Success seemed to come easily to Lori Esker. She was class president at Wittenberg-Birnamwood High School. Growing up in
rural Hatley, about twenty-five miles east of Wausau, she also served as
president of the high school chapter of Future Farmers of America. She
was a member of the National Honor Society and a runner on the girls'
track team. Pretty and smart, young Lori was as popular with administra-
tors and teachers as she was with fellow students. For three years, she held
a part-time job in the school office.

After high school, she enrolled at the University of Wisconsin-River
Falls. In June 1989, everything seemed to be going right for Lori. She
won the title of Marathon County Dairy Princess and was making plans
to marry Bill Buss, a tall, strong, dark-haired and handsome Wausau-
area farmer. Her college friends said she talked constantly about Bill and
often window-shopped for a wedding dress. Lori told her friends they
were engaged, although she never showed them a ring.

"I would say that she was bright, articulate, competent and a very
attractive girl," said Jean Flefson, her faculty advisor. Lori and Bill were
business partners, too, because Bill kept seventeen head of cattle Lori
owned at his farm. Lori no doubt viewed this arrangement as a prelude to
their marriage, when all of their possessions would be mingled.

The way Buss viewed his relationship with Lori, however, was far
different than her fantasies of marriage and family. And on June 23, when
he told her he wanted to end the relationship because he was getting back
together with his long-time girlfriend, Lisa Cibaski, it would unleash a

chain of events resulting in Lisa's violent death. Buss was unaware that Lori apparently had become obsessed with him in a fatal attraction.

Buss and Cibaski dated for about three years before she decided to cool the relationship, telling him she needed "some space." Buss began dating Esker but, by January 1989, he felt the romance with the dairy princess beginning to sour. He renewed his acquaintance with Cibaski and they talked on the phone more than a dozen times before that fateful June night, when he took Esker to a street dance and told her their relationship was over.

Lori was devastated. The end of her relationship with Buss set her emotions on a roller coaster. She hated him but she loved him. Her friend, Tammy Zack, tried to console her.

"She just didn't want to break up," Zack said. "Sometimes she cried."

Lori wasn't used to losing and she wasn't about to give up her man that easily. Twice she visited Buss after his midnight milking chores, stripping off her clothes and climbing into his bed dressed only in a skimpy nightgown. She called him frequently and once reached him at a friend's house.

"How could you do this to me?" she cried. He hung up on her. She called Alan Andrus, a friend of Bill's, and pleaded with him to intercede and help get them back together. "I could just kill her," she said of Lisa. "Just kill her."

That summer was miserable for the dairy princess. As the weeks went by, her obsession only deepened. Her friends noticed that the Lori they knew — the intelligent, well-rounded Lori with diverse interests — could focus only on her lost boyfriend and how to win him back. In September, someone told Lori that Lisa was pregnant and that rumor may have been what finally set her on a course to murder. The pregnancy, if true, could put Buss out of reach. Even worse, it would be concrete evidence of his relationship with Lisa.

Lori called Buss to confront him about Lisa's pregnancy. He denied it, telling her the rumor was false. During the conversation, he mentioned that Lisa would be working late on the night of September 20.

"I just want you to know that I have accepted the fact that Lisa and you are back together and I am going to leave you alone now," Lori told him. But it was a lie.

On September 20, Lori left this message on a friend's answering machine: "Hi. This is Lori. I am going to the library. Maybe I will talk to you later." Then, she got in her car and drove 150 miles from River Falls to Wausau. She later told detectives she came to Wausau "to get things straightened out."

Knowing that Cibaski was working late, Lori drove to the Howard Johnson's Motor Lodge in Rib Mountain, where Lisa held a job as assis-

Marathon County Dairy Princess Lori Esker

tant sales and catering manager. They got into Cibaski's car to talk. When Lori asked her about being pregnant, their conversation grew more heated.

"I thought she was going to kill me or really hurt me," Lori later told investigators. She reached into the back seat of Cibaski's car and grabbed a belt, wrapping it around her neck.

"I pushed on her," Lori later said. "I don't know if it was the belt or my elbow."

When Cibaski passed out, Lori began to panic. She grabbed Cibaski's purse and pulled out a mirror. She held it to the other woman's face to see if she was still breathing.

"Oh, my God!" Lori said to herself. "I killed her."

Lisa Cibaski's body was found the next morning by her mother, Shirley, who had become worried that her daughter was missing. The body was found in Lisa's parked car, where Lori had left her.

It didn't take investigators too long to figure out who might have wanted Lisa Cibaski dead and, eight days after the murder, Lori was arrested. She made her initial appearance in Marathon County Circuit Court October 2 on a charge of first-degree intentional homicide.

Although they were aware of Lori's obsession with Bill Buss, her friends at UW-River Falls were shocked that she would be accused of killing her romantic rival. It certainly was out of character for the bright, articulate dairy princess. Counselors worked with students to help them cope with the emotional stress of their classmate's crime.

Esker agreed to take a lie detector test and then, with the encouragement of Bill Buss, she confessed to the crime. It was a confession that her attorney, Stephen Glynn, later would claim was coerced.

On June 15, 1990, jurors deliberated for more than seven hours before finding Lori guilty of first degree murder. Members of the Cibaski family reacted with glee, hugging each other and shouting "Yes! Yes!" outside the courtroom.

"She always had to be number one and she got number one," said Vilas Cibaski, Lisa's father.

But Bill Buss wasn't joyful about the verdict.

"My life will never return to normal because Lisa will never be back," he said.

At her sentencing hearing, Lori pleaded for leniency, saying she was "so sorry" for all the pain and suffering she caused.

"If I could trade places with Lisa, I would in a minute," she said, asking for a "chance to start paying back all the people I hurt so bad.

"I will be punishing myself for as long as I live. There isn't a day that goes by that I don't think about what happened."

It was ironic that Lori also had wanted to trade places with Lisa a year earlier and, in fact, that's what drove her to kill.

Judge Michael Hoover sentenced Lori Esker to life in prison but, due to her clear criminal record, he made her eligible for parole in thirteen instead of twenty years.

"It's as much a tragedy that has befallen the defendant's family as the Cibaski family," the judge said. "No one expects the Cibaski family to understand that, at least not today. I know this sentence leaves them wholly unsatisfied and perhaps that much farther away from healing."

In September 1995, a TV movie based on the case and titled "Beauty's Revenge" was shown by NBC.

Lori Esker killed for love. But that motive and the judge's sympathy were little comfort to the Cibaskis, who lost their daughter to a jealous killer.

"Lori Esker took something very precious from me," Shirley Cibaski testified at Lori's sentencing hearing. "She took something and destroyed it and it can never be replaced."

While the deep wound to the Cibaski family left by Lisa's death may never fully heal, Bill Buss at least has been able to move on with his life. In 1993, he announced his engagement to Linda Gritzmacher, a Wausau legal secretary with a five-year-old son. Buss continued to operate his 440-acre farm and tended fifty-four head of cattle.

"It's not totally behind me," he said. Perhaps it never will be.

2

Arsenic in his Drink
Waunakee, 1938

Farming during the Depression was a tough and lonely business. As it is today, a farmer's wife often worked alongside her husband, sharing his hard labor and the loneliness of a rural lifestyle. Some women thrived on it; others did not.

Florence Peters farmed with her husband, John, near Waunakee during the summer of 1938. The thirty-eight-year-old Mrs. Peters was a slim, plain-looking woman. When Edward Harvey, who used the alias of Elmer Johnson, came to work on the Peters' farm, it wasn't long before the thin and bony twenty-three-year-old young man attracted the older woman's eye. They soon became involved with each other.

She was experienced with men but it apparently was his first affair. Her husband was oblivious to the stolen kisses behind the barn or how their hands softly caressed as she drew water from the well and he brushed past her, going about his chores.

One day in mid-July, Florence told Edward she could stand it no longer. They must get rid of her husband. She sent Harvey to the garage for a package of arsenic, which was used for rodent control. Harvey didn't argue with her or protest but went wordlessly outside for the poison. For her, it was a chance to be free of a man she no longer loved. For him, it was an opportunity to have the woman he loved all to himself.

While Peters was busy milking in the barn, his wife took the arsenic and mixed it into a drink for him. After imbibing the lethal mixture, Peters got sick and soon was confined to bed. His wife pretended to nurse him back to health and, a few days later, he asked her for something to

Wisconsin State Journal archives

John Peters   **Florence Peters**

make him feel better. She mixed another dose of arsenic into milk and gave it to him with some medicine.

But Peters got sicker and authorities became suspicious of the relationship between Harvey and Mrs. Peters. The lovers had not been as discreet as they imagined. The young farm hand was brought in for questioning but he was uncooperative. He was charged with resisting a Waunakee police officer, then released on a promise to leave the state.

Peters finally became so ill that he was admitted to a Madison hospital. Mrs. Peters and her children moved to a Rutledge Street apartment in Madison to be closer to her sick husband. But she and her lover could not stand to be apart and Harvey secretly moved in with her. On September 28, police raided the apartment, arresting Mrs. Peters and Harvey on charges of lewd and lascivious conduct because they were found living together. In his defense, Harvey told police he was engaged to Mrs. Peters and they would marry as soon as she divorced her husband.

Peters' illness, which still remained a mystery, revived rumors about the suspicious death eight years earlier of Henry Kessenich. In 1930, Kessenich and his wife lived on another rural Waunakee farm with their two young children.

After Peters was hospitalized, relatives asked the district attorney to investigate Kessenich's death. The body was exhumed and toxicology tests showed high levels of arsenic in hair roots and tissues. Dr. F.L. Kozelka, state toxicologist, found that the poison couldn't have come from the embalming fluid or ground contamination. Kessenich had been poisoned deliberately.

Kessenich's wife wanted a divorce but he had refused. She said she wanted to be free. Like Mrs. Peters, she said she had fallen in love with a young farm hand.

As the harvest season neared that August of 1930, she had gotten some arsenate of lead from the barn and put less than a quarter teaspoonful in Kessenich's tea. Within two days, he became ill and started vomiting. He died shortly afterward. Doctors determined that the cause of death was pneumonia and wanted to do an autopsy but respected the wishes of the widow, who opposed it. Rumors circulated around Waunakee that the death may have been unnatural but no one investigated and Mrs. Kessenich collected $1,000 in life insurance.

Three years after her husband's death, she married John, then a

Wisconsin State Journal archives

Edward Harvey

farm hand himself, and the widow, Florence Kessenich, became Florence Peters. She moved in with him at his town of Westport farm. They had two children together besides the two children from her previous marriage.

During the exhumation and autopsy on Kessenich's body, Mrs. Peters was held in jail on the lewd and lascivious charge. She laughed when she heard police suspected her of killing her first husband.

"Whoever would think I did that?" she asked incredulously. But after intense questioning and learning of the laboratory findings, she tearfully confessed to the murder. When investigators told her a green and white bag of arsenate of lead was

found at the Peters farm, she also admitted poisoning her second husband.

Lloyd Paust, an assistant district attorney who prosecuted the case, later served as Columbus city attorney. He recalls questioning Mrs. Peters, but said the confessions came in a different order.

"As I recall, she was in the hallway at the D.A.'s office. She admitted then that she had fed her existing husband arsenic. That led me to wonder if she didn't kill her first husband that way."

Paust said he suggested exhuming Kessenich's body, although at the time he said he didn't have any idea how to exhume anyone. He also recalls that the slim and meek Mrs. Peters certainly didn't fit the stereotype of a killer.

"Criminals don't necessarily took like criminals. From that experience, I learned that criminals don't look any different than anyone else."

Wearing a light-gray coat, Mrs. Peters buried her face in her hands as she sat before the judge. She pleaded guilty to both crimes in a low, tense voice, barely audible more than a few feet from the bench. She was called to the stand and walked haltingly up to the witness chair. As she sat down, the proceedings apparently overwhelmed the simple farm wife and she fainted. Policewoman Pearl Guynes tried to help her down the steps from the chair but Mrs. Peters lost her balance and fell. Paust carried her from the courtroom. Later, she sent a message from her cell asking Judge Roy H. Proctor to "get through with it."

He scheduled a sentencing hearing the following day, interrupting another case.

"Have you anything to say before the court imposes sentence?" Proctor asked. Mrs. Peters whispered to Guynes.

"Only what she told me this morning," Guynes said, referring to Mrs. Peters' request for a swift sentencing.

"As the district attorney has stated, it is mandatory upon this court to sentence you to imprisonment," Proctor began, his words echoing in the nearly empty courtroom. "Do you hear, Mrs. Peters, that the assistant district attorney has moved to amend the complaint that the charge occurred in 1930? Is your plea guilty?"

Paust had amended the original complaint, which incorrectly listed Kessenich's death in 1929 when he actually died a year later. Mrs. Peters whispered "yes" to Proctor, then rested her head on her arms folded in front of her.

"Do you want to listen?" Guynes asked her sympathetically. "We're just about through." Guynes then turned to the judge. "She'll try to finish, your honor."

Proctor continued. "No good purpose would be served to recount the incidents leading to the discovery of the crime. I am satisfied that you were fully aware of what you were doing. You have committed the most serious of all crimes and it is the duty of this court to impose the penalty set in the statute."

The judge paused.

"In view of your plea to the amended complaint and information, it is the duty of this court — " At that point Mrs. Peters moaned, "Oh!" She straightened up in her chair and collapsed, failing to hear the rest of the sentence.

" — for the rest of your natural life," Proctor said. He also imposed a sentence on Edward Harvey of one to ten years for the poisoning of Peters to run concurrently with the life sentence. The lewd and lascivious charge was dropped. Proctor rapped his gavel and ended the hearing.

Mrs. Peters was taken back to her cell, where she picked up a picture of her ten-month-old boy and sobbed. "I wish I could see my baby again!"

Her husband had moved into the Rutledge Street apartment after his release from the hospital. He agreed to provide a home for the children from his wife's first marriage as well as his own. But later, after he divorced his wife, the older children moved in with Kessenich relatives near Waunakee.

During her fainting spell, Mrs. Peters had failed to hear part of the sentencing and when she arrived at Taycheedah state prison, she was under the mistaken impression that Proctor had given her only one to ten years. And the three police officers who accompanied her to prison didn't have the heart to tell her otherwise, that she would be separated from her four children for the rest of her life.

Meanwhile, Harvey brooded alone in his jail cell, waiting to go to trial for his role in the poisoning. No good-byes passed between the lovers and Harvey was upset by the news that Mrs. Peters had received a life sentence. While Harvey apparently moped over his lost love, Mrs. Peters didn't feel the same. Her cellmate told reporters prophetically: "She's through with him for life." After a few days, Harvey finally asked to be taken before Elliot N. Walstead, the assistant district attorney, to confess his part in the attempted murder.

In court, the gaunt Harvey wore his shirt open as he described how Mrs. Peters suggested it would be a good time to get her husband out of the way. He told about how he went to get a sack of poison. Even the prosecutor, Walstead, was moved by the young man's innocence and he asked the judge for leniency.

"It is possible that this young fellow was more sinned against than sinned. I certainly feel that the woman was the moving force in the act."

Walstead said Harvey either lacked imagination or was unfamiliar with the consequences of his act. Perhaps he was too much in love.

"I noticed that he showed a peculiar disregard for human life. There was no discussion on that day in July — he simply went out to the garage for the poison."

But Proctor disregarded Walstead's plea, saying that if Peters had died, Harvey could have been charged with murder.

"The court feels that it would be derelict in its duty in imposing a nominal sentence," the judge said. He gave Harvey one of the same sentences as his lover, one to 10 years in the Green Bay Reformatory. Unlike Mrs. Peters, Johnston showed no emotion during the sentencing.

Mrs. Peters eventually learned of her longer sentence. Her pleas for executive clemency were denied in 1942 and 1943. A prison psychiatrist described the woman who had fainted twice in court and evoked the sympathy of police officers as "a tigress whose confinement for the remaining period of her natural life should be effected" and "absolutely no argument whatever could be advanced in any way favorable to her cause."

She was paroled in 1951. Waunakee residents familiar with the case say she remarried and moved out of the area. Prison records show she was discharged from parole on Sept. 15, 1969, more that 40 years after the first poisoning.

As in many cases of this kind, the poisonings by Florence Peters remained a family secret from many of her descendants until the *Wisconsin State Journal's* Crimes of the Century series was published in August, 1985.

3

A Carefree Bird is Caged
Platteville, 1927

Earlier in the day, William Coffey and his new wife, Hattie, had toured Galena, Illinois. Then the honeymoon couple had driven to Dubuque, where they bought box lunches, crossed the bridge into Wisconsin and stopped to eat along the roadside.

Coffey remembered that a friend lived in Shullsburg and the newly-weds debated whether to visit him. Finally, they decided to camp right there in Bratton's Woods about five miles south of Platteville. In the evening, they sat by the campfire singing a few hymns — a fitting end to a perfect day. After a spirited rendition of "Goodbye Sweet Day," they went to sleep about nine p.m. Coffey later would describe their mood as "like two carefree birds."

As the cool of the fall night moved in, Hattie slept soundly next to her new husband. While she slept, Coffey knelt next to her and smashed her head with a baseball bat. Then he grabbed a hammer and beat her repeatedly until she was dead. He used a knife to cut her body in fifteen pieces and buried them in several scattered shallow graves.

In the morning, on October 10, 1927, Coffey went to the Joe Tansy home for water, then returned to the campsite. The next day, a Monday, he called a local garage and asked an employee to send someone out with a new battery for his car. When Raymond Spink arrived with the battery, Coffey told him it was his hobby to camp alone.

The killer was born in the Blue Ridge foothills of North Carolina to a poor farm family. The Coffeys later moved to Topeka, Kan., and, while young William still was in grade school, his father was stricken with an illness that later would force his commitment to an institution and ultimately cause his death. Coffey's mother wanted him to become a minister so he enrolled in a theological seminary. While in the seminary, he did odd jobs for an elderly widow in exchange for room and board. The widow had survived three husbands and Coffey thought she viewed him as a son until one day he claimed she came to his room with a leather wallet crammed with bills and gold pieces.

"I'm going to give you some of this money to help you out," she told him. "You know, I love you very much."

Coffey said she pressed sixty dollars into his hand, put her arms around him and kissed him.

"I do love you very dearly indeed," she said. "And one of these days, I'm going to marry you."

Coffey was shocked at the widow's feelings for him but, when he was broke again at the beginning of the next semester, he went to her for money. This time, she dropped a wad of bills — $540 in all — into his lap. He lived with her for a month without having to work until finally the day of reckoning came and the widow asked Coffey to marry her. When he refused, she accused him of stealing the money. He was charged with grand larceny and sentenced to three years in prison. Coffey's version of these events made an unlikely story but he said his conviction and prison term embittered him and he vowed to take revenge for how the widow had framed him.

"When I came out of the big house, my hopes blasted, my future ruined, it was with the determination that I would collect from the world — from the world especially of women — all and more than this woman had taken from me.

When he was released from prison on good behavior in February, 1902, Coffey had a tough time landing a job until he was hired by the Howard Association, a charitable organization based in Chicago. He began skimming money off the top of contributions to the association, collecting as much as $20,000, for example, and turning in $4,500. And, as he wrote later in a copyrighted story in the *Wisconsin State Journal*, women became his prey:

"There was a matronly little woman in a small town in Iowa. She gave me her life savings to invest for her and never uttered a peep when I told her later that the investment had been unfortunate. There was a waitress in Nebraska. She didn't have much money, but what she had she gave to me. I never saw her again.

"I remember one old banker's wife who simpered like a school girl of sixteen when I told her how maturely beautiful she was. And, with one arm around my neck, her free hand was busy signing a check that represented a full year's income of her husband's money. For the association, of course! But, then — Women! Women! Women! There are

Wisconsin State Journal archives

William Coffey   **Hattie Sherman Hales**

scores of them who will remember me now. They believed anything, everything. It was a huge joke and a very pitiful commentary on fife. Starved, most of these women were, for the romance of living. Crazy about men, crazy to be admired, petted, flattered, sympathized with. And every one of them sure that she was beautiful, attractive, irresistible."

Coffey married a Kansas woman and they had three children, two girls and a boy. But the marriage didn't put a damper on his philandering ways. He took a job with an advertising agency but lost it when his new employer found out about his criminal record. Leaving his family behind, he roamed from town to town in search of work and generous women, finally scraping together enough money to open a collection agency with a partner. A real estate deal fell through, driving the agency out of business. Coffey moved his family to Madison and went back to work for the Howard Association.

It was on a trip for the association that he met the widow Hattie Sherman Hales in La Crosse at a church picnic. He found out she lived in Winona, Minnesota and, more important, that she had money. They began a whirlwind affair. Still married to his first wife in Madison, Coffey married Hattie in September 1927, and they plunged blissfully into their fateful honeymoon, traveling first to Rockford, Illinois to visit Hattie's aging mother and her sister, Anna Holdridge. Anna didn't like her sister's new husband from the start. There was something too slick and insincere about him. The family's police dog didn't take kindly to him either, growling and baring its teeth when Coffey was around. He tried in vain to impress his new in-laws with boasts about his job as a bond salesman and his wealth. A few days later, the honeymoon couple left Rockford, passing through Dubuque and camping at Bratton's Woods.

After the murder, Coffey carried on the honeymoon by himself so he wouldn't arouse suspicion among Hattie's relatives. She had written letters from Dubuque, discussing the route the newlyweds would take through Illinois.

Coffey forged letters to his in-laws after her death, signing them with her initials and later with a rubber stamp that had a facsimile of her signature. A bundle of clothing was sent to Hattie's sister without explanation. Later, a letter supposedly from Hattie mentioned the clothing and talked about the growing attentions of a new acquaintance, a Mr. St. Claire. More letters also mentioned St. Claire and the tone indicated she was falling in love with him. From North Carolina, a letter signed by Hattie said she had left Coffey for St. Claire and had given Coffey fifty shares of her stock in the Elroy Service Oil Co. as compensation for his broken heart.

It was an ingenious scheme but not clever enough to fool Hattie's shrewd sister. She didn't buy Coffey's ruse and began her own quiet investigation. Anna realized she hadn't talked directly to Hattie in two months. Meanwhile, Coffey spent Christmas with his family in Madison. He gave expensive clothing and jewels to his first wife, Alberta, and their two daughters. The gifts were the leftover property of Hattie Sherman Hales.

To transfer Hattie's oil company stock to his name, Coffey had to attend a January meeting in Elroy of the stockholders. His cool demeanor offered no hint of the murder and swindle when he arrived at the meeting. In a low, cultured voice and adopting a casual tone, Coffey asked that the routine stock transfer be confirmed as he presented a letter signed with Hattie's rubber-stamp signature. But Anna anticipated that Coffey might show up at the meeting and alerted her brother-in-law, Ernest Rosier of Elroy, to watch for him. Rosier arranged for Coffey's arrest on a forgery charge.

At first, Coffey said he didn't know where Hattie was, sticking to his story that she had run off with St. Claire. But detectives found women's clothing at Coffey's Madison home that Anna identified as belonging to her sister. Coffey was held on $5,000 bail, pending further investigation of Hattie's disappearance.

For three days, Coffey sat in the Juneau County Jail, pacing his cell and protesting his innocence during long interviews with investigators. Then he came up with a new story. He admitted he'd killed his second wife but claimed it had been an accident. While camping at Bratton's Woods, he said, she woke him up and accused him of being unfaithful.

She had tried to hit him with a baseball bat and Coffey fought to fend off the attack. While trying to throw the bat out of the tent, he accidentally hit her on the head. When he saw Hattie was dead, Coffey said he panicked and threw her body off the Mississippi River bridge at Dubuque.

Police suspected the story was a lie but couldn't get the truth out of him. In those days before the rights of criminal defendants were protected and before reporters exhibited ethical standards about respecting them, a group of Madison reporters conspired to find out what really happened to Hattie. The *State Journal* described the scheme:

"Finally, by what is rather vulgarly known as a frame, the real story came out. Coffey wanted a lawyer. The reporters offered to get him one. They did — one of their own number who had just arrived and had never seen the slayer."

Coffey then told the whole story — that is, most of it — how he dismembered the body, etc., after killing Mrs. Hales at the camping place by the river.

The reporter posing as Coffey's lawyer shared the story with his accomplices and the true story of the murder hit the Madison newspapers. A spade and pickax were found by Madison police at Coffey's Blount Street home and were taken into evidence. But murder charges against Coffey were a problem because it wasn't clear whether Hattie was killed in Wisconsin, or Illinois, especially if her body was thrown off the Mississippi River bridge as Coffey had claimed. The Dubuque County district attorney and sheriff interviewed Coffey at Mauston but couldn't develop enough evidence to seek his return to Iowa. G. F. Hayne, superintendent of the Eagle Point auto park at Dubuque, positively identified a picture of Coffey as the man who camped with a woman at the Iowa park on October 11-13. But Coffey denied he'd ever been to the Eagle Point Park, insisting that the crime occurred in Wisconsin, a state without capital punishment. If he were found guilty in Iowa, after all, he would be executed.

"I have confessed to a terrible deed in Wisconsin," Coffey said in a statement to the Iowa authorities. "And now I wish to remain silent until Wisconsin is through with me. You may go ahead and ask all the questions you want to when Wisconsin is through with me. Whatever Wisconsin has against me, I am willing to pay the price."

Coffey said he bought the baseball bat in July at La Crosse just to have fun with it. He said Hattie kept it by her side for protection when they slept outside. He agreed to go to Grant County to point out the place where he and Hattie camped. The day after Coffey was tricked by the reporters into confessing, he led detectives to the woods south of Platteville.

But a heavy snowstorm forced Coffey and his guards to spend the night in Mineral Point, arriving in Platteville on a Friday to begin the search. At the same time he was leaving Mauston, a divorce suit was filed in Madison on behalf of his first wife, to whom he had been married for twenty years. Later, Coffey's daughters refused his request to see them and Alberta said the family was through with him.

"He has been wiped out of our lives," she said.

More than seven hundred cars lined the highway near Bratton's Woods, where three thousand people had gathered to watch Coffey lead investigators on their grisly treasure hunt. He was shackled and heavily guarded, more to protect against mob violence than to prevent escape. Coffey pointed out the campsite and several mounds were found nearby, but the hard frozen ground made digging difficult.

Frank Olson, a farmer, shouted to the detectives that he'd found a mound under the snow where he was standing, about fifty feet from where Coffey said he'd pitched the tent. Diggers cleared away the snow, then used a pick to break through the frozen earth. A few feet below the surface, they struck a gunny sack. Inside was the rotting torso of a woman. Other body parts were found buried under similar mounds but the dead woman's head couldn't be found.

Coffey continued to insist he'd thrown it from the river bridge. By nightfall, the diggers were tired and cold but they continued their search, hoping to unearth the head that would positively identify the dead woman as Hattie. From the last hole they dug, the diggers carefully lifted a bundle wrapped in a partly burned newspaper. Inside was Hattie's head, her face crushed and the skull fractured with a hole in it made by a sharp instrument.

The teeth matched Hattie's dental records and her courageous sister, the single person most responsible for Coffey's undoing, came to Platteville to make a positive identification. Police also found the butcher knife Coffey used to cut up the body.

The gruesome nature of the crime and Coffey's cold-blooded execution of it led investigators to believe it probably wasn't his first murder. They grilled him for hours that night about the triple murder five years earlier of a rural Sauk City family. Like Hattie, Mary Balzer and her two brothers, Julius and William, had been clubbed over the head by a brutal killer who then ransacked their farm home. The Balzers were deeply religious and had modest investments in the stock and bond markets. Coffey, a bond salesman, preyed upon religious people like the Balzers. He had been near Sauk City at the time of the Balzer murders and said he'd read details of the case in the newspapers but would not admit to the crime.

Nationwide publicity about Hattie's murder led to a flurry of letters from abandoned women who identified Coffey as their missing husband. The letters came from as far away as Texas and New Jersey, where he was mentioned as a possible suspect in another murder. Coffey denied any connection with these women and said he'd never been to New Jersey. Juneau County Sheriff Lyall Wright received a telegram from Plymouth, Indiana, asking him to question Coffey about the disappearance there of a woman the previous October. Coffey also denied involvement in that case and retraced his route on a map to show he couldn't have been near Plymouth when the woman vanished.

But Coffey could no longer deny the murder of Hattie. Faced with incontrovertible evidence of his wife's dismembered body, Coffey finally gave a full confession:

"I killed her in Bratton's Woods. I did it because I was afraid news of the (bigamous) marriage would leak out. She was there beside me asleep. I struck her with the baseball bat. I think that killed her but then I lost my head, seized a hammer and struck her again and again. She was dead. Then I did the rest and buried it there in the woods. The hammer is in my car in Madison. You have the knife. It was deliberate."

Despite the confession, Coffey still wasn't finished trying to lie and manipulate his way out of a murder conviction. He tried to make a case for insanity, revealing that his father had died in an insane asylum and suggesting maybe he'd inherited the mental illness from his father. Coffey said he'd fallen from a horse at age eighteen, suffering a head injury and he said the fall probably affected his mental condition. Two alienists, predecessors to today's forensic psychiatrists, interviewed him for about three hours. Coffey told them a theory he had about good and bad spots on the brain and that the good spots fought to subjugate the bad ones. But the alienists weren't impressed. They found that his conversation showed no trace of a mental disorder and that he was sane when he viciously beat his wife to death.

Coffey pleaded guilty to Hattie's murder and was sentenced to life imprisonment at Waupun state prison. As he awaited the trip to prison, he comforted himself in his jail cell at Lancaster with a Bible that had been purchased for him. He pledged that his work at trying to rehabilitate prison inmates wouldn't stop just because he was one of them. He also vowed to continue working on his book, which he called *Hardscrabble*, a history of North Carolina mountain people featuring Coffey's father as the central character.

But Coffey, the Madison bond salesman, budding author, traveling minister and social worker who found it easy to swindle vulnerable women by playing to their vanity, never finished his book. He spent the rest of his life without the company of women, dying at Waupun in 1962.

4

Bambi's Flight to Freedom
Milwaukee, 1981

As Sean Schultz awoke, he felt something tighten around his neck, perhaps some kind of rope or wire. He opened his eyes just in time to see a large gloved hand slam down across his nose and mouth. Young Sean screamed, awakening his younger brother, and both boys began to struggle with the assailant. Shannon would say later that the assailant had a reddish ponytail and wore a fatigue jacket.

Suddenly, the figure bounded from the room and across the hall to their mother's bedroom. The boys were still shaking as they heard their mother's voice: "Please don't do that!" They heard a noise that sounded like a firecracker and the boys ran to the other bedroom. They caught a glimpse of the dark figure hunched over their mother's bed before the assailant fled from the room and down the stairs.

Christine Schultz, the boys' mother, had been fatally shot in the back. A scarf also was wrapped around her neck. Her death about 2:00 a.m. on May 28, 1981, touched off one of Wisconsin's most fascinating murder mysteries: the case of Lawrencia "Bambi" Bembenek.

Elfred Schultz, Christine's ex-husband, was on duty as a Milwaukee police officer at the time his wife was shot. When he received word of the shooting, Schultz rushed home to comfort his two terrified sons, then joined in the investigation. His colleagues quickly ruled him out as a suspect. After all, he was on duty when the mysterious assailant broke into his ex-wife's home.

Based on the description given by Sean and Shannon, police began a manhunt for an assailant with a red ponytail who wore a green Army fatigue jacket. A neighbor told detectives someone had broken into his garage on the night of the murder and stolen a green jogging suit and a .38-caliber revolver.

At the time of the murder, Lawrencia Bembenek, the current wife of Elfred Schultz, said she was home alone, sleeping. She was awakened shortly before 3:00 a.m. by a call from her husband, who said he had just found out that Christine was murdered. About 4:00 a.m., two detectives rang her doorbell. They asked if she owned a gun or a green jogging suit. She said no and they left.

An hour later, Elfred arrived with his partner, Michael Durfee. Durfee checked Schultz' off-duty revolver and found that it hadn't been fired. Later, a spot of blood was found on Schultz's regular service revolver. He took a polygraph test and passed, but Bembenek refused to take the test. Her husband told investigators he had seen her playing with the bullets in his service revolver a few days before the murder.

Within three weeks, the focus of the case shifted to Lawrencia Bembenek. A woman named Judy Zess, a former roommate of Bembenek's, came forward and told investigators she had heard Bembenek threaten to kill Christine Schultz. Bembenek was angry, according to Zess, that the murder victim demanded so much alimony from Elfred Schultz. Bembenek also was jealous of her husband's first wife, police were told, and wondered whether Elfred still spent time with her.

The case seemed circumstantial until a reddish brown wig was discovered in the plumbing of the building where Bembenek and Elfred Schultz shared an apartment. On June 24, Lawrencia Bembenek was arrested for the murder of Christine Schultz. Her attractiveness made that case an instant worldwide sensation. She had worked as a model and as a waitress at the Playboy Club in Lake Geneva, Wisconsin. She also was a former Milwaukee police officer.

Investigators decided Bembenek probably put on a green jogging suit and grabbed her husband's off-duty revolver. Then, she jogged to Christine Schultz's home about two miles away. After trying to strangle Sean and killing his mother, she jogged back home.

The case was solved, or so it appeared. Bembenek spent three days in a holding cell. She was represented at her initial appearance by Richard Reilly, her husband's divorce attorney. But she soon hired Donald Eisenberg, a flashy Madison attorney who enjoyed notoriety and high-profile cases. He promised Bembenek the case would be dismissed at the preliminary hearing. He requested a $25,000 retainer to take the case.

But the charges against Bembenek would not go away that easily. Two startling bits of testimony ensured that she would stand trial for murder. Judy Zess, her neighbor across the hall, told the court that Bembenek once told her she would pay to have Christine Schultz "blown

Madison Capital Times file photo

Lawrencia "Bambi" Bembenek in a 1983 photo.

away." And Bembenek's husband was granted immunity from prosecution in exchange for his testimony against her.

At the time of her arrest, Bembenek was working as a Marquette University security guard. Before that, however, she had worked for the Milwaukee police department. At the time, the chief was Harold Brier, who didn't have a reputation as a progressive law enforcement leader. In fact, Brier's department came under fire from the African American community when Ernest Lacy, an African American, died while in police custody on July 9, 1981. Police had taken him into custody for a rape it later was determined he didn't commit.

Under Brier, the department was equally insensitive about women officers as it was about African American suspects. During one week in August 1980, Brier fired three women officers. Among them was Lawrencia Bembenek. When Bembenek finally was allowed to read her file, she discovered the reason for her dismissal was that Judy Zess had signed a statement accusing her of smoking marijuana at a concert.

Out of work, Bembenek landed a job as a waitress at the Lake Geneva Playboy Club. Despite the testimony of Zess that cost her her police job, the two women remained friends. She discovered other Milwaukee police officers weren't so pristine when she saw nude photos taken of officers at a picnic sponsored by a local tavern. One of the officers posing naked was Fred Schultz.

Bembenek continued to fight to get her police job back, even showing some of the nude photos to one of her old friends on the force. She also began dating Schultz after he broke off a relationship with one of her friends, Marjorie Lipschultz.

Later, as she sat in jail charged with murder, she may have wondered whether the charges against her were in retaliation for her battle against the department. Although the testimony of Elfred Schultz wasn't as devastating as the testimony of Judy Zess, she felt betrayed. Fred cried at the preliminary hearing, appearing distraught over his ex-wife's murder. Zess testified that Bembenek once told her she would pay to have Christine Schultz "blown away." The testimony was enough to bind Bembenek over for trial, despite the assertion by Sean Schultz that his mother's assailant that night was a man in an Army fatigue jacket, not a woman in a jogging suit.

After the hearing, she was free on bond and tried to patch things up with Fred but too much damage obviously had been done to the relationship. The way Bembenek later told it, the tension between them erupted into a shoving match and Fred kicked her, knocking her to the ground. The police were called and Bembenek went home with her father. The story about Milwaukee's most glamorous murder suspect made the papers the next day.

Bembenek's trial began February 23, 1982. Her attorney, Donald Eisenberg, moved to dismiss the case for lack of evidence — a routine motion that is routinely denied.

In his opening arguments, prosecutor Robert Kramer described how Bembenek had jogged to the Schultz house that night, started to strangle Sean and then went to Christine's bedroom and shot her. Defense attorney Eisenberg said his case would hinge on the testimony of Sean Schultz, whose description of the killer did not match Lawrencia Bembenek. He also asked why it took police twenty-one days to arrest his client.

During his testimony, young Sean again insisted that his mother's murderer was a man. But Judy Zess again told of Bembenek's comment of having Christine Schultz killed. This time, she even provided more detail, saying that Bembenek actually asked her once about having a murder contract taken out on Schultz.

Day after day, the media circus trial dragged on. Fred Schultz testified that he accused his wife of playing with his bullet pouch but added he didn't think she had access to his off-duty revolver. Eisenberg scored a point against Schultz's partner, Michael Durfee, who claimed to have destroyed all of his records on the case.

On March 4, Lawrencia Bembenek took the stand. She testified for five hours, providing details about how she met Fred Schultz, the nature of their relationship and her actions on the night of the murder. She also testified about harassment from the Milwaukee Police Department related to the fight to win her job back.

On cross examination, Kramer tried to portray Bembenek as a greedy woman driven to kill so her husband would no longer have to pay child support. But the cross examination wasn't nearly as devastating as two additional witnesses who would follow. Marilyn Gehrt testified that, a year earlier, she sold Bembenek a wig. Annette Wilson, a security guard at the Boston Store, testified that Bembenek once stole a green jogging suit from the store. The damaging testimony of Gehrt and Wilson tied Bembenek directly to the evidence in the circumstantial case.

After weeks of testimony, it wasn't surprising that closing arguments would be lengthy. Kramer repeated his theory that Bembenek killed Schultz so Fred could stop paying child support and they could sell the Ramsey Street house for more money. Eisenberg spent five hours reviewing his case in intricate detail. Jurors also took their time. They asked to visit the apartment complex where Bembenek and Fred Schultz lived. Kramer refused the request. The jury also requested portions of the trial transcript to review. On March 9, after several days of deliberations, the jury found Lawrencia Bembenek guilty of the first-degree murder of Christine Schultz.

The public reaction to the verdict was double-edged. Some people viewed Lawrencia Bembenek as a black widow spider, beautiful but deadly.

Others could not believe such an attractive woman would commit such a horrible crime. In February 1983, the Appeals Court upheld the conviction.

Like many inmates, Bembenek began immediately to prove her innocence. She was supported by hundreds of letters from sympathizers throughout the nation. Public pressure also was brought on the Milwaukee County District Attorney to reopen the case, especially after Eisenberg was accused of impropriety in the Barbara Hoffman murder case for representing two conflicting clients.

The interest of Milwaukee investigator Ira Robins in the Bembenek case apparently began with a 1984 tip from his mechanic, according to an account in *Run, Bambi, Run*, a book by Oconomowoc teacher and writer Kris Radish. The mechanic said he had heard that a wig was planted as evidence that would tie her to the Schultz killing.

The tip piqued Robins' interest in the case so much that he began a one-man crusade to free Bembenek over the next eight years. He was so tenacious and unflagging that Bembenek referred to him affectionately as "my personal bulldog."

What really motivated Robins isn't clear. Perhaps the forty-two-year-old investigator developed a secret infatuation for the beautiful convict. Maybe he sought the notoriety of an association with her. He may have identified with her struggle with the Milwaukee police since he was an former officer himself who suffered discrimination over his Jewish heritage. It could have been he truly was convinced of her innocence and sought justice. In any case, Robins became Bembenek's man on the outside, using his detective skills to follow up her leads and try to find another suspect.

The motives of Jacob Wissler were easier to figure out. He was infatuated with Bembenek and devised a hit-man theory to get close to her. He offered $20,000 to Joey Hecht, convicted of the 1983 murder of Carolyn Hudson in Madison, if Hecht would confess to killing Christine Schultz. From prison, Hecht had bragged that the Hudson murder wasn't his only contract killing. Wissler also offered Michael Durfee (Elfred Schultz's partner) a $25,000 bribe to retract his testimony. Meanwhile, Wissler was writing a series of love letters to Bembenek in prison. Later, Wissler moved to California and became involved in the computer business.

About the time Wissler was writing his love letters, Bembenek had hired a new attorney, Thomas Halloran. Halloran was replaced in 1986 by Martin Kohler. Robins continued to plod along in his effort to find something that would shake the state's case against Bembenek. He spotted similarities between the Schultz murder and a robbery at Judy Zess' apartment. In prison, Bembenek worked on a bachelor's degree and became interested in inmate rights.

Based on Robins' research and Eisenberg's improprieties, Kohler filed a motion for a new trial in 1987. After some delays and a hearing, Judge Michael Skwierawski denied the motion in November 1988. Several months later, Kohler filed an appeal of Skwierawski's ruling. That, too, was denied.

Despite repeated rebuffs in court, public fascination about the Bembenek case continued to build. In 1989, the first of many movies about the case was made by a small-time filmmaker. In the public mind, her character was dramatic and exciting. She was an innocent woman framed for murder and beaten down by the judicial system. Robins and Bembenek's parents formed a group to raise money for her defense.

Nick Gugliatto was visiting his sister at Taycheedah state prison when Bembenek first saw him. Soon afterward, they began writing letters back and forth. Their correspondence turned to romance and they planned to marry. On July 15, 1990, less than a month after the Court of Appeals denied Bembenek's request for a new trial, she climbed over the prison fence and fled with Gugliatto to Canada.

The escape rekindled the public's fascination with the case. In Milwaukee, Robins tried to capitalize on the renewed interest, organizing a rally and enlisting public support for a new trial. Her picture was splashed across TV screens until, finally in October, a tip to the program "America's Most Wanted" led police to her in Thunder Bay, Ontario, where she was working as a waitress under the name of Jennifer Lee Gazzana.

Bembenek's fight against extradition piqued the interest of Canadian authorities. Her dramatic escape and capture also generated more than a little interest from U.S. authors and moviemakers. In the bright eye of publicity, Bembenek seemed to forget her romantic promises to Gugliatto, who was sentenced to a year in the Fond du Lac County Jail for his role in the escape. Mary Woeherer had replaced Kohler as Bembenek's latest attorney in Milwaukee. Woeherer filed a motion for a secret John Doe investigation into the case and it was granted by Judge William Haese.

On November 30, 1991, Frederick Horenberger shot and killed himself after committing an armed robbery. Horenberger had evolved as Robins' prime suspect in the Christine Schultz murder. Just before he died, Horenberger denied killing Schultz. But Robins couldn't give up the notion that easily. He reasoned that Horenberger committed suicide rather than become the target of the John Doe probe.

During Bembenek's stay in Canada, she negotiated a publishing deal to write a book titled *Woman on the Run*. In this country, Son of Sam laws, named after the notorious New York City serial killer, often prohibit convicted criminals from profiting by their crimes. She got around

Wisconsin State Journal file photo
Bembenek at a 1993 speaking engagement in Madison.

those laws, in part, because the book was published in Canada.

At one time, more than a half dozen authors had books in the works on the Bembenek case. Only two, however, were published. Books that argued in favor of her guilt never saw the light of print because they didn't fit the public's popular conception of the case.

After more than a decade behind bars, Bembenek finally won her freedom in 1992. Ironically, it wasn't because a jury or judge finally decided she was innocent. Instead, she agreed to plead no contest to a reduced charge of second-degree murder.

Three TV movies later, some cracks began to appear in the Bembenek fable. Nick Gugliatto complained that he was abandoned by his lover immediately after their arrest. He said her parents helped in the escape. Ira Robins also had become disenchanted with his heroine. He hoped some of the big movie money might help defray some of his expenses over the years in trying to win Bembenek's freedom. Like Gugliatto, she apparently dropped Robins when he wasn't useful to her anymore.

The movies and books on the Bembenek case haven't really cleared up the mystery of who killed Christine Schultz. They have only reinforced the public perception of Bembenek as an unfortunate victim of the judicial system. In *Run, Bambi, Run,* author Kris Radish speculates that perhaps the women on the jury resented of Bembenek's beauty. But her beauty clearly was a double-edged sword. If she were unattractive, it's likely she still would be in prison because she may not have inspired men like Gugliatto to help her.

A case still can be made for Bembenek's guilt. The two people who stood to gain the most from the death of Christine Schultz were Bembenek and her husband, Fred. But would Fred try haphazardly to strangle his son? Despite the portrait of him as a moral degenerate painted in books about the case, that's unlikely. The judicial conspiracy against Bembenek also appears unnaturally broad. Did the entire Milwaukee Police Department conspire to frame her for murder because she protested her firing? Were the jury and several judges in on the plot? That seems incredulous.

E. Michael McCann has been Milwaukee County district attorney for over a quarter century. His office has prosecuted many high-profile cases, from Bembenek to Jeffrey Dahmer. After all the evidence unearthed by Robins, all the appeals and all the TV movies, McCann remains convinced of her guilt. "I believe she committed the homicide and that she's left a tragic wake of sorrow," he told the *Milwaukee Journal* in May 1993.

After her release as part of the plea bargain, Bembenek went on a speaking tour. She proclaimed her innocence and, to her credit, also spoke in favor of educational opportunities for inmates. She said education would help inmates successfully build a life away from crime upon release. But she had difficulty finding a job, working for an accounting firm until it closed and then for temporary employment agencies.

In February 1996, Bembenek was back in jail. This time, she was picked up in a drug investigation that resulted in a drug-dealing charge against fifty-three-year-old Robert North of Shorewood, who was arrested with her. She was held on a parole violation. A drug test showed she had used marijuana.

After two weeks in jail, she was released but required to wear an electronic monitoring bracelet. She was diagnosed with hepatitis C, a liver ailment, and underwent treatment for depression.

In July 1996, she boarded a plane to Washington, where her parents lived, with the permission of her parole office, Colleen Frey. By this time, Bembenek, then 37, had tired of the notoriety — the books and public speaking — and looked forward to living "someplace where nobody knows who I am."

Her mother, Virginia, said the move was a matter of life and death due to her daughter's depression and suicidal thoughts.

The nickname "Bambi" was assigned to Bembenek by the media. It is a nickname she neither sought nor particularly likes. It characterizes her as an innocent victim caught in the headlight glare of the criminal justice system. Charged suddenly with a horrendous crime, she reacted like a deer, too frozen to move while the justice system rumbled over her like a two-ton truck. Whether she is guilty of murder or not, it's clear that Bembenek is no Bambi. When the murder occurred she was a street-wise cop. The alienation of those who helped win her freedom demonstrates a strong dose of self-centeredness. But self-centeredness and street wisdom do not necessarily add up to murder.

The most telling evidence against Bembenek came from her own attorney. During an interview with TV host Geraldo Rivera, Eisenberg said, "Everything that I know about points to the fact she did do it."

That comment provided part of the basis for Bembenek's appeal. It also led to the revocation of Eisenberg's license to practice law in Wisconsin in November 1989.

Did Lawrencia Bembenek, the former Playboy Club waitress and police officer, put on her green jogging suit and kill Christine Schultz that night? It's a mystery that may never be resolved definitively.

5

A Literary Spinster's Revenge

Waukesha, 1917

The fatal love triangle involving the dairy princess wasn't Wisconsin's first, nor last, crime of passion. A similar case involving a love triangle ended the same way in 1917 in Waukesha, when a woman killed her rival for a man's affections.

On a warm day in May that year, Grace Lusk sat at her writing desk, trying to compose a letter to Mary Newman Roberts. The act of writing itself wasn't a problem, for Grace Lusk was a brilliant school teacher. But the deep passions involved made the words come hard.

"It has been a desire with me for a long time," she began, "to tell you frankly about the state of affairs between Dr. Roberts and myself. I have asked him repeatedly to tell you the whole story, but you seem to have him terrorized to a pitiful degree. If I have to blame you for one thing, it would be for that. You must have known for many years that there did not exist between your husband and yourself the honest confidence that is essential in the higher state of marriage."

It was a brave letter for Grace Lusk but, after all, she was nearing the end of her rope. She had met David Roberts four years earlier at a party in the home of Mrs. S.B. Mills. Roberts, in his fifties, ran the David Roberts Veterinary Co., which manufactured cattle preparations and other animal medications. He also operated a dairy and breeding farm.

Grace Lusk was in her thirties and, in her era, she was nearing the end of marriageable age. She had been teaching since she was nineteen. Her first principal in Menomonee Falls described her as "wonderfully mature in mental attainments and a splendid teacher, a most loyal friend, a young woman of pure and noble character, a brilliant girl." She had attended the teachers' colleges known then as Milwaukee Normal and Whitewater Normal. She left her teaching job in Menomonee Falls for a job in Waukesha. As part of her duties as a Waukesha teacher, Grace was required to teach agriculture, a subject she didn't know much about.

Despite her brilliance as a teacher, Grace Lusk never had taken the time to learn much of practical value, especially in relationships between men and women.

At the party, she asked Dr. Roberts about how to distinguish among various breeds of cattle. He gave her one of his books on the subject and recruited her to help him write a veterinary book. Perhaps across the desk after a long night's work, he stole a kiss or two. As part of the seduction, he told her his wife no longer loved him and Grace, inexperienced, was easily seduced.

For four years, David Roberts told Grace repeatedly that he loved her but he couldn't leave his wife. Despite what she perceived as his weakness in this area, Grace still loved him and, now, had decided to matters into her own hands with her letter.

"You must have known," she wrote, "for a long time that your husband's affections had passed from you; that he cared for someone else. That is sufficient annulment of any marriage vow that ever was given."

Despite what many of her contemporaries would call a tawdry affair, Grace had assumed the high moral ground. She was having an affair with a married man, yet it was justified because of her lover's failing marriage. Now, she grew poetic about her situation:

"That is the way you respectable folk — good, normal women — do things in order to keep your reputation and live lives of ease," she went on. "In the eternal triangle our souls require for their solution the elimination of one character. The two who should remain are the two whose affection is mutual. There is no use in my telling the details of our 'case.' I am sorry that it even started. It has wrecked my life and hurt those who are dear to me. Will you some time read Ellen Kay on *Love and Marriage?*"

Ever the teacher, Grace Lusk could not resist suggesting some reading material for her rival. Regrets? Of course she had them. Like Lori Esker, Grace Lusk was out of control. She was obsessed with her doctor lover so much that her passions clouded her very capable mind.

But unlike Bill Buss, the target of Lori Esker's affection, David Roberts wasn't an innocent party in this love triangle. He clearly had taken unfair advantage of Grace's inexperience in the ways of love. He had no intention of leaving his wife or marrying Grace as she wistfully dreamed. He was too comfortable with his wife at home and a doting mistress on the side.

David and Grace had arranged their clandestine love trysts at locations away from Waukesha, where a mutual acquaintance might discover them. They often traveled south to Illinois, finding out-of-the-way hotels in Peoria or Chicago. David had managed to make lame excuses to his wife for his absences.

When the lovers met in mid-May at the Hotel Wisconsin in Milwaukee, Grace told David about the letter. In desperation, she also brought along a revolver.

"Never in my life have I done anything which even bordered on unconventionality," she told Dr. Roberts, "and this episode has almost killed me."

Grace demanded more from David. She demanded that he tell his wife everything and leave her. Grace tied herself to the writing desk and pulled out her revolver. She pointed it at David and made him swear on the Bible that he would confess to his wife.

Of course, at that moment, David agreed. Later, after they had made love, he hedged a bit. He told Grace he couldn't tell his wife right away because they were leaving the next day on a business trip. Maybe after that... Grace said she would give him until June 15.

"I want you to ask her for your freedom, David. I want you to arrange this so we can all understand each other."

The letter Grace sent to Mrs. Roberts might have created a serious problem for David if he hadn't been such an expert philanderer. He merely told his wife that the letter was from a woman who was pursing him relentlessly and making a nuisance of herself. But Mrs. Roberts wasn't totally convinced. Grace seemed to offer too many details in her letter. During the trip, Mrs. Roberts decided she must speak to this woman in person to find out the truth.

An hour after David and Mary Roberts arrived home from their trip, Grace appeared at the door. Mary Roberts encouraged her to come in but her husband quickly pushed Grace back outside and walked her home. The next morning, Mrs. Roberts called Grace and arranged to meet at her school office.

Naturally, David Roberts was upset about the idea of his wife and mistress getting together. Comparing notes by them could only be dangerous for him. He tried to talk Mary out of it and, when that failed, he cut the telephone lines to his house so his wife couldn't call Grace.

Although she didn't keep the appointment, Mary Roberts remained determined to confront her husband's pursuer. On June 21, she walked over to Mills House, the rooming house where Grace lived. Grace came downstairs to meet her in the lobby.

"I came here to get an explanation of your conduct last night," Mrs. Roberts began. "I think it was the most asinine performance I ever saw."

Grace swallowed hard but didn't respond, so Mrs. Roberts went on:

"He said you are the damnedest fool he ever saw. He said that you were actually chasing him, that he did not care anything about you."

"You don't mean that he said that, do you?" Grace was getting upset now.

"What else could you expect when you chase a married man?"

Mrs. Roberts demanded that Grace get out of town. She threatened to go to the school board and try to get her fired.

"My friends will put you out of town," she threatened. "They will tar and feather you!"

Mrs. Roberts demanded that Grace break off the affair with her husband. Grace, of course, refused, saying that she was David's true love. Grace said she would prove it, too. She said she would go upstairs and get the love letters from David to show Mrs. Roberts.

While Grace was getting the letters, Mrs. Roberts called her husband, asking him to come over and verify one story or the other.

Upstairs, Grace opened a dresser drawer. Instead of letters, her eyes fell on her revolver.

David Roberts reluctantly obeyed his wife's request. Earlier, he had asked a business partner to watch his house, so he knew already that Mary had gone to see Grace. He and the partner, W.D. Blott, drove over to Mills House. He was terrified. Despite his best efforts to keep them apart, the two women had gotten together. What if they compared notes and decided to turn on him? As he approached Mills House, he was too nervous to stop and drove on by. He came around the block and, on the second pass, he heard a shot.

David stopped the car and asked Blott to go take a look. Blott peeked in a window. He saw Mary Roberts lying on the floor with blood staining her side. He saw Grace coming down the stairs. Instead of bothering to check on his wife or Grace, David fled to a phone some distance away. He called the police and Dr. R.E. Davies.

When Davies arrived, he saw that Mary Roberts had been shot twice. The wounds were fatal. Grace stood at the top of the stairs, bleeding from a self-inflicted wound to her chest. Davies started up the stairs.

"If you come up, I'll shoot!" Grace warned. "Where's David?"

David, of course, was still too frightened to go anywhere near the place.

"Where's my heart?" Grace wanted to know.

"What?"

"Where's my heart?"

"Why, right here," the doctor said, placing his hand over his chest. "You'd better let me tend to that wound."

Without a reply, Grace turned and went into the bedroom. Davies heard another shot and bounded up the stairs. Grace had shot herself once again in the chest and passed out. But once again she had missed her vital organs. As she was carried out on a stretcher, she regained consciousness.

"That was the most unfortunate miss I ever made," she mumbled, referring to her last shot.

At her trial, Grace's attorneys tried to portray her as neurotic and caught in the grip of an uncontrollable passion. They presented evidence that she had frequent migraine headaches and often worked too hard. They brought witnesses who said her father sometimes swatted flies away from his face in the winter and talked to his hat. Her father testified that her mother once tried to hurl herself into Niagara Falls. But three psychiatrists examined Grace and found her sane.

When the guilty verdict was returned on May 29, 1918, Grace found it hard to bear. She jumped out of her chair and grabbed prosecutor D.S. Tullar around the neck in a choke hold. Several spectators, clearly sympathetic to the defendant, tried to vault the rail to help. Grace was hauled out of the courtroom shrieking as the judge rapped his gavel and restored order.

On June 18, almost exactly a year after the murder of Mary Roberts, Grace was sentenced to nineteen years in prison. She also was sentenced to spend every June 21 in solitary confinement so she might reflect on her awful deed.

But Judge Martin Lueck didn't view Grace as the only culprit in the case.

"I want to say that I have one regret, a sincere regret, that I cannot mete out to Dr. Roberts the punishment I think he ought to have."

Dr. Roberts served a brief term in the Milwaukee County House of Corrections after he was convicted on a morals charge for his affair with Grace. He later remarried, proving that even the worst philanderers sometimes land on their feet.

Grace Lusk didn't recover as well as her lover from the ordeal. She was paroled in 1921 and went straight into a sanitorium at Oconomowoc. When she was pardoned two years later by Gov. John J. Blaine, she vowed to devote the rest of her life to prison reform. When *Atlantic Monthly* carried an article on prison reform written by an "Alice Thornton," many people assumed the author was Grace.

A few years later, Grace claimed to have married a "Mr. Brown," but no one ever saw him and some people thought he was a figment of her imagination, although she once bought some furniture and had it shipped somewhere in the South. She died in Milwaukee, still apparently alone, in 1930.

Did she ever wonder in her later years what might have been? Did she ever think about David Roberts and imagine what might have happened if Mary Roberts had obeyed her wishes in the letter and surrendered her husband? That remains one of the secrets of the heart that, in this case, will never be known.

6
The Gang's All Here
Oshkosh, 1990

Twenty-year-old Jennifer liked to dance. Six-year-old Emily ate crayons. Thirty-two-year-old Franny liked to spend money. Brian was a body builder. Ginger liked to get drunk and hang out at a place called Just Pete's. Shadow was very violent, once pushing her hand through a window. Others included Eleanor, Justin, Richard, Gerald, Evan and Sam.

They were among forty-six separate personalities said to reside in the body of a twenty-six-year-old Oshkosh woman. When Mark Peterson, a married grocery store bagger, met the woman in June 1990, he liked Jennifer best.

Two days after they met in a park, he took her out for coffee. Then he asked the woman's personality called Jennifer to come out.

"Can I love you, Jennifer?" he asked. Jennifer later told authorities that she agreed, even though she didn't know quite what it was. They had sex in the front seat of his car.

But six-year-old Emily was "peeking" and reported the incident. Peterson was arrested on August 6 and charged with second-degree sexual assault in one of the most bizarre Wisconsin cases of the century.

Peterson, who faced up to ten years in prison and a ten thousand dollar fine, was released on a five thousand dollar signature bond. He said he didn't know the woman had a mental illness. But prosecutors claimed he violated a Wisconsin statute that says people with mental illnesses are incapable of giving permission to have sex.

The woman's friends said they had told Peterson that she suffered from multiple personality disorder when he met her and, two days later, when he took her out for coffee.

"I think it speaks for itself," Winnebago County District Attorney Joseph Paulus said of the case. "I have never seen anything like it."

Peterson's attorney, Edward Salzsieder, claimed his client was guilty only of an immoral act because the woman was faking her medical condition. He questioned whether the woman actually was mentally ill or whether it was just "a big show."

At Peterson's preliminary hearing on August 16, Judge Robert Hawley required each of the woman's personalities to take the oath separately when they were ready to testify. The lawyers also introduced themselves to each personality.

The woman was born in Seoul, South Korea and her father was an American soldier. As an infant, she was taken to an orphanage.

"I had no maternal or paternal care of any kind," she told the *Appleton Post-Crescent*. "I was not touched or picked up, except to be changed or fed. I was a very angry, lonely, sad baby."

She was adopted at eight months of age by parents who picked her out of a catalog. She came to the United States in a cardboard box with a blue blanket. She said her father physically abused her, which brought on her multiple personalities. She heard voices and suffered mood swings. Later she earned an associate degree in law enforcement from an Iowa college.

When another personality took control, the woman said her real personality went to "a dark place, a place of nothingness."

Dr. Inam Haque, a psychiatrist at Winnebago County Mental Health Clinic, treated the woman for four years before diagnosing her with multiple personality disorder in February 1990. In his notes later subpoenaed for Peterson's trial, Haque indicated he was troubled by the fact that his patient seemed intrigued by the diagnosis, seemed to enjoy "flaunting the new-found disease and having fun with it." He said she also switched personalities so quickly that he wondered if she was faking it.

Despite those reservations, Haque, who said he treated four cases of multiple personality disorder during his 20 years at Winnebago Mental Health Institute, was a key witness for the prosecution.

"She couldn't appreciate her conduct because her real personality was not there," he testified.

In early October, while awaiting her case to go to trial, the woman called police and reported that one of her personalities was threatening another with a knife.

"I'm an MPD (multiple personality disorder) and she's got a knife at my stomach," the woman told a dispatcher, who broadcast the call as a potential suicide attempt. When officers arrived, they found her sitting quietly in a chair.

Peterson's trial became a media circus as reporters from the television tabloids and newspapers flocked to the courtroom. The *Oshkosh Northwestern* described the reporters descending on the courtroom like "flies to a Dumpster full of week-old pizza."

Dr. Bennett Braun, an expert on multiple personality disorder at Chicago's Rush-Northside Medical Center, said the apostle Luke in the Bible may have referred to multiple personality disorder when he recounted how Jesus healed a "demoniac." Paulus, who was expected to call at least six of the woman's personalities as witnesses, said Peterson took advantage of her.

"What it comes down to is he manipulated a mentally ill woman into having sex with him in the front seat of a car in a small park in Oshkosh in broad daylight," Paulus said. "That's simply a question of what's right and what's wrong."

But Salzsieder compared the case to Richard Nixon's involvement in the Watergate scandal: "What did the president know and when did he know it?"

Dr. Darold Treffert, a psychiatrist called by the defense, said people with split personalities do not lose touch with reality and she would have maintained control of her body even when switching personalities. Treffert was not permitted by the court to examine the woman

"What you see is not someone who is pretending to have a disorder," he said. "What you have is a therapist-induced illness."

On November 8, a jury found Peterson guilty of raping the woman. Six weeks later, however, Hawley dismissed the charge against Peterson and said he deserved a new trial because the defense psychiatrist was not allowed to examine the woman. Paulus said he would not bring the case to trial a second time because it would be too hard on the victim.

But the case was far from over. In January 1991, Paulus' wife, Janet, who had filed for divorce, claimed he was actively pursuing a movie deal with a CBS producer during the trial.

"The producer called our home many times during the trial and after," she said. "Joe was excited about hearing who would play whom in the movie. The man called weekly and sometimes daily."

Sheila Carmichael, the county's victim-witness coordinator, said Paulus knew during the trial that she planned to write a book about the case. Carmichael, the first cousin of Janet Paulus, was fired from her county job on November 21 after allegations that she had signed a contract with the victim for movie, television, radio, record and publication rights.

Paulus discounted the charges against him by Carmichael and his estranged wife.

"With regard to Sheila's comments, all I can say is she seems to be getting more desperate as time goes by," he said. "The next thing you know, she'll accuse me of kidnapping the Lindbergh baby. With regard to my wife, we are in the middle of a divorce right now and it seems obvious why she is making these comments."

In June 1993, one or more of the woman's personalities led Oshkosh police on a high-speed chase. She pleaded no contest by reason of insanity to resisting arrest and was found innocent by reason of mental disease or defect. She was committed as an outpatient to the state Department of Health and Social Services.

Her probation agent reported she later disappeared for a week and could not account for her whereabouts when one of her personalities apparently took over. The woman believed she may have been traveling with a truck driver.

7

Hunter of Young Lovers
Eau Claire, 1948

Harry Truman was embroiled in his nip-and-tuck campaign against Thomas Dewey. In Eau Claire, the weather on October 23, 1948, was clear and mild. And Trudy Baumann was happy. At seventeen, life is uncomplicated and it's easy to be happy with the little things in life. Trudy had a new camera and a new boyfriend.

Her new boyfriend was Raymond Smith, also seventeen, who had moved to Eau Claire from Duluth three weeks earlier. He had worked at a Duluth bank so, when his family came to Eau Claire, he got a job at the American National Bank & Trust. Trudy was a high school senior, an honor student who was gifted in art and music. She was a dedicated member of the Lutheran Church of St. Matthew and had called the parsonage a week earlier to ask if it was too early to begin the annual fundraising campaign for tuberculosis patients.

On this beautiful fall Saturday, Trudy took her new camera on a walk with her new boyfriend. They left her house about 3:00 p.m. and headed for the country club golf course at the end of Main Street east of Highway 53. It was an area favored by hunters in search of squirrels and rabbits. Ray was an avid bow hunter and had planned to bring his bow along, but the string was broken so he left it at home.

Trudy and Ray set out, laughing and snapping pictures of each other, holding hands and stopping for a kiss behind a tree as young lovers do. They walked across the golf course and sat down under the east end of a railroad bridge that goes over the Eau Claire River. That's where fifteen-year-old Jack Hanson saw them as he walked along the other side of the river. Hanson kept walking and lost sight of the couple behind some bushes and trees.

Meanwhile, Marshall Johnson had gone to the country club area from his home on the city's west side to hunt squirrels. He roamed the bushy untended areas around the golf course, hoping to flush out the varmints and nail them with the .22-caliber automatic rifle he carried.

The thirty-two-year-old Johnson, who was married with a six-month-old son, had an extensive criminal record, mostly for burglary. In 1942, he had been sentenced to four years in prison on a burglary charge. That came after a one-to-three-year sentence in 1939 for breaking and entering. He had served another prison term for burglary beginning in 1937 and six months in jail the previous year on a Chippewa Falls larceny charge. In 1933, he was sentenced to three years probation on a federal forgery conviction.

As he walked around the outside of the golf course, Johnson met a couple he knew, Arthur Thompson and his wife, and stopped briefly to chat with them. Thompson noticed a squirrel's tail sticking out of a bag Johnson carried. The Thompsons continued on their way and Johnson approached the railroad bridge. From the cover of bushes near the bridge, Johnson spotted Trudy and Ray. He circled slowly toward the young couple, quietly edging closer to his prey. When he got to the end of the underbrush by the bridge, he broke into the clearing and confronted them.

"I saw a young man and girl sitting there," he later told detectives. "I started toward them. The man got up and started toward me and we started scuffling. I kicked him and got away from him a few feet and then fired the first shot that struck him. The girl started to scream so I shot her in the chest. She went down and continued to scream. The man tried to get up so I shot him two or three more times. Both of them were dead."

Johnson dragged Smith's body down to the river and pushed it into the water. He went back for the girl's body but saw two men coming and panicked. He picked up his rifle and ran across the railroad bridge toward Eau Claire, making it across just in time before the four o'clock train came roaring by.

Johnson threw the rifle into Dells Pond, then went downtown and bought an apple turnover at the Barstow Street Bakery. He bought a pair of work shoes at the Huleatt Clothing Store and then went home. His day of hunting hadn't turned out quite the way he'd expected. He also had missed the 4:00 p.m. bus bound for the West Coast so he hitched a ride to St. Paul, then to Jamestown, South Dakota, where he caught up with the bus.

About 4:25 p.m., Hanson, the teenager who'd seen the couple sitting under the bridge, heard several shots fired and a woman screaming. But he didn't report it until much later. When the couple didn't return home, a search party was organized. Firefighters combed the river until dark. They found trousers, shoes and a hat but no sign of Trudy and Ray.

The search resumed on Sunday, with the couple's relatives and friends joining the police effort. On Sunday afternoon, Trudy's body was found in some bushes by James Smith, Ray's older brother, and a cousin, Carl Wuesteneck. A short time later, Ray's body was found in the river. Both had been shot to death with a .22-caliber rifle.

Two days after the murders, Trudy's camera was found in the river about twenty feet from shore. Police hoped the water-damaged pictures would provide a clue to the killer's identity. But when the film was developed, the killer's mug wasn't on the roll. Five pictures were taken on the hike and six previously. Three shots were of Smith, two of Trudy and one inexplicable.

The killer apparently dragged Smith's body down the riverbank to the water's edge and rolled it into a shallow stream. The victim's pants and shoes probably came off, police theorized, while the body was dragging, then the clothing was thrown into the water. Or, had Johnson come across the two young lovers in a compromising position and then tried to take advantage of Trudy? Scratches on her face, arms and one hand indicated she had struggled with her assailant.

Police began a wide search for possible suspects. A youth who knew Trudy was picked up for questioning after he ran from police. Detectives traveled to Streator, Illinois to interrogate two sailors and a .22-caliber rifle owned by one of the sailors was brought back to Wisconsin for analysis. Police interviewed a Minneapolis man and a teenager living in Chicago. But these leads went nowhere. St. Paul Police Chief Charles Tierney came to Eau Claire to confer on the case. On October 17, Wisconsin Assistant Attorney General William Platz took over the investigation with the blessing of Gov. Oscar Rennebohm.

Rumors abounded that the bodies of the young couple had been mutilated by the vicious killer but the *Eau Claire Leader* quoted authorities who said it wasn't true. Hundreds of people showed up to see for themselves at a wake in the Stokes & Sons Funeral Chapel. Trudy was buried in Eau Claire but Ray was taken to Superior for burial.

As detectives reviewed the evidence and reconstructed the killings detail by detail, Johnson began to emerge as a strong suspect. They knew he had been near the golf course at the time of the killings. They found out he'd left town shortly afterward. They also knew about his extensive criminal record. On November 1, a week after the bodies were found, Johnson was arrested in Seattle, Washington as a suspect in the slayings of Trudy and Ray. Johnson insisted he was innocent and waived extradition. He denied he fled Eau Claire after the murders and, in an interview with a Seattle reporter, said the police were making him a scapegoat.

"I had been working as a roofer in Eau Claire but it got kind of slack," he said. "Then, they brought me up for window peeping not so long ago and I had to pay a fifty-dollar fine although I pleaded not guilty. That's why I wanted to get out of Eau Claire. They were blaming everything on me."

Johnson told the police he'd sold his rifle to a Mondovi farmer. He said the trip to the West Coast had been planned three weeks earlier and had nothing to do with the murders. Eau Claire Sheriff Lloyd Thompson and Detective Harold McLaughlin went to Seattle to pick up Johnson and return him to Wisconsin. On the long drive back, a camaraderie developed between the guards and their prisoner. They stopped for breakfast at a Minnesota restaurant.

"Marshall," McLaughlin said, "I want to know all about it."

"I'm no killer," Johnson replied. "I don't know why I did it."

Then Johnson told McLaughlin and Thompson his version of the crime. He told them how he'd confronted the couple under the railroad bridge and shot them both when a scuffle developed. He described how he'd tried to dispose of the bodies but panicked and fled across the bridge.

"Johnson whimpered and gulped frequently while he told his version of the murders but there was nothing in the way of a complete emotional breakdown," McLaughlin said later.

Despite the confession, Johnson pleaded innocent to the murder charges in court, in a voice that was barely audible. About one-hundred-fifty people jammed the courtroom and an overflow crowd waited outside. Johnson passed a lie detector test about his possible involvement in the rape of a fifteen-year-old Colfax girl who had identified Johnson as her assailant. He refused to take a lie detector test, however, in the sexual assault of a twenty-one-month-old Eau Claire toddler. Johnson was held without bail and ordered to stand trial on two charges of first-degree murder.

Investigators had evidence and a likely suspect but a problem still remained. The murder weapon hadn't been found. Johnson had given three stories about the gun. First, he said he'd sold it to a farmer. Then he told police he dropped the rifle into Dells Pond. Later, he said he sold the gun to two men. A one-hundred-dollar reward was offered by Eau Claire Police Chief Chris Laursen for recovery of the weapon, but that failed to turn it up so a search of Dells Pond began.

By this time, cold weather had set in and the pond was frozen. Firefighters chopped holes in the ice so divers could search the cold bottom underneath. Professional divers from Milwaukee were called in. They found a boy's cap pistol and a golf ball. More than six hundred high school students joined in the search. Authorities concocted a scheme to withhold water upstream so the pond could be drained. The dam was closed twice to lower the water level and the pond was swept with a large magnet but still the rifle couldn't be found. Police brought Johnson to the scene four times, once in a driving rain, to point out where he'd tossed the murder weapon. He was given another lie detector test with truth serum and afterward the search resumed at Dells Pond. Even Johnson's attorney advised his client to help locate the weapon.

On December 1, two six-year-old boys found a rusty .22-caliber rifle in a grassy area near Dells Pond. But tests showed the rifle was the wrong one. The next day, another .22-caliber rifle was found in ten feet of water.

On December 3, Walgreen's and Sears stores were destroyed in one of the worst fires in Eau Claire's history. The same day, Dr. John Dalton, a St. Paul police criminologist, confirmed that the rifle found in the pond killed Trudy and Ray.

Johnson was held in jail through the holidays and his case was scheduled for the court's spring session in March. Despite the earlier confession, he stood by his innocent plea until March 1 when he was taken at his request to Minneapolis for more truth serum tests. After taking the serum, Johnson confessed again. Then, at a March 10 hearing, he retracted his confession and repeated his plea of not guilty.

The on-and-off confessions may have been a ploy to set up a case for insanity. But that hope fizzled after Johnson was sent for a mental exam to Mendota Mental Health Institute, where both Dr. Walter Urben, the Mendota superintendent, and Dr. Fritz Kant, a UW-Madison psychiatrist, pronounced him sane.

The sanity finding apparently was such a blow to his case that Johnson stood March 22 with his head bowed before Judge Clarence Rinchard and changed his plea to guilty. But District Attorney Victor Tronsdal presented fifteen witnesses anyway so the guilty conviction would be protected if Johnson later sought a pardon or parole.

"I have listened to this testimony carefully," Rinchard said. "If Wisconsin had capital punishment, it would be my duty to impose such a sentence. It is now my duty to pronounce the sentence made mandatory by the law."

As Johnson's face flushed slightly, Rinchard gave him two consecutive life sentences. H.C. Vermilyea reported in the *Eau Claire Leader* that the one-day trial was boring:

"There were few dramatic moments and little testimony of a sensational nature. The greater part of the afternoon was taken up by experts who testified (about) ballistics tests."

But Johnson's third confession to the murders wasn't his last. Two days before he was taken to Waupun State Prison on March 25, Johnson admitted he had sexually molested the twenty-one-month-old Eau Claire girl in her crib and then he'd fled the toddler's trailer home after the girl's mother came home. The woman had watched him run away into the underbrush — similar to the weeds and bushes where he later stalked Trudy and Ray.

8

Sexual Monkey
Weyauwega, 1977

As usual, Robert Patri drove his truck up to the Weyauwega farmhouse about 7:30 a.m. that Friday to pick up his two daughters, ages ten and twelve. His estranged wife, Jennifer, let him in the house and then told him his daughters weren't there, that she'd taken them to a relative's home. That set him off and he exploded, raging at her, calling her a pig and a slut, threatening her. She let him scream for a while, taking his verbal abuse in silence. When he'd quieted down a little, she asked him to check the furnace in the basement because she thought she smelled a gas odor. Still grumbling about his children not being there, Patri grudgingly agreed and walked to the basement door. When his head was turned, Jennifer Patri reached behind a chair and picked up a 12-gauge shotgun she had loaded and readied, perhaps just for this moment. As her husband walked down the stairs, she fired into his back.

"Oh God, Jen," he cried, stumbling down the rest of the way. She calmly put another shell into the gun and fired a second blast close to his head, blowing off his jaw.

Later, Jennifer Patri would say that her husband came at her with a knife. She would claim she confronted him about sexual advances toward their daughter.

"I told him I thought he was sick and he needed help," she would say on the witness stand. "That's when he became enraged."

The shotgun slaying of Robert Patri brought a brutal close to the couple's stormy thirteen-year marriage. Jennifer had ordered the shotgun by phone two weeks earlier and picked it up on March 23, 1977, two

days before the murder. She told Robert Montgomery, the store manager, that she was buying the 12-gauge Remington as a gift for her husband and, in a way, she was telling the truth. She had test-fired the weapon
a couple of days before firing the fatal shot into Patri's back.

After killing her husband, Jennifer Patri got into his pickup truck
and drove to Waupaca, later saying she intended to turn herself in. Instead, she parked the truck on Sessions Street, threw the keys on the floor
of the truck and went over to a supermarket, where she tapped on the
window of a taxicab. She asked driver Charles Kealiher to take her to
Lind Center, which wasn't far from her farm home. During the ride,
Kealiher noticed she seemed quiet and preoccupied, never once looking
at him.

When she got home, Jennifer called her husband's business partner,
John Melberg, and told him she was worried that Patri hadn't come yet
to pick up the kids. Patri and Melberg operated Bob's Body Shop in
West Bloomfield, where Patri also lived with a woman, Cherie Mercer.
Patri had met Mercer a year earlier and they'd been involved with each
other since the previous October. Jennifer, who naturally wasn't on great
terms with Cherie, called her and asked that she come over to the farm.
Jennifer told her husband's lover that she was afraid to do her chores
alone with Patri missing. While Patri's body was hidden in the basement
below them, the two women talked in the farm kitchen. "I sat at a table
and Jennifer paced," Cherie said. When Cherie went to the bathroom,
she noticed some blood on paper towels but didn't think anything of it at
the time. When Jennifer's brother showed up, Cherie left and decided to
search for Patri's truck, finding it on the Waupaca street. Cherie Marie
Mercer held Social Security cards under five different names, including
Cheri Deshaney, Cheryl Lee, Cheryl Todaco and Cheryl Barraca. A week
after the murder, she changed her name once again to Cherie Patri because, she said, she and Bob had been engaged even though she technically still was married to her third husband. She'd been arrested three
times between 1971 and 1972 on suspicion of heroin possession but none
of the charges stuck. Her third husband was a bank robber and heroin
addict for twenty-seven years and Cherie admitted she'd been addicted to
the drug for a few years herself.

About midnight, Jennifer crept down to the basement and carefully
wrapped her husband's body in Viscene plastic. She dragged the body up
the stairs, then outside to a shed, where she buried it in a shallow grave,
piling lumber and cardboard on top. She had hidden the shotgun in the
basement rafters over the cistern room. After burying the body, she returned to the house and lit several fires, waiting until they got going
before she called the fire department. Firefighters arrived about 3 a.m.
and battled the farmhouse blaze for seven hours.

Jennifer told Deputy Fire Marshal Leslie Mayer that her husband, who still was missing, had threatened her and she was afraid so she sent the kids away and slept on the couch. She said she heard a truck with a loud muffler that sounded like her husband's pickup drive by the farmhouse. She heard a crash and then the fire broke out. But there was something about her story that didn't quite ring true. When Waupaca County Chief Deputy Sheriff Robert Andraschko found blood and tissue in the basement, Jennifer told him she had bought a large amount of ground meat to make sausage and that it must have left some residue. Deputies searched the farmhouse and found the gun. In the shed, they saw a human hand protruding from the pile of lumber. Removing the lumber and freshly turned earth, they found Patri's body. With her scheme unmasked, Jennifer confessed to the murder as she walked from a car to the sheriff's department that Saturday afternoon.

Wisconsin State Journal file photo
Jennifer Patri

"I couldn't take it anymore," she said. "I killed him. No, Bob never hit me. But I couldn't take the mental anguish. He wasn't satisfied with anything. He wanted the kids and the farm."

By the time of her trial, defense attorney Alan Eisenberg had painted the case with a different hue. He also was criticized by Philip Kirk, Waupaca County assistant district attorney, for freely discussing the case with reporters.

No longer was Jennifer a woman driven by her husband's persistence to get the farm and her daughters in the divorce settlement, as she'd said in her confession. Eisenberg now characterized her as "the classic case of the battered woman," who killed her husband after years of torture and abuse. He compared the case to the Joan Little trial, where a black North Carolina woman was acquitted of murder charges after trying to kill a white jailer who attempted to rape her. Women's groups across the nation were stirred by Jennifer's case and flocked to her defense.

She told Associated Press reporter Timothy Harper how Patri had slapped, pushed and struck her several times a week. She talked about how, before they were married, her husband struck her so hard she had to have a rib surgically removed. She said Patri served jail time for fighting and stealing. He had L-0-V-E tattooed on the knuckles of his left hand and H-A-T-E tattooed on the knuckles of his right hand — the fist he repeatedly slammed into her.

She told how her husband came at her with a knife in her kitchen and how she picked up the new shotgun and fired at him. She said she set the house ablaze in a suicide attempt.

"I was just out of control, operating from some subnormal rage," she said. "It was both rage and fear."

Eisenberg described Patri as "a violent hellraiser" and maintained "the world is better off without him."

Outside the Waupaca County courthouse, about fifty women attended a rally on November 16, 1977, sponsored by the Jennifer Patri Defense Committee. Inside, at a hearing on the case, Eisenberg asked Wood County Judge Frederick Fink to allow Jennifer to attend the Women's International Conference in Houston but the judge refused, saying she would forfeit her $60,000 bail if she left the area.

The murder trial began December 5 and the court had some difficulty selecting a jury. Fink excused sixteen prospective jurors during the first two hours of selection. Finally, a jury of nine men and three women was assembled.

In his opening statement, Eisenberg characterized the difference between Patri and his wife as a struggle between good and evil. Patri was a "turbulent, reckless, ruthless, physical person whose estranged wife killed him in self-defense," the attorney argued, adding that Patri was "first a weekend alcoholic, then a full-time alcoholic, then a philanderer."

On the other hand, he described Jennifer as "an exemplary mother dealing with a difficult situation." She was a Sunday school teacher and former PTA president "devoted to her children, her church, her God, her community."

Kirk's opening remarks were more brief and less flamboyant than those of the Milwaukee defense attorney. He simply said he planned to introduce Jennifer's March 26 confession.

As testimony got underway, Mayer, the deputy fire marshal, said Jennifer had told him she'd argued with her husband about money after she'd actually shot him early that morning. Store owner Montgomery testified about Jennifer buying the gun.

During the testimony, Jennifer watched intently from her seat beside her attorney, wiping away a tear from her gray eyes now and then or jotting on a legal pad. She had lost eighteen pounds since the murder and spent 105 days in jail before she was released on bail. Scars still showed on her face from when she was burned in a fire at age four.

Bill Knutson, a reporter who covered the trial for the *Appleton Post-Crescent*, interviewed Jennifer in a hallway outside the courtroom.

"Those 105 days were very important to me," she said. "I had time to rest. I read a lot. I went to jail a bigot and that changed. I am grateful for the true and the meaningful things that happened to me there."

The support of women's groups, she said, "helps to know I am understood as a human being."

Witnesses who knew Patri well supported Eisenberg's theme that he wasn't a nice man. His body shop partner, Melberg, said Patri was a big spender who often paid his employees with bogus checks. Melberg said Patri sometimes spent $500 a week in taverns.

Patri's sister-in-law said she'd once caught him peeking in a bathroom window where her daughter and his daughter were bathing. He'd also once made a pass at her.

Even Patri's own mother, Hildegarde, testified that Jennifer Patri had a reputation for being peaceful and truthful.

In all, twenty-one defense witnesses testified to Patri's bad qualities. They said they'd seen him "twist and squeeze" his wife or dig his fingers so hard into her arm that it left the skin marked and reddened. They said Patri often made her arm-wrestle with him against her will.

In the climax to the defense case, Jennifer Patri took the stand and told the jury about repeated beatings she'd suffered since 1963, when she met her husband. She told about being hospitalized for the broken rib in Cedar Rapids, Iowa, where he knocked her against the corner of their bed. She told about a miscarriage after a beating in 1969.

"Why did you marry him?" Eisenberg asked.

"Because we already had a child and I was pregnant a second time. And I loved him."

"Why didn't you turn him in?"

"I always understood that whatever a husband does to his wife is acceptable."

Eisenberg said Jennifer became her husband's "sexual monkey" and he did with her as he pleased.

The defense attorney argued with the judge over the testimony of fire marshal Mayer because the murder charge was to be tried separately from the arson charge. Fink accused Eisenberg of theatrics and denied his motion of a mistrial.

Eisenberg concluded his case with the testimony of psychiatrist Ann Campbell of Elm Grove. She agreed with earlier testimony of psychiatrist Kathryn Beummann of Waukesha that Jennifer was incapable of first-degree murder.

The jury deliberated about two hours before finding Jennifer guilty of manslaughter, an alternative to a murder conviction permitted by Judge Fink. Eisenberg said his client couldn't ask for anything better.

"If Jennifer Patri goes free, the jury will return to society a person who deserves it," he'd argued in his four-hour closing statement. Kirk had said her memory lapses were "convenient" and that she never mentioned the beatings to investigators.

With tears in her eyes, Jennifer pleaded with Fink for probation at her sentencing hearing on February 22, 1978. She told the judge that her daughters needed her at home more than the state needed to send her to prison. But Fink disagreed and sentenced her to ten years at Taycheedah Correctional Institution.

"Probation would unduly depreciate the seriousness of this crime," Fink said. Eisenberg accused the judge of being "erroneous and anti-female." The defense attorney said Fink committed more than a hundred legal errors and that he planned an appeal to the Wisconsin Supreme Court.

As jury selection began in June for Jennifer's arson trial, the first list of fifty prospective jurors was nearly exhausted as many said they couldn't understand that she was innocent until proven guilty. Fink ordered twenty-five more Waupaca County residents be summoned for jury duty but ultimately the frustrated judge moved the trial to La Crosse County.

As the arson trial began in December, Eisenberg asked for another change of venue, arguing that "the embers of time have not cooled." The defense attorney who'd been so willing to discuss the case with reporters before the murder trial now said he wanted the judge to move the arson trial to another city, bar reporters and issue a gag order. Fink turned down the request.

On December 11, 1978, a jury of nine women and three men — the exact opposite gender balance of the first jury — found Jennifer innocent of the arson charges by reason of insanity. She appeared stunned and confused when the jury ruled she was mentally ill and in need of medical treatment.

"It means you're out of Taycheedah," Eisenberg told his client, later observing that the jury was "a lynch mob with a conscience." Kirk said the second verdict contradicted the first jury's ruling in the murder trial, which found her sane.

Two years later, the state Court of Appeals upheld Jennifer's murder conviction and the 10-year sentence, rejecting Eisenberg's argument that she didn't receive a trial by a jury of her peers because Kirk used his juror challenges only against potential women jurors.

The eighty-eight-acre Patri hog farm was sold in 1979 to pay off the land contract. The contract holders filed suit, saying they received no payments on the $51,000 farm since Jennifer's arrest in March 1977. She spent nearly a year at Winnebago Mental Health Institute but was transferred to Taycheedah in November 1979, after Fink held a sanity hearing and found she was no longer a danger to herself or others.

Women's groups continued to rally in support of Jennifer. Four times she asked for parole and was denied. In January 1981, an advisory panel recommended that Gov. Lee Dreyfus deny her pardon request. But six months later, she was paroled.

"It was the unanimous judgement of the board that she had served sufficient time considering the crime and her sentence," said parole board chairman Fred Hinicke. "Her conduct and program participation have been exemplary. In the judgment of the board, there is no likelihood of criminal behavior in the future."

In January 1982, U.S. District Court Judge Myron Gordon denied a request to overturn Jennifer's manslaughter conviction, rejecting the defense arguments that instructions to the jury shifted the burden of proof to the defense.

Despite the strong support of women's groups for her cause as a classic battered wife, Jennifer didn't become a women's rights activist upon her release. Instead, she remarried and took a job as a nursing assistant at the Wisconsin Veterans' Home in King. In 1986, she took a leave of absence from her job to put the events of 1977 in better perspective, she said. In an interview published by the *Appleton Post-Crescent*, she described her feelings at the time of the murder:

"I didn't have the words to explain what happened to me. The things Bob did to me, I just locked them away. The memories are tripping over each other to get to the forefront on my conscious mind.

"He would call every day to needle me, to harass me. He said he would take the girls, get the farm and I would get nothing. And I believed it because he always got his own way. I believed no one was going to help me.

"I knew things would get worse if he had free rein with them (the children.) All of that was just weighing so heavily on my mind. We were in this life-and-death struggle over the kids. The only thing on my mind was to stop him from hurting them anymore."

Jennifer's story was sold for book and movie rights to brothers Steve and George Englund of California. In writing his book called *Man Slaughter*, Steve Englund, who grew up in Waupaca, began with the premise that Jennifer was a classic battered woman, but his research changed his mind. Relying heavily on interviews with Cherie Mercer, Patri's lover, Englund said he began to see the abusing husband as a decent man. He suggested Eisenberg used the battered woman image as a ploy, first asking Jennifer to list all of her husband's failings.

"On material such as this, carefully molded by the media, Bob Patri shortly became synonymous with Satan the length and breadth of Wisconsin," Englund wrote. "It seems to me that her journey toward wholeness is severely impeded, not so much by the murderous violence of March 25 as by the systematic duplicity thereafter.... Jen is thus in profound ways ever with her Bob; the myth of his meanness is the necessary prop to her mythic role of 'classic case,' which is paradoxically both her emancipation and her imprisonment."

By the early 1990s, Jennifer Patri had changed her name and moved to Madison. She resurfaced briefly in an unsuccessful effort at getting more publicity for her case and she still seemed to have difficulty coping with life.

In his book, Englund quotes Jennifer as saying the trial was "just a game and the side that played the best won but it didn't have much to do with truth or justice." Was Jennifer Patri a classic battered woman driven to murder to escape years of torture and abuse? Or was the battered-woman image merely the creation of an effective defense attorney?

9
Poison and Lies
Madison, 1977

She was beautiful and knew how to get her way with men. She worked at a massage parlor and studied biochemistry. Those diverse interests would merge in one of the strangest murder cases in Wisconsin history.

On Christmas morning of 1977, Gerald Davies had a gift for Madison police officers. He walked into the City-County Building about 10:30 a.m. and told officers he had helped a twenty-five-year-old woman named Barbara Hoffman dispose of a body.

The thirty-one-year-old Davies, a shipping clerk at the University of Wisconsin-Madison, led detectives to the Blackhawk Ski Club northwest of Middleton, where they found the nude body of Harry B. Berge Jr., age fifty-two. He had died of head injuries. Davies told detectives that Hoffman had shown him a sheet-wrapped corpse behind her State Street apartment building about 4:00 a.m. on Christmas Eve day. They dragged the body to his car and he helped her take it out in the country.

Hoffman, a student and keypunch operator who also had worked at a Madison massage parlor, had told Davies she found Berge's body in her apartment three days earlier. But Berge, who worked at the Uniroyal plant in Stoughton, had attended a work Christmas party on December 22. He told his coworkers he had an appointment later.

In 1975, Hoffman had sued the city over its sexual massage ordinance, which she claimed violated her constitutional rights of freedom of expression and privacy. Her boss, William Grover Garrott, was the first massage parlor operator prosecuted under the ordinance.

By mid-January, detectives had discovered the motive. Hoffman had taken out a $34,500 life insurance policy on Berge under the alias of Linda Millar. She had Millar's mail sent to Davies' Park Street address. Hoffman also was joint owner of property Berge owned in Stoughton.

On Valentine's Day, Davies slipped a valentine's card under Hoffman's door. Two days later, he testified against her at a preliminary hearing.

Detectives appeared to have an open-and-shut case. They had a body, a motive and a key witness. But it wouldn't be that easy. Before Hoffman's scheduled arraignment on April 6, Davies was dead in his bathtub of an apparent self-inflicted drug overdose. Worse yet, he wrote letters before his death that retracted his prior confession.

"I want to write these letters because I want to set the record straight," he wrote in letters to the *Wisconsin State Journal* and his lawyer, Donald Eisenberg. "I was scared, I was jealous, Barb is innocent and I wrecked her life. All those stories I told about Barb are false.

"She never had anything to do with a body at all. She never did. I went crazy, I was so scared, the police scared me. I was crazy and I didn't know what I was saying.

"Then I had to keep telling the same story or they would charge me with a crime. Now they did it to Barb instead and I don't know what to do anymore except tell the truth.

"I'm not crazy anymore and I'm not scared. I want to tell the truth, I'm not afraid of going to jail. Barb never had anything to do with a body at all. I swear it and they can do what they want to me."

An empty bottle of Valium, an antidepressant drug, was found in Davies' apartment. His body was found by a building manager checking a neighbor's complaint about a noisy fan in Davies' bathroom.

Eisenberg moved for dismissal of the murder against his client due to extensive pre-trial publicity. The motion was denied by Dane County Circuit Judge P. Charles Jones.

Within weeks, however, a new development seemed to tie together the deaths of both Berge and Davies. Autopsy results indicated both men had died of cyanide poisoning. Berge apparently had swallowed thirty-seven times what is considered a lethal dose while Davies had ingested twice the amount required for a lethal dose.

Dane County Coroner Clyde Chamberlain said the blows to Berge's head, face and neck originally thought to have caused his death could have been caused by violent convulsions in reaction to cyanide poisoning.

When Davies died, Hoffman was free on $15,000 cash bail posted by her parents. A year earlier, she had bought a $750,000 insurance policy

Wisconsin State Journal file photo

Barbara Hoffman sits next to attorney Donald Eisenberg at her June 1980 trial.

on his life. That policy lapsed in March 1978. but later that month Davies took out three new policies totaling $20,000 on his life and naming Hoffman as his fiancée and beneficiary. He had asked about policies for $3 million and $1 million.

In January, shortly after Hoffman was charged with Berge's murder, Madison attorney Charles Giesen told the district attorney's office he had information about the murder that he would trade for reduced charges against four of his clients.

The previous year, Hoffman, who maintained a 3.9 grade point average, had taken a biochemistry course at the UW-Madison that included discussion of the toxic effect of cyanide on humans. A quarter pound of potassium cyanide was missing and presumed stolen from the university's biochemistry building between November 1976 and March 1978.

In May 1977, Garrott, the operator of the massage parlor where Hoffman worked, told Giesen of Hoffman's murder plot. Garrott said she planned to marry Davies, take him to Mexico, poison him on their honeymoon and cremate the body. Then she would collect the insurance money. Her plan was to use the cyanide to grow botulism spores. Garrott told her she would never get away with it.

On May 10, 1977, a shipment of cyanide was sent from Laabs Inc., a Milwaukee chemical company, to Davies' apartment.

In November 1978, courthouse observers were stunned when the district attorney's office dismissed the first-degree murder charge against Hoffman for killing Berge. Outside the courtroom, Eisenberg shouted at a police officer who immediately arrested her on two new charges of killing both Berge and Davies. The charges came after a lengthy secret John Doe investigation.

In Feburary 1980, Jan's Health Studio, the massage parlor where Hoffman worked, had reopened on Regent Street as a sexual counseling service. It quickly was shut down again by restraining orders.

After repeated delays, the trial finally began in June 1980. Garrott was a key witness but his cooperation came at a price. He had agreed to cooperate as part of a plea bargain for Samuel Cerro, who was convicted of dealing cocaine and sentenced to six months in jail. He was allowed to plead guilty to four commercial gambling charges for football bets and fifty-one other gambling counts against him were dropped. Eisenberg's law firm represented both Cerro and Hoffman, a conflict-of-interest that ultimately would lead to Eisenberg's disbarment in Wisconsin.

A key piece of evidence was blood matching that of Berge found in a snowbank behind Hoffman's State Street apartment. No blood was found inside the apartment.

Hoffman's parents testified she was with them when he supposedly poisoned Berge and Davies. Robert Hoffman, a mechanical design engineer from Park Ridge, Illinois, testified he picked up his daughter on Dec. 22 to take her home for Christmas. He said she returned on Christmas Day.

After deliberating nearly nine hours, jurors found Hoffman guilty of Berge's death but not guilty of killing Davies. Eisenberg filed an appeal based on the fact that she was tried for both murders simultaneously.

"She's a tough lady," he said. "She doesn't give up and neither do I."

On July 1, 1980, Judge Michael Torphy sentenced Hoffman to life in prison for killing Berge. Hoffman broke her silence to declare her innocence.

"I did not commit the crime of which I was accused and of which I was convicted," she said. "That's all I can say."

Torphy denied a motion by Eisenberg that she be freed pending appeals.

"A first-degree murderer is the best parole risk there is," Eisenberg argued. "Murderers don't run."

Tension between prosecutors and the defense attorneys over the difficult case didn't end with Hoffman's conviction and sentencing. Doyle said Eisenberg should be investigated for representing clients with conflicting interests.

"I think the district attorney should investigate his facts before he flows with oral diarrhea of the mouth," Eisenberg shot back.

But Doyle, who later became attorney general, was proven right when Eisenberg was disbarred for his actions in another case.

Buoyed by their daughter's acquittal of killing Davies, Hoffman's parents filed a claim for the $20,000 in life insurance he had put in her name.

In 1981, Eisenberg argued before the Appeals Court that it was prejudicial to try Hoffman on two murder charges at once. But the court disagreed and upheld her conviction.

Three years later, Eisenberg's license was suspended for six months by the Wisconsin Supreme Court and he was ordered to pay nearly $10,000 for his ethical conflict in representing both Hoffman and Cerro. It had been Cerro's plea bargain that led to Garrott's testimony against Hoffman.

In 1989, Eisenberg's license to practice law in Wisconsin was revoked because he speculated in a television interview that another client, Lawrencia Bembenek, was guilty.

In a 1996 effort to reinstate his license, Eisenberg, then 63, was no longer the cocky, flamboyant defense lawyer he once had been. He had battled cancer and operated a private investigation and process-serving business in Orlando, Florida. Before the Board of Attorneys Professional Responsibility, Eisenberg argued that he had changed.

"I was a bad winner, let's face it," he said. "When I won, and I loved to win, I would crow. I wish I hadn't done it."

But the board wasn't convinced and, based upon its recommendation, state Supreme Court rejected Eisenberg's plea for reinstatement. The board said he had failed to repay any of the fee he charged Hoffman despite the conflict of interest.

In 1991 after serving 11 years in prison, Hoffman's application for parole was denied. The beautiful former student and massage therapist still was buying a lot of cosmetics at Taycheedah. She had become a born-again Christian and continued her education in prison through independent-learning courses.

10

The Keys to her Heart

Lac du Flambeau, 1930

San Francisco Police Detective James Johnson was thumbing through the July 1931 issue of *True Detective* magazine when he came across a story about George "Jiggs" Perry written by *Rhinelander Daily News* reporter Jack Cory. Perry, it seemed, was wanted for murdering one of several women he married. Johnson read part of the story but stopped when he spotted a picture of Perry. He motioned for inspectors Robert Hughes and A.P. James to come over and take a look.

"That's the same man we questioned two months ago in connection with an automobile accident," he said, pointing at the picture. "I'm sure of it."

The detectives checked an address and then rushed out to arrest a man they believed could be a Wisconsin killer. But they didn't find Perry. Instead, they arrested Frank Moran, who claimed he knew nothing about the Wisconsin slaying.

During the year he had been on the run, Perry had gained notoriety as "the marrying brakeman." A former railroad employee, he had married and deserted more than a half dozen women from Cleveland to California.

On September 30, 1930, Henry St. Germaine, a watchtower attendant at the Lac du Flambeau Indian reservation, was walking in the woods when his dog led him to what looked at first like a pile of rumpled clothing.

"I didn't want to believe it was a body," he said later. "It looked more like a scarecrow."

But it was a body — the body of Cora Belle Hackett, in fact — one of the many wives of Jiggs Perry. A warrant was issued a week later for Perry's arrest. He was tracked to Cleveland, where another wife was discovered. The trail then led to southern Illinois, where still another wife turned up. Authorities lost Perry's trail, however, in Blytheville, Arkansas, where they found yet another woman he had married.

Cora Belle had disappeared July 6, 1930, while she and Perry, her new husband, were honeymooning at the Crawling Lake Resort, owned by William Parker in Vilas County. Perry borrowed a rifle from Parker, then the couple left for a while. Perry returned without his bride, paid the bill and left with her luggage in her car.

Katherine Gebhardt, his wife in Cleveland, got a call from him the next day asking if he could come home. He was in Racine and had car trouble. He told her that his Aunt Cora had given him some belongings and her car. Gebhardt reluctantly agreed that Perry could return home but she didn't get along very well with him. By the end of July, Perry left Cleveland and was on the run again.

Cora Belle, who worked selling lifetime memberships to Chicago's Art Institute, had been widowed twice. She had been married to a Milwaukee banker and, later, to a U.S. Secret Service agent. She met Perry by an-

Wisconsin State Journal archives

George "Jiggs" Perry

swering his blind ad in a Chicago newspaper for a traveling companion. Perry told her he was the outcast son of a wealthy family and asked her to marry him. She agreed to finance their honeymoon.

When the inspectors in San Francisco came to arrest Moran that day in July 1931, they weren't willing to take Moran's word for it that he wasn't the fugitive Perry. They contacted the Vilas County sheriff at Eagle River to tell him of the capture. The sheriff began the process of trying to determine whether Moran actually was the missing killer.

After viewing a photo of Moran, the sheriff was convinced the man in custody probably was Perry. He sent a warrant by air mail to San Francisco, then arranged a train trip to the West Coast. Accompanying him to aid in positive identification was resort owner Parker, who knew Perry well.

When he was taken into custody, Moran was employed as business manager for the International Brotherhood, a welfare agency. He had married Anna Gutiérrez after a whirlwind courtship.

The sheriff and Parker visited Moran's cell and he still denied that he was Perry. Parker noticed, however, that Moran kept referring to his California jailers as "them guys," a midwestern expression. When Parker pointed it out, Perry admitted his true identity.

"I did not kill Cora Hackett," he said. "It's bad enough to be guilty of bigamy, non-support and many other crimes without being guilty of murder."

Reporters contacted Perry's only legal wife, Mary Perry of Milwaukee, and she could not believe her husband was guilty.

Several reporters were among the entourage escorting Perry by train back to Wisconsin and he was willing to give interviews, although for a while he insisted the reporters call him Moran.

"Oh, what's the use," he said finally. "I'm Perry and you know it. There's nothing I can do but take the raps. I'm guilty of bigamy, plenty guilty, but not of murder."

In fact, Perry had married seven women illegally within a little more than a year. On January 3, 1930, he married Katherine Gebhardt in a secret ceremony in Chicago. Using the same ruse, he would later use to lure Cora Belle Hackett, Perry told her he was heir to a fortune. For several months, she supported him with income from her seamstress job while he lounged around their Cleveland home and read the newspaper. In early June, he left for Chicago, saying he had some family business to settle.

On June 16, Perry married Cora Belle Hackett. In several letters to Gebhardt, he talked about his Aunt Cora and said he would be traveling with her to northern Wisconsin. In a letter to her best friend in Chicago, Cora Belle said she was extremely happy with her new husband.

When Perry called her on July 7, Gebhardt said he could return home. He arrived with Hackett's clothing, luggage and car. He seemed "extremely irritable," she said.

In late July, Gebhardt received a call from another woman who asked if she was married to Perry. Gebhardt told the other woman Perry was her husband.

"Why, he can't be!" the woman said. "He proposed to me and promised me $18,000 after we were married in Chicago."

The phone call led to a bitter argument between Gebhardt and Perry and Perry departed. He landed in Eldorado, Illinois, where he married Lida Downey. That ceremony was quickly followed by another marriage to Elizabeth Manson of Harrisburg, Illinois. Perry began to worry that he had two wives living too close together so he was on the run again.

In Blytheville, Arkansas, Perry put Hackett's car in storage as collateral for a $150 loan and married Dorothy Davis before moving on to St.

Louis, where he married Harriet Milligan after one of his trademark whirl-wind courtships. Perry still used his own name but claimed he was from New Orleans. Milligan noticed Perry's name mentioned in a newspaper article about the Hackett case. She pointed it out to him and he was on the run once again, this time to San Francisco.

In Milwaukee, the original Mrs. Perry hoped the sheriff would bring her husband by to see her and their three children on the way back to Eagle River.

"I would like to see him," she said. "Only then would I believe it is really Jiggs. I have been awake for every hour of the night for the past two weeks, worrying."

But the entourage bypassed Milwaukee and Perry was placed in the Vilas County Jail. On June 5, he pleaded innocent to first degree murder.

The master philanderer turned to his stable of wives for help, asking each of them to come up with his bail. "Write me, and if you can, help me," he wrote to Anna Gutiérrez. None of the wives responded. In Cleveland, Katherine Gebhardt filed for divorce.

Perry appealed to Milwaukee attorney John Dolan to represent him. Dolan and Perry once worked together at a moving and storage company.

"Am not guilty of this crime I am accused of and, with the help of a good attorney, can be freed," he wrote. Dolan agreed to take the case.

"Perry may be the world's greatest lover but he certainly is no killer," Dolan announced after meeting with his new client. Accompanying him to Eagle River were Mary Perry and her children.

"Mary, Mary, Mary," Perry greeted his original wife, who carried their twenty-one-month-old daughter, Grace, in her arms. "Hello, Dad," said son Danny while their other son, Johnny, bragged to his father about fistfights he had with reporters and photographers who lurked outside the family's Milwaukee home.

"Why did you marry all those women?" Mary wanted to know. Perry just hung his head. "Well," he said, followed by a long silence. Finally, she decided to change the subject. "I brought you some oranges, George."

With his head held high and shoulders back, Perry strutted into the courtroom when the trial began on July 30. He had an ironclad alibi, he had bragged to reporters. But Perry soon became shaken when Dr. E. W. Miloslavich, a Milwaukee pathologist, held up Cora Belle's skull, describing how she had been shot once through the left side of her head. Perry's face twitched and he clenched his fists. The ironclad alibi fell apart when witnesses from Minocqua refused to testify on his behalf.

The most damaging testimony was provided by Mrs. Michael Dever, wife of a Chicago police officer, who said she recognized Perry as the man she saw on July 6, 1931, standing next to a car parked along the roadside near where the body was found. Katherine Gebhardt also testified for the prosecution and Perry shifted nervously when she described his claims of great wealth.

Perry took the stand in his own defense and the courtroom went into an uproar with the first question by Dolan.

"Are you married?" the attorney asked.

"Yes," Perry replied.

Perry claimed he had told Cora Belle the truth, that they weren't really married, and she was disappointed, not angry. She said they couldn't live together anymore. But she generously agreed to give him her car and some of her clothing for his real wife. They parted on the roadside at the Indian reservation and someone else must have killed her, according to the story.

"I didn't know Cora Belle was dead," Perry said, feigning great sincerity. "I cried and paced the floor because I was married to Katherine. I was sorry for that mix-up and wanted to get home."

During his testimony, of course, Perry must have lost track of his wives, forgetting that he actually was married only to Mary, who maintained a vigil with the children in the courtroom to show support for him. The all-male jury didn't buy Perry's flimsy tale. He collapsed in his chair when the jury returned a guilty verdict, then went on a petulant hunger strike in jail.

He was sentenced to life in prison and carted off to Waupun state prison, handcuffed to insane killer Phil Block and John Adams, a convicted burglar.

"I'm sure Mr. Perry is innocent," said the faithful Mary after the trial. "Someone else killed her, not Mr. Perry."

Mary Perry said she would have to remain on welfare because the children were too young to work and she couldn't leave them alone.

Like William Coffey, Perry bragged of his power over women to get them to do his bidding. He once invited his nephew to join him in the love scam business.

"It's all a game," he said. "Easy money. Women fall for the love stuff and then you can get their money. Give me two weeks with any woman and she will give me the keys to her heart."

11

Body in a Hot Furnace
Stoughton, 1983

Ruth Homberg knew something was amiss with her marriage. The loving relationship she had just a couple years earlier with her husband, Gary, had deteriorated. The palatial home they shared in the town of Dunkirk near Stoughton seemed cold to her now and the dreams they had nurtured were just a distant memory. Ruth had heard rumors that Gary might be having an affair with another woman.

During the summer of 1983, Ruth sometimes burst into tears on her job at Millfab in Stoughton, a business in which she and her husband shared a minority ownership. Gary Homberg also was company president.

"She was very upset with domestic problems and the way things were going at work," said her co-worker and friend, Bonnie Sampson.

On Friday night, November 4, 1983, Gary and Ruth Homberg spent the evening with friends, Carlton and Kenlynn Pokrandt. They had dinner and danced at the Essen Haus, a German restaurant in Madison. Gary, a German immigrant, felt comfortable in surroundings that echoed some aspects of his native land.

The evening went better than most, but didn't ease Ruth's concerns about her husband. The two couples returned to Stoughton and the Pokrandts invited the Hombergs inside their Stoughton home for a drink. When Carlton and Gary left the room for a moment, Ruth seized the opportunity. She asked Kenlynn whether she knew anything about Gary's possible involvement with another woman.

"I have to know what's going on," Ruth pleaded with her friend. Kenlynn told Ruth she had heard rumors that Gary was having an affair with Sharon Jacobson Nordness, Ruth's daughter-in-law. Despite her suspicions, Ruth was stunned by Kenlynn's confirmation of them. To Kenlynn, Ruth looked shocked and tears welled in her eyes.

When the Hombergs arrived home, Ruth decided to confront her husband directly. While he was in the bathroom, she confronted him, demanding to know if the rumors were true. . . .

What happened next is known only to Gary Homberg. But the outing with the Pokrandts would be the last time anyone saw Ruth alive. Homberg would say later that his wife left him. Although her body never was found, a jury later convicted Homberg of murdering his wife — the first murder conviction without a body in Wisconsin history.

Wisconsin State Journal file photo

Ruth Homberg

About 6:30 a.m. the following morning, Sharon Jacobson Nordness received a call from her lover, Gary Homberg. He told her to meet him at the Dane County Regional Airport in a half hour.

Nordness circled the parking lot twice before she spotted Homberg driving into the lot in his wife's car. Homberg parked the car in a long-term parking area, then got in Nordness' car and told her to drive him home but to take a circuitous route in getting there.

On the drive back to Stoughton, Homberg told Nordness about the confrontation he had the night before with Ruth. He told her: "Ruthie's gone and she's not coming back."

"She said she was going to call Dan Wahlin," Homberg told her. Wahlin was the majority owner of Millfab and Ruth threatened to tell Wahlin about the hundreds of thousands of dollars she knew Gary had embezzled from the company.

Gary warned Nordness to keep Ruth's disappearance a secret because she was now an accomplice to the murder. "You're an accessory," he told her. "If I go to jail, you go to jail."

"What are you going to do with Ruthie's body?" Sharon asked. "Throw her in the furnace?"

"You don't need to know that," he snapped. "They (the police) don't have a body. There is no body."

Gary Homberg was four years old when his father, a German shoemaker, was killed in the Allied bombing of Berlin. He went to vocational school, where he studied to be a tailor, but dreamed of seeking his fortune in America.

He immigrated to Canada, where he worked as a lumberjack. He eventually came to the United States to take a job training horses in Ohio. He joined the Air Force and was stationed at Truax Field in Madison.

After his discharge, Homberg decided to settle in Madison, where he met and married his first wife, Sara. They divorced in 1973 and Sara blamed the breakup on Gary's devotion to his career. He had been hired as a salesman for Millfab, a wood processing company in Stoughton. In three years, Homberg was named company president.

Later, Homberg would express an intense vindictiveness toward his first wife, often referring to her as "The Pig."

After Ruth Nordness came to work at Millfab in 1975, it wasn't long before she fell in love with the company president. Like Gary Homberg, she was divorced. He had two children by his first marriage; she had three from hers. They married a year later and received forty acres of land near Stoughton as a wedding gift from her parents.

A year before the disappearance of Ruth Homberg, the affair between Homberg and Nordness began with a simple kiss in the office. Nordness was unhappy in her marriage and began to envy Ruth Homberg's lifestyle. She could barely conceal her jealousy when she and Ruth's daughter, Roxanne, accompanied Ruth on a Florida vacation. Sharon found Gary attractive and didn't repel his advances.

By the fall of 1982, the two were lovers and often arranged secret rendezvous at hotels in the Madison area and traveled secretly to Denver. They rented rooms at the posh Edgewater Hotel and, later, after Sharon separated from her husband, Homberg rented a condominium for her in the upscale Foxwood Hills development along Moorland Road in Madison.

Nordness wanted more than just their illicit affair. She urged Gary to divorce Ruth or get rid of her somehow. Gary said a divorce was out of the question.

"Ruthie could nail me to the cross," he said, with information about the money he was stealing from the company.

But Gary began to fantasize about killing his wife. He became intrigued with how he could commit the perfect crime.

"It kind of intrigued him," Sharon later would say at Homberg's murder trial. "It was a challenge. He thought he could do it."

He decided the best way would be to grind up an overdose of sleeping pills and put them in a drink. When Ruth passed out, he would put her in the driver's seat of her car in the garage and turn on the engine, making her death look like a suicide.

When he actually tried the scheme, however, the plan failed because Ruth didn't pass out.

The second time, however, Homberg's plan to get rid of his wife succeeded and now all that was left was to cover up the crime. Later that Saturday, about 5:00 p.m., he called the police to report his wife missing, saying he was supposed to meet her for lunch and was worried when she didn't show up.

Relatives of Ruth Homberg found it odd that Gary didn't call them to ask if they had seen Ruth before reporting her disappearance to police. And the night before, Ruth had made plans with Kenlynn Pokrandt to take Ruth's mother to lunch and a church bazaar on Saturday afternoon.

On Monday, Beverly DeGront was scheduled to make her regular visit to clean the sprawling Homberg home. Before leaving home, DeGront received a call from Sharon Nordness.

"You don't have to come and clean today," Nordness told her. "Ruth is out of town and we don't know when she'll be back."

Ruth Homberg often told the cleaning lady that she knew the house better than its occupants. When DeGront arrived to clean a week later, she couldn't help making a careful inspection.

"I was convinced in my mind that Ruth would not just leave," DeGront said later. The cleaning woman knew that Ruth was close to her parents, Art and Sally Nelson, and planned to take care of them as they grew older.

When she walked into Ruth's bathroom, DeGront said, "I was frightened. I felt like someone was with me."

But more than just an eerie feeling confirmed DeGront's suspicions that Ruth had met with foul play. The only thing missing was Ruth's jewelry, which she usually kept on a vanity. DeGront knew Ruth was very particular about her appearance and couldn't believe she would leave behind her make-up, curling iron and hair dryer.

When she looked out the window, the cleaning woman saw the ground was covered with leaves except in one area. She wondered whether Ruth was buried there. Police later checked the area but found nothing.

In 1984 Sharon Nordness was divorced from her husband. Both she and Gary now were free to marry but it would never be. Instead of enhancing their relationship, the murder became a weight upon it. Nordness began to fear Gary.

"I felt I would be harmed if I talked," she said. "Just like Ruthie was."

Sharon and Gary split up. Sharon eventually remarried but Gary left Millfab and headed west. Ruth Homberg's jewelry had been missing since her disappearance and Gary told police she must have taken it with

Wisconsin State Journal file photo

Deputies take Gary Homburg into custody at the Dane County Regional Airport.

her. A year later, however, Gary sold her bracelet on consignment to a Madison company and gave a gold choker to a woman in Denver.

The same year, he testified at a hearing to appoint a receiver for Ruth's property that she owned no expensive jewelry and that he made no profit from selling anything she owned. In 1987, Homberg sold the 40-acre estate on Leslie Road.

Although there was no hard evidence that Ruth Homberg had been murdered, Dane County Detective Merle Ziegler became convinced she had met with foul play. As the years went by, the inconsistencies about the case began to grow.

Ziegler and other deputies searched the Homberg estate for Ruth's body. They pumped the septic tank and also searched the grounds of the

Stoughton Conservation Club and the shores of the Yahara River.

"We looked everywhere we could think of," Ziegler said. "It was an almost insurmountable task but we did our best. But we couldn't come up with anything."

By the spring of 1987, however, Ziegler had amassed circumstantial evidence that pointed to Homberg as a possible suspect. But that wasn't Homberg's only problem. In 1986, the state Department of Revenue began a probe of Millfab's finances and investigator Donald Murphy eventually uncovered evidence that Homberg embezzled more than $600,000 from the company.

A secret John Doe probe was conducted in April to gather evidence in the murder case. Among the witnesses called to testify was Sharon Jacobson Nordness, Homberg's former lover. Sharon said she knew nothing about Gary Homberg's possible murder of his wife.

Without any physical evidence and with Sharon's testimony, the murder case against Homberg remained weak. But the embezzlement case was stronger. Days after the John Doe investigation ended, papers were filed to extradite Homberg from California to face tax fraud and embezzlement charges in Madison. At the time, Homberg was managing a lumberyard in Fontana, earning an annual salary of $100,000.

The lengthy investigation had discovered that Homberg, between 1982 and 1986, issued himself 48 Millfab checks ranging in amounts from under $2,000 to more than $27,000, then disguised the checks in the company's record books as payments to suppliers from the raw materials account. The embezzlement of more than $600,000 helped Ruth and Gary Homberg finance their extravagant lifestyle.

"No wonder the company was broke," said a shocked Dan Wahlin when he learned of the massive embezzlement scheme.

Ruth Homberg's son, Richard Nordness, was pleased that his ex-stepfather and ex-wife's lover finally was in custody.

"At last, maybe we can get some answers," he said.

Richard Nordness had known about his wife's affair with Gary long before his mother found out about it. He had discovered a letter from Gary to Sharon in his wife's purse, extolling her virtues as a lover.

Homberg was jailed on $300,000 cash bail until the amount was lowered several months later and he was permitted by the court to resume his job managing the California lumberyard.

By the end of the year, Homberg pleaded no contest to reduced charges of two counts of embezzlement and two counts of tax fraud involving about $245,000 in company funds. Dane County Judge Robert Pekowsky ordered a pre-sentence review and allowed Homberg to remain free on bond. With the convictions, he faced fines up to $40,000 and thirty years in prison.

Homberg was sentenced to seven years in prison on the embezzlement and fraud convictions and he returned to Wisconsin. Police finally had Homberg cold on the embezzlement but Ziegler wondered whether he would ever come to trial for the murder of his wife. He conferred with veteran prosecutor John Burr. How could they charge him with murder without a body? It was unprecedented.

Yet Ziegler and other sheriff's investigators had done everything humanly possible to find Ruth Homberg's remains. One thing the detective was sure of: She definitely was no longer alive.

By spring, however, a major break in the case caused Ziegler and Burr to bring Homberg to trial even without a body. Sharon Jacobson Nordness had agreed to talk under a grant of immunity from prosecution. Despite her earlier lies to the John Doe grand jury, now she changed her story about her ride with Homberg back to Stoughton that Saturday morning.

"He said something to the effect that he killed her and that she wasn't coming back, that it happened quickly," Nordness testified at a preliminary hearing. Homberg was charged with first-degree murder and held on $100,000 bail.

It would be more than a year, however, before the case came to trial in October 1989. Prosecutors offered Homberg a deal, saying they would reduce the charge if he pleaded guilty. "I didn't do it," he replied.

In January 1989, assistant public defender Dennis Burke moved for dismissal of the murder charges against Homberg. Burke charged prosecutors with unreasonable delays in providing him with evidence about the case. He said seven months had passed since the district attorney's office agreed to provide more than 3,500 pages of police reports about the case.

As expected, the key witness at the trial was Sharon Jacobson Nordness. She described her ride with Homberg and the events on that Saturday morning. During cross-examination, however, Burke launched a severe attack on her credibility, pointing out that her testimony was inconsistent with earlier testimony she had given about the case.

Other important witnesses included Ziegler, Richard Nordness and cleaning woman Beverly DeGront.

To refute Sharon's testimony, Burke called Gary Lintvedt, who dated her during the summer of 1984 when she was breaking off her relationship with Homberg. Lintvedt said she never expressed any fears of Gary.

Lintvedt said he had heard that Ruth Homberg once walked in to discover Gary and Sharon in bed together. But Lintvedt said he couldn't recall whether Sharon had told him that or whether it was a rumor he had heard.

Prosecutor John Burr also brought out the inconsistencies in

Homberg's behavior concerning his wife's jewelry and in reporting her disappearance. Witnesses were asked if they saw Ruth Homberg at the funerals of her parents, who died in 1988.

But the state's case clearly rested on the testimony of Sharon Jacobson Nordness. Prosecutors could offer absolutely no physical evidence. There were no hairs or fibers linking Homberg to his wife's murder and, without a body, some doubt remained about whether she actually had been killed.

Would the jury believe Sharon's story? Or would they give weight to Burke's argument that she had lied before about the case? Burke decided not to call Homberg to testify in his own defense.

In the end, the testimony was enough for the jury to convict Homberg of first-degree murder in the unprecedented case and he was sentenced to life imprisonment.

Despite the conviction, a major loose end remained. Judge Gerald Nichol offered to reduce Homberg's sentence if he revealed the location of Ruth's body.

"I haven't killed Ruthie and I haven't killed anyone else," Homberg told the judge. "How can a person show remorse when he hasn't done anything wrong?"

Two years later, the Appeals Court upheld the conviction, ruling that "the jury heard overwhelming evidence that Homberg intended to get rid of his wife, and that he did."

If the jury's decision was correct, Gary Homberg had dreamed about committing the perfect crime. He had planned how to kill his wife and dispose of her body where no one would find it, But the flaw in his perfect scheme came when he had to dispose of her quickly and in his failure to cover up the crime. Many Stoughton residents believe Ruth's body ended up in the furnace at Millfab, capable of generating heat of more than 2,500 degrees.

12

A Stick and a Haystack
Portage, 1922

His sister's autumn romance didn't set well with Hartwell Farwell. Why couldn't she leave well enough alone?

Farwell and his sister, Alice, had lived together on the Dane County farm in the town of Vienna for decades. They both owned the farm equally. He couldn't understand why a woman in her fifties suddenly would want a beau.

Besides that, Farwell had a particular dislike for Theophil Hosten, the man Alice had decided to date. Hosten had worked on the Farwell farm for nine years and left only after frequent arguments with Farwell, his boss. Hosten, who called Alice "my girl," had told his friends that Alice was tired of living on the family farm and wanted to leave. She and Hosten planned to buy a chicken farm of their own.

Farwell had disdain for all his workers and that one would have the audacity to begin dating his sister particularly infuriated him. What if Hosten married his sister and moved in with them? Would he then have equal rights to the farm?

These thoughts no doubt were running through his head one evening in early January 1922 when Hosten stopped by the farm to see Alice. Several versions of the events that followed were offered by Farwell and his sister but there's no question that Hosten ended up with two fatal .32-caliber bullet wounds in his head.

A few days later, Dr. Charles Curtiss of Portage was driving by a deserted marsh about three miles from Portage when he noticed a burning haystack. When he stopped to take a closer look, he noticed a section of hay fall way to reveal some kind of object in the stack. Curtiss managed to drag a body from the flames.

The body appeared almost impossible to identify. Part of the face was burned away and one leg had been consumed by flames. Although the body was charred, investigators could tell the victim hadn't died in the fire. He was killed by a bullet that passed through his right eye into his head. Another bullet wound was found in a cheek.

He was wearing a sheepskin coat and khaki shirt, indicating he may have been a soldier. The body had been placed in gunny sacks.

The *Wisconsin State Journal* called the case "the most baffling mystery in that section of the state." But authorities wouldn't be baffled very long.

A key with the inscription "E.1.6." matched a padlock on a small garage in the town of Windsor owned by Hosten, who by this time had been reported missing.

After authorities questioned acquaintances of Hosten and his two roommates, it wasn't difficult to pinpoint a suspect. When they found tire tracks in the snow matching the tires on Farwell's car, it clinched the case and they brought Farwell in for questioning.

He readily confessed, admitting that he shot Hosten about 7:00 p.m. or 8:00 p.m. on January 10. He left him in a wooded area across the road for a couple hours, then carried the body to his barn. The next night, he moved the body again to a tobacco shed. On January 12, Farwell loaded the body into his car, intending to dump it somewhere in Madison. Instead, he headed in the other direction. When he spotted the haystack, he decided that was as good a place as any to get rid of Hosten once and for all. Farwell even admitted he had Hosten's watch and chain in his room. A spot of blood was found near the doorway of Farwell's hog barn and marks on the floor indicated something had been dragged across there.

Farwell spent his fiftieth birthday confined in the Dane County Jail and Sheriff William McCormick was congratulated on a quick resolution of the case.

For a short time, authorities thought Farwell might have had an accomplice. A pair of youths had been skating on a pond near Poynette. They claimed to have seen Farwell and another man drive up. They said Farwell got out of his car and peered through a hole in the ice, perhaps looking for a place to dump the body. The story proved to be mere gossip.

The confession might have cleared the case easily but Farwell added a bombshell. He said he had shot Hosten in self-defense. He said he heard a noise outside and went out to investigate. He saw Hosten move toward him carrying a stick, making it look like he had a gun. Hosten fired three times, missing on the first shot.

Meanwhile, Alice Farwell offered several versions of what occurred that night to police.

"I don't know why I said no before (but) I did see Phil," she said. "I was washing dishes when I heard a tap on the window. It was about 7:00 or 7:30. I looked out but saw nothing and then went into the front room without seeing anything.

"I went back and washed the dishes. Then I took the dish water and went out through the kitchen door to throw it out. I saw Phil just around the corner. I went on toward him and told him to go away because my brother was here. He did not embrace me and we did not touch either.

"My brother was upstairs. I heard the door on the opposite side of the house open and I went back in the way I had come. I didn't hear any shots fired. I know that my brother saw Phil had come but don't know what happened.

"I did tell the sheriff that I didn't remember a time when five shots were fired at Phil as he passed the house. But now I'll admit I heard the shots at that time. Of course, I can't say for sure that it was my brother."

Farwell's self-defense ploy didn't hold up very long because, at his preliminary hearing, Alice offered a different version. She said she had seen her boyfriend running away

Wisconsin State Journal archives

Hartwell Farwell

from her brother just before he was shot. Farwell was charged with first-degree murder.

The stick that looked like a shotgun was explained by Joe "Belgian Joe" Carlier, a friend of Hosten.

"Phil had a homemade cane, (made) out from some brush, that he always carried when he went to see his girl," Carlier said. "There was a bad dog along the way and it was for this reason that he carried the stick that night, the same as he always did."

By the time of the trial, Farwell was considering an insanity plea. He didn't fare well in jail and tottered into court, almost like he had trouble walking. He was suffering from lumbago, stomach trouble and a general breakdown.

Alice and her brother had tried to coordinate their stories. But District Attorney Ted Lewis had a more convincing version: He said Farwell had gone upstairs to fill an oil lamp. He looked out in the front yard and saw his sister with Hosten. He walked to a dresser, pulled out a loaded revolver and walked outside to shoot Hosten. After dragging the body to the woods, he milked the cows, apparently undisturbed by what had just occurred.

When Alice took the stand, she said Hosten had tapped on the window and motioned for her to join him outside. She said she warned Hosten that her brother was angry and he should leave, then went back inside and resumed her chores. Refuting her earlier testimony, she said she didn't see Hosten running away or the actual shooting.

Farwell continued to maintain that the shooting was in self-defense. But the stick Hosten was carrying had mysteriously disappeared. Farwell said he had cut it up because it was "strange" and he didn't want it around.

The prosecutor noted another inconsistency in Farwell's testimony. Farwell said he could see the eyes of his victim yet he couldn't distinguish a stick from a gun.

Alice, who had tried her best to help save her brother, once again came forward with damaging testimony. She told the court how Farwell once had chased Hosten with a pitchfork. In that incident, Hosten had returned and threatened Farwell with a shotgun.

The jury deliberated for forty-eight hours before finding Farwell guilty of the murder of Theophil Hosten. Farwell, a prominent farmer and trustee of the Windsor Congregational Church, was sentenced to seven years in prison.

Hartwell Farwell came by his protective attitude toward his sister naturally. His father, James, had discouraged Alice and her sisters from marrying. John Butler, another hired hand, earlier had set a date with Alice to get married but James Farwell intervened.

"I've got money enough to support my daughters and they don't need to marry for support," he told Butler. One of Alice's sisters married Ole Anderson despite her father's opposition. She wasn't allowed to attend James Farwell's funeral when he died a decade before the Hosten murder.

The murder didn't dampen Alice's romantic ardor nor did it cure her brother's jealousy. She married Harry G. Phillips but they were divorced in 1932. Her brother didn't shoot Phillips but he didn't like him any more than Hosten.

Before the divorce, Alice and Phillips fought in court three times, once over a bay horse that Phillips said was his. Phillips said that her brother Hartwell, then known as the "gray deacon of the township of Vienna" had put her up to it. Phillips, who acted as his own attorney, accused Hartwell of stealing produce from his farm and selling it but the judge said Hartwell had a right to visit the Phillips farm if his sister invited him.

13

Lessons out of School
Jefferson, 1994

For seventeen-year-old Douglas Vest Jr., it was a lesson he never expected to get in study hall at Jefferson High School.

A teacher's aide, Diane Borchardt, befriended him. Like many people going through the throes of a disintegrating marriage, Borchardt had to talk about it. Despite his youth, Vest could sympathize because his parents also had divorced. Worse yet, she kissed him and played on his emotions to get him to do what she wanted.

Not only was the marriage on the rocks, but Diane Borchardt was angry in early 1994. The previous fall, she had learned of her husband Ruben's longtime affair with Judy Frantz, the wife of the city manager. Now, a court had ordered her to move out of the family home on Bear Hole Road. She wanted revenge for the hurt that Ruben had caused her. She wanted more than revenge. She wanted to kill him.

The teacher's aide recruited Vest and two of his companions, seventeen-year-old Josh Yanke and sixteen-year-old Michael Maldonado in a plot to murder her husband. She promised them $20,000 in life insurance she would collect after his death, two cars and jewelry.

In the days before Easter, which fell on April 3, the Borchardts' marriage continued to grow in anger and violence. On Saturday of that weekend, she yelled at him as she pushed him out of her silk-screening shop known as Diane B's. According to the account of an employee, she told him he was scum and that she didn't want to see him. One time, she whispered, "You're dead."

After the shoving match, Diane Borchardt went to the police and reported that her husband was violent and had threatened her. Then she left town with her daughter, Regan, age fourteen.

Early the next morning, the three teenagers she recruited entered the Borchardt home on Bear Hole Road in the town of Jefferson. Diane Borchardt had given them six hundred dollars, a map of the home and instructions on how to get in. The assassins couldn't find the shop door that Diane Borchardt said would be unlocked so they entered the garage. They found Ruben Borchardt, a self-employed cabinet maker and screen printer, in the basement and shot him several times at close range. He died two hours later at Fort Atkinson Memorial Hospital.

Diane Borchardt wasn't in town but her alibi didn't hold up for long. Despite their marital differences, Diane Borchardt demanded to attend her estranged husband's funeral as a grieving widow. But Ruben Borchart's relatives already suspected she had a role in his death. Regan's half-sister, Brook Borchardt, age nineteen, immediately accused her stepmother of the murder. And Diane Borchardt refused to cooperate with investigators.

Over the summer, the probe into Ruben Borchardt's death moved slowly as Jefferson County District Attorney Linda Larson launched a John Doe investigation. Coroner Mark Schoenleber requested an inquest and detectives listened carefully to a 911 call from Borchardt's home, trying to isolate background noises. Divers searched a pond on the Borchardt property for the murder weapon — a sawed-off shotgun.

Larson's investigation focused on the teenagers, whom she believed had done the actual shooting and the effort ultimately paid off. Josh Yanke agreed to cooperate and was charged with second-degree intentional homicide in exchange for his testimony against the others. He told detectives that Maldonado was the triggerman, using a sawed-off shotgun he had bought in Milwaukee.

By fall, Vest, Maldonado and Diane Borchardt were charged with first-degree murder. Borchardt's uncle posted her $150,000 bail and she was free until the trial early the following year. Maldonado surrendered in early October in Harlan, Texas and was extradited to Wisconsin to face murder charges. A social worker described Maldonado, who had dropped out of school in seventh grade, as "a paid assassin" and "a moral deviant."

On October 10, Diane Borchardt was released from the Jefferson County Jail after her $150,000 bail was posted by Dean Pfister, an uncle from Bluffton, Indiana.

Investigators also arrested Shannon Johnson, an intimate friend of Borchardt's who was described as her lesbian lover. Johnson reportedly threatened the teenagers not to tell anyone about the murder plot or she would kill them. But the charges quickly were dropped against her, although she was a key witness during the trials.

Young Regan Borchardt was her mother's only defender. The girl had angrily made hang-up calls to Judy Frantz when she had learned

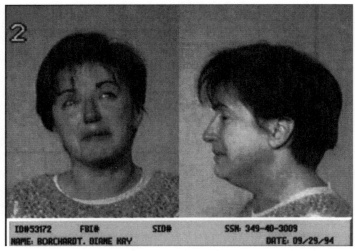

ID#53172   FBI#   SID#   SSN: 349-40-3009
NAME: BORCHARDT. DIANE KAY   DATE: 09/29/94

Jefferson County Sheriff's Department

Diane Borchardt's mug shots.

about her father's affair. Her father had been murdered and, now, she was about to lose her mother to prison.

"Please, Judge Ullsvik, believe my mom's innocence and send her home as soon as possible to be with me," she pleaded, sobbing in court.

After an emotional trial and despite her pleas of innocence, a jury convicted Diane Borchardt of the first-degree murder of her husband.

"I swear that I never did this," she told Judge John Ullsvik at her sentencing on August 1, 1995. "There's all kinds of evidence that would prove that I didn't."

But the jury already had decided her guilt and the judge agreed with the verdict.

"Evidence of her aiding and solicitation was overwhelming," he said, calling it "the greatest crime possible" and commenting that she was "more dangerous than Douglas Vest."

She received an automatic life sentence and Ullsvik set her earliest parole eligibility at forty years, when she would be 86 years old. Larson had requested that she not be eligible for parole until 2094, a century after Ruben Borchardt's murder. Maldonado's earliest parole date is in fifty years while Vest received an earliest parole date of twenty-five years.

"I think she should have gotten life without parole or the death penalty, that's what she gave my dad," said Brook Borchardt-Fisher — still bitter over losing her father.

The Borchardt slaying was similar to an East Coast case in which a teacher recruited teenagers for murder and Hollywood smelled potential. A TV mini-series, "Seduced by Madness: The Diane Borchardt Story" starring Ann-Margret was shown by NBC in early 1996. Larson and other key figures in the case said the four-hour series was mostly factual with a few overly done dramatic effects.

Critics said Ann-Margret gave more physical glamor to Borchardt than she may have deserved. A magazine writer once described Borchardt as "plump and looking frumpy in her middle age."

In December 1996, Diane Borchardt's request for a new trial was denied. Her motion claimed ineffective counsel, errors by the trial judge and abuse of the John Doe process. The same month, an agreement was reached that she wouldn't receive any part of her husband's estate. The agreement settled a wrongful death lawsuit filed against her by Ruben Borchardt's children.

"Mrs. Borchardt maintains her innocence," said her new attorney, Thomas Monogue, "but she realizes that continuing (her claims on the money) will only build up lawyers' expenses and result in less money being turned over to the children."

14

Her Last Groceries

Madison, 1949

For Sadie and Julius Jackson, it was just a routine trip to the grocery store on the fateful day of July 10, 1949. Julius, a paralyzed World War I veteran, rarely got out of the house. It was just too difficult to move him in and out of the car.

The couple decided to stop at the Norris Court grocery on Madison's East Side after dining at the Park Motor Inn on the Capitol Square for dinner. Julius Jackson recalled the dinner as a particularly memorable evening.

"We enjoyed ourselves so much and we were very, very happy," he said.

And so, Sadie Jackson wanted to stop at the grocery store for a few items after dinner on their way home. Julius Jackson had no objection. He would wait in the car.

While Sadie was inside the store, however, George "Butch" King came up to the Jacksons' parked car.

"Do you mind if I get in?" he asked. Julius recognized King but, before he could reply, King climbed in the back seat.

"He was talking something about my wife running around with other men and he was all incoherent," Jackson said.

Unaware of King's presence, Sadie Jackson paid for some radishes, a cantaloupe and a head of lettuce, then went outside and crossed the street to where her car was parked. When she got near the car, she saw King get out of the back seat.

"You get out of there!" she said. Still mumbling, King complied, then pushed Sadie against the car.

"You've been running around with too many other men," he said. "I'll teach you a lesson." He pulled a small handgun out of his pocket and fired twice, about eight inches from her chest.

Arthur Fetterhoff was sitting in his car a few feet away. Hearing the shots, he jumped out of his car to come to the aid of Mrs. Jackson while King disappeared in the crowd that had begun to gather.

Sadie Jackson staggered back across the street to the grocery store. She fell to her knees and crawled up the front steps. She got to the counter where she had bought her groceries moments before, where Bernard McDermott still stood.

"Shot," was all she could say, clutching the wound oozing blood on her chest. "Shot," she repeated before collapsing to the floor.

To Robert McDermott, Bernard's father and the grocery store owner, the shots from the .25-caliber automatic sounded like firecrackers but his son, Bobby, insisted that McDermott go downstairs to the grocery to investigate. When he got downstairs, he saw several people huddled over Sadie Jackson's body on the floor of the store. She died there, before the ambulance arrived. Outside, a stunned Julius Jackson sat in the car, clutching the bag of groceries and his wife's purse.

It wasn't the first time King had pestered the Jacksons. The previous Saturday night, he had approached them while Mrs. Jackson was pushing her husband's wheelchair near Mifflin and Baldwin streets. Jackson told King to stay away from his wife and wanted to call the police but his wife talked him out of it, saying she was afraid of King because she knew he had a gun.

After the shooting, King, a carpenter, drove back and forth past the murder scene several times before speeding away in his red-panel truck. He abandoned the truck at his daughter's Monona home and fled in his son-in-law's car, a blue 1941 Plymouth sedan. In a daze, he drove for four hours, stopping at the farm of Charles Hull near Stoughton, looking for his daughter. Hull was his daughter's father-in-law. At the farm, King told Hull he had just shot a woman before driving away. Hull immediately notified police. Police found King's truck parked on the Capitol Square, where his daughter and son-in-law had driven it to attend a movie.

Police staked out his home in rural McFarland until they spotted a car that matched the description of the one King was driving. They followed with their police lights and radioed to other units. Police set up a roadblock at Edwards Park, where King was stopped.

"What's this all about?" King said, stepping from the car. He was handcuffed and taken to jail.

Before the shooting, pharmacist Clifford Olson noticed King was acting strangely when he visited his Monona Drive pharmacy.

"He was very, very much upset, hysterical and acted just like a maniac," Olson said. "He ran from one end of the store to the other, looking out the front and back windows. He definitely acted rather insane."

Olson had known King for about sixteen years. He remembered when King was "a friendly man who you liked to hunt and fish with and liked to be around." That was before he met Sadie Jackson.

King met the pretty, dark-haired waitress a year earlier while he was working on a job near the restaurant where she worked. She had worked at the Park Motor Inn, and at the Orin Rime Tavern and Steak House outside the city.

Wisconsin State Journal archives

Sadie Jackson

Most people considered Sadie Jackson a dedicated wife who took good care of her invalid husband and supported him. He had worked as a bartender at the Loraine Hotel but was forced to give it up due to his disability.

Whether Sadie Jackson pursued King or vice versa was an issue at King's trial the following year. But it was clear from her love letters to him that they had had a sizzling affair. In the letters, she referred to gifts he had given her such as a sweater and garden produce.

"Never can tell when J.J. (her husband) might take off, so don't think anything of it if I say wrong number," she wrote. "Love you, dearest, much too much."

"I sure did enjoy those two days with you, dearest," she wrote in another letter. "Call me Sunday if you get a chance about 2:00 p.m. I'll be home all day but be sure and ask if I can talk."

When King left town for a carpentry job in Minocqua, she wrote him again: "I'm glad you got on your heavy undies because I know it's cold up there."

"I have you on my mind almost all day," she wrote in still another letter. "This morning, the first song I heard on the radio when I got up was 'My Happiness' and then the one called 'Pretty Eyes.' I'll never forget those songs."

While Sadie Jackson appeared to enjoy the clandestine affair, it took a heavier emotional toll on King. He fell hard for Sadie and was angry when she wanted to break off the affair eleven months after it began.

Wisconsin State Journal archives

Butch King is arrested.

William King, the grown son of the killer, noticed a dramatic change in his father after the affair began. Sadie Jackson apparently was the first woman Butch King dated after his wife, Molly, died several years earlier.

"He became very thin and sullen and he was not happy," William King said.

King's pharmacist friend, Clifford Olson, also noticed the change.

"He became very snappy, nervous and had a bad temper," Olson said. King also began suffering severe headaches. One time, he took an entire twenty-four-tablet bottle of aspirin to ease the pain. Another time, he asked Olson to give him the same yellow capsules he'd been given by Sadie.

"He said he took twelve or fifteen of them at a time and they were the only ones that helped the pains in his head," Olson said.

King's carpentry work also began to suffer. Once known as the best carpenter in Dane County, he built an addition to Clarence Hoyt's Sun Prairie home shortly before the murder and the job was five inches off center.

When Sadie decided to break off the affair, it only aggravated King's problems. He brooded for several weeks before confronting the couple on the sidewalk that Saturday night. The argument only charged his anger. He vowed to himself to punish Sadie somehow. King often packed a small pistol for protection because he carried sums of money from construction jobs in his truck.

On Sunday, the day after the argument, the obsessed, spurned lover spent most of the day driving back and forth in front of the Jacksons' home on East Johnson Street. His thoughts ran to murder-suicide. He would kill Sadie, then turn the gun on himself.

King's murder plot was drawn from a fictional story he had read in a detective magazine called "Bullets Claim Secret Bride." King scrawled a note to his daughter on the magazine page, possibly on Saturday night or Sunday morning: "Leaving to look for her. Hope I have better luck today."

About 5:00 p.m., he followed the couple to the Park Motor Inn and then to the grocery, where he seized the opportunity to get even.

"She was two-timing me," King later said in a confession to police. "I shot her. I was jealous of her."

King's sensational trial began in late May 1950. At some points, the testimony was so steamy that it offended Judge Alvin Reis.

"There's no necessity for this sort of detail, Mrs. Witness," he warned Muriel Thorson, who had spotted King and Sadie in a lover's tryst through the window of King's Blooming Grove home. "Stop that stuff right there."

The trial also featured a touch of controversy when defense attorney Darrell MacIntyre demanded a mistrial because prosecutor Robert Arthur had hired court bailiff John Arnold to help him screen potential witnesses.

"It is reprehensible that the district attorney would use an officer of the court to go out and find a jury that would bring in a conviction," MacIntyre told the judge.

Arthur defended his employment of the bailiff, saying it had been done by other district attorneys.

"Jack is a former sheriff and knows almost everybody," the prosecutor said. "He could do the job quickly and economically and I didn't think there was anything wrong in hiring him."

Arnold had been hired as a special investigator by previous district attorneys but never when he also was serving as court bailiff.

The mistrial motion was denied and the trial went on for nearly four weeks. On a hot Memorial Day afternoon, about 300 people packed the courtroom and a nineteen-year-old university student fainted from the heat.

On the nineteenth day, the controversial trial was transferred to the bedside of Dr. Walter Urben, where he lived on the grounds of Mendota State Hospital. Dr. Urben's wife had appeared in court with an affidavit declaring that he was too ill to testify.

But Urben was a key witness because he had conducted a court-ordered mental examination of King the previous fall. The deposition was taken by the judge, bailiff and attorneys without the jury or usual throng of spectators. At one point during the informal proceeding, Dr. Urben stuck his foot out from under the sheet and wiggled it around.

King was convicted of first-degree murder. Due to the mores of the time, Sadie Jackson was viewed as a villain in her own murder. MacIntyre tried to paint a portrait of his client as a good man, misguided by an evil woman who pursued him, then spurned him. Arthur, however, maintained that it was King who chased Jackson, a decent woman devoted to her disabled husband.

The truth probably was somewhere in between. At the time, Sadie Jackson would have been considered a tramp. Today, her actions wouldn't be viewed a justification for her murder.

15
The Brutal Thing
at Cad's Tavern
Wisconsin Rapids, 1952

The oppressive heat of summer was bad enough, but Edward Kanieski operated a jackhammer, his sweat-soaked body vibrating with the machine as it cut through the sizzling pavement.

He got off about 4:30 p.m. and it was a half hour drive home to Wisconsin Rapids from Nekoosa, where he was working on a job for Meyers Construction Co. It was a Monday, June 30, 1952, and Kanieski's pregnant wife, Mildred, had an early supper ready. Kanieski told her he was going for a ride after supper to check the fishing on Lake Wazeecha, southeast of the Rapids, and she asked to ride along with their son, Eddie, 7. Cruising with the car windows open at least whipped up a breeze that offered some relief from the heat.

Kanieski figured he'd dig some angle worms and then go fishing. They drove past the swimming pool and out on the bridge, where he spotted a fisherman.

"Any luck?" he asked, stopping his car near the man.

"Yep," the fisherman replied.

Kanieski drove on, past a new church under construction where Mildred wanted to see how the building was coming. Eddie started complaining he was thirsty and hungry. Kanieski told the boy he'd drive to Highway 54, where they'd find a place to get something to drink and maybe some hot dogs. On the way, they passed Cad's Tavern near Kellner.

"I feel as if I would like a beer," Kanieski told his wife as he pulled into the tavern driveway. "Would you want anything?"

She said yes, some orange pop and some for the boy, too. Kanieski got out of the car and walked to the tavern's front door. It was locked. He went around to the outhouse at the rear. On the way back, he slipped and fell on the sidewalk. As he got up and straightened his clothing, he heard a funny noise, muffled from inside the tavern.

"It sounds like somebody crying," he told his wife as he returned to the car.

"Maybe somebody left a kid alone," she said.

Kanieski went back and rapped on the tavern door. Dogs began to bark.

"Let's go over there to this fellow who lives in the next place and ask him if he knows who runs the place," he suggested.

They drove about 200 feet down Highway U to the home of Alvin Phipps, who said Clara, or "Cad," Bates ran the tavern. Phipps agreed to return with Kanieski to the tavern to find out if anything was wrong. They knocked on the tavern door, shouting "hello." Phipps stooped and peered under the garage door, discovering that Cad's car was still there. They went around the back, found the door ajar and went inside. When the two men opened the door, two dogs came bounding out, an Irish setter and a beagle. Phipps later recalled he'd seen the dogs earlier in the day lying on the steps outside the tavern.

Inside, Phipps found Bates dead in her bed. Under the circumstances, Kanieski appeared very calm to him.

"Don't you think we better get out of here?" Kanieski asked Phipps. "This is no place for me. We should make a phone call. Who should we call?"

"We will have to call the Wood County sheriff," Phipps replied. "That would be the proper thing." Kanieski made the call because Phipps said he couldn't hear very well on the phone.

When Sheriff Arthur Boll arrived, he found the body of Cad Bates nude except for shoes and stockings. The bedroom was orderly and two wine glasses were on a bedside table next to a nearly empty bottle of Christian Brothers brandy. A blood-soaked towel was wrapped around the dead woman's neck and a chenille rug was on the bed. Under the towel, a cord had been fastened tightly around her neck. Clothing was stacked neatly on a chair and Boll noticed there was no sign of a struggle. Blood was splattered on the walls and ceiling with some spots on the floor. The tavern's till hadn't been touched and Cad's jewelry hadn't been removed but a collection of Roosevelt dimes was missing. The rear screen door was slit and the hasp had been ripped off. Tests later determined that seventy-six-year-old Cad Bates had sexual intercourse shortly before she died.

Cad had operated the tavern near the Wood-Portage county line for five years. She was born December 27, 1875, in Burlington, Iowa but spent forty years in the Wisconsin Rapids area. Her tavern had a reputation as a sporting place, where Cad was happy to supply her male customers with prostitutes. In back, where she lived, Cad also let her sporting customers use the bedrooms. Besides the cord around her neck, her skull also had been crushed with a heavy object. Boll, who faced a tough three-way Republican primary in September, called the murder "a brutal thing, probably the work of a sadist." Community pressure was on the sheriff to find the killer quickly.

Kanieski's presence when the body was found didn't look good for him because of his criminal record dating back twenty years. In 1950, he had been sentenced to one to two years in prison for breaking and entering at a town of Saratoga home. He had cut the telephone wires and forced his way into the house, where he was shot in the neck by the victim, Linda Eberius. On the Fourth of July, five days after Cad's body was found, Kanieski was arrested for the rape of a ten-year-old Grand Rapids girl. Then detectives learned Kanieski wasn't at all unfamiliar with Cad's Tavern and the slain proprietor. In fact, he had known her well.

He had been to the tavern several times since the previous April, even spending time with a woman there once or twice. He had told Cad Bates he was an aviator, working as a crop duster at nearby cranberry marshes. He promised to fly Cad to Iowa, where she wanted to visit relatives. A few weeks before the murder, he'd shown up at the tavern with a bandage on his head, the result of a fall outside a funeral home. But Kanieski told Cad he'd been injured in a plane accident. At first, Kanieski denied he'd been to the tavern on the Saturday night of June 28, two days before the body was found. After several witnesses placed him there, he admitted the truth — that he'd stopped by for a drink.

On that Saturday, Kanieski and his family went to a carnival in the city. About 9:00 p.m., they stopped by the Cyril Dunn home, where they waited with Dunn's daughter for her father to arrive. Dunn came home drunk a few minutes later and Kanieski helped put him to bed. After having coffee with Dunn's wife, the Kanieskis went home. It was a hot summer night and Kanieski ate a piece of cantaloupe to cool off. He went back to Dunn's house and drove Dunn to work at the Green Bay & Western Railroad roundhouse on the north side of the Rapids. Then, he drove to Cad's Tavern, arriving a little after midnight.

Two groups of younger people were in the tavern and members of one group shouted loudly to each other as they played a pinball bowling game. Kanieski talked to Cad Bates a while before he left. After he was gone, patrons said Cad appeared agitated and upset. She began clearing glasses away and said she was tired and wanted to close up early.

Photo from The Tangled Web

Linda Eberius demonstrates how she shot Edward Kanieski.

Kanieski's black 1940 Chevrolet had problems with the mechanical shift. When the shift wouldn't move out of first gear, he had to stop the car, lift the hood and move the shift linkage with a screwdriver. Several witnesses said they saw a black Chevrolet like his parked along the road about a hundred yards from the tavern. But when they left Cad's that night, the car was gone. If he had parked there, Kanieski said, it was only to fix the shift.

After leaving Cad's, he stopped at another tavern and stayed until about 1:00 a.m., arriving home about an hour later. But the distance from the second tavern to Kanieski's home was only a twenty-minute drive. Where was he during the extra forty minutes? Did he have time to return to Cad's Tavern and kill her?

The Kanieskis lived in an eighteen-foot by twenty-foot home originally built as a garage. When he got home, Kanieski found his wife upset that he'd stayed out so late. He lay down on the couch and tried to sleep. But it still was hot and he began sweating so he went outside and slept in the back seat of the car, where it was cooler. On Sunday morning, he had breakfast, then picked up Dunn at the round-house. At Dunn's house, he said he picked some blueberries, getting scratches on his arms. Were the scratches actually from his struggle with Cad Bates? In the afternoon, Kanieski chatted with visiting in-laws, read some magazines and napped. After a Sunday-evening drive past Cad's Tavern, he went to bed early and got up for work the next morning at 5:30 a.m. on the day Cad's body was found.

The day after Kanieski's Fourth of July arrest on the rape charge, a search warrant was served at his home but authorities couldn't find the shirt and shoes they sought. A blackjack was found July 6 in a woodpile outside Cad's Tavern. Traces of blood were found on the blackjack but, although it could have been the murder weapon, it mysteriously disappeared. The Rev. Paul Bicket interceded for the sheriff and asked Mrs. Kanieski for her husband's black oxford shoes. She told the minister they were in the attic so Bicket got a trunk and put a chair on top of it to reach into the attic, where he found the shoes behind a basket.

The shirt was another matter. Mrs. Kanieski said she'd scorched it while ironing on the day Cad's body was found. Afraid her husband would find out, she said she threw the shirt away. Detectives found the shoes recently had been resoled. Hoping to find traces of blood, hair or fiber that could tie him to the murder, they ripped off the new soles. They found holes in the old soles along with grooves Kanieski had put in them to make the glue hold better. No blood was found.

In fact, as Kanieski's attorney later reminded the jury at his murder trial, no blood had been found on any of Kanieski's clothing despite the fact that Cad's room was splattered with blood. A bartender at Worzella's Tavern testified that Kanieski had been there until 1:00 a.m. as he said. Mrs. Kanieski testified that she was a light sleeper and would have heard the car if her husband had left again after coming home that Saturday night.

These witnesses weren't enough to derail the prosecution's case, which was built on the new science of microscopic fiber examination by the Wisconsin Crime Lab. Crime lab expert Laurin Goin repeatedly took the witness stand, connecting Kanieski to the crime through similarities between the hair from one of Cad's dogs and one found on his jacket, between fibers taken from his purple wool trousers and those found on the chenille rug and among the fibers of the rope around the victim's neck. Kanieski had submitted a sample of pubic hair and Goin found an apparent match there too.

"Using the microscope, I found no discrepancy to be present between the hair removed from the bedspread and that submitted as coming from Mr. Kanieski," Goin said. Insulation material found on Cad's bedspread also matched similar material found on Kanieski's trousers.

During the December 8-10 trial, prosecutor John Potter also presented Kanieski's earlier testimony during a John Doe investigation, demonstrating that he'd lied several times about knowing Cad Bates and being in her tavern that Saturday. The jury deliberated six-and-a-half hours before reaching a guilty verdict.

Asked if he had anything to say before the sentencing, Kanieski replied: "I will say I am innocent."

"Do you have anything further to say?" the judge asked.

"Mr. Potter did not prove — he claims they were not the pants I wore at the time of the murder. He claimed I wore a different pair of pants. Why were those pants not brought if those were the pants I wore at the murder?"

"Anything further?"

"No, that is all."

Despite one final protestation of innocence by Kanieski, Judge Herbert A. Bunde sentenced him to life imprisonment. Bunde was a former law partner of Harold Billmeyer, Kanieski's attorney.

Kanieski served his sentence at Waupun State Prison and later at Fox Lake Correctional Institution. He steadfastly maintained his innocence through the years and appealed the case six times to state and federal courts. Six times his appeals were rejected and Kanieski later said he was denied parole because he wouldn't admit to the murder. During the fall of 1971, he suffered a heart attack and was hospitalized at University Hospital in Madison, where he underwent open heart surgery in December of that year. Three month later, his conviction was overturned by the Wisconsin Supreme Court after he had served nineteen years. Two justices dissented.

Writing for the court's majority, Justice Horace Wilkie said the circumstantial case presented against Kanieski didn't justify a conviction. He also rejected the microscopic fiber evidence.

"We find that the only established fact is that defendant (Kanieski) took forty minutes too long in getting home. There is no fact to support the proposition that he went back to the Bates tavern, that he had some reason to kill Miss Bates or that he committed the crime."

Wisconsin State Journal file photos

Edward Kanieski Sr.   **Edward Kanieski Jr.**

Kanieski, still recovering from heart surgery, was overjoyed at his release.

"I want to go fishing in the spring," he told a *Wisconsin State Journal* reporter, saying he also planned to settle in Stevens Point. Kanieski filed a claim against the state for compensation under the innocent convicts law but it was denied because he hadn't proven his innocence beyond a reasonable doubt. He died in April 1975.

After Kanieski's death, his son, Eddie Jr., set out to prove his father's innocence. The younger Kanieski, who'd been with his father that day a quarter century earlier when the body of Cad Bates was found, wrote letters to major figures in the case and searched court records. The effort was complicated by the fact that Eddie Kanieski Jr. is blind from an eye disease he has had since shortly after birth. His wife had to read court documents to him and Kanieski had to be driven to interviews.

Besides Kanieski's blindness, the family suffered in other ways during the time the elder Kanieski was in prison. Eddie's mother had frequent hospital stays as she tried to recover from a mental collapse some say was brought on by the murder trial and her husband's imprisonment. Her youngest son, Dan, was sent to live in a Milwaukee foster home. The family lived on welfare in dilapidated houses with secondhand clothing, Christmas baskets for the poor and harassment from Eddie's classmates.

Eddie Kanieski said the memory of his early life drove him on to prove his father's innocence and make life easier for the families of those who are wrongly convicted. In letters to John Potter, Harold Billmeyer and others, Kanieski asked some hard questions about the case:

Why wasn't the blackjack introduced as evidence? Whose finger-prints were on the bottle of brandy and drinking glasses by Cad's bed-side? If the elder Kanieski was cut while committing the crime, why was the blood found on the floor of Cad's bedroom and outside the tavern of the wrong type? Why didn't Billmeyer ask for a change of venue to counteract pretrial publicity, especially since he was a long-time acquaintance of the judge? Why were the investigators so inter-ested in a pair of wire cutters or pliers his father owned? Why weren't other suspects investigated more thoroughly, including one who ad-mitted he had sexual intercourse with Cad Bates, submitted a sample of pubic hair and had failed a lie detector test?

During his research on the case, Kanieski found the other sus-pect apparently had a weaker alibi than his father, although both failed the tests. The suspect said he had been painting his porch and went to bed early on the night of the murder.

Kanieski wrote to Potter:

"It is my feeling that you had a moral and ethical obligation to bring it to Judge Bunde's attention that my father was not receiving a defense that he was entitled to."

On January 18, 1979, Potter drafted an impatient and weary reply to the son's inquiries:

"The death of Miss Bates occurred over twenty-six years ago and the facts are not exactly clear in my mind. However, I do not recall any blackjack involved in the case. I do not recall any wire cutters. I do not recall a bottle of brandy and two drinking glasses. I have no recollection of inferring during the trial that your father was cut or that blood was dripping from his arm.

"As to Mr. Billmeyer's capabilities, Judge Bunde must have been fully aware of them. They had practiced law together here for many, many years before I ever commenced a practice.

"You have called me on several occasions and I have always attempted to give you whatever information you requested. I would suggest that in the future you search the record yourself. It should be able to furnish you with the most factual information available."

The Kanieski case, along with that of Kenny Ray Reichoff, prompted the state to change its innocent convicts compensation law in 1980. Reichoff was convicted of double murder in Adams County and served three years in prison before he was freed. In March, 1980, Gov. Lee Dreyfus signed legislation that said convicts later found innocent need only provide clear and convincing evidence rather than proving their in-nocence beyond a reasonable doubt. The new law also increased the amount of compensation innocent convicts could collect from the state.

In 1993, *The Tangled Web,* a complete account of the Kanieski case by Potter, was published by Waubesa Press. Potter wrote about how the case had haunted him for years, especially after the Supreme Court ruling, and he wondered whether he had done the right thing by pursuing Kanieski so vigorously. The book not only concludes that Kanieski was the killer but a chapter by noted forensic psychiatrist Dr. Frederick Fosdal postulates that Kanieski would have gone on to become a serial killer if he weren't stopped. Fosdal never interviewed Kanieski and his analysis was done entirely through court records and newspaper accounts of the case.

Two years later, Waubesa Press published *Please Pass the Roses* by Colleen Kohler Kanieski, the wife of Eddie Jr. While professing the elder Kanieski's innocence, that book focuses on the love and family of Colleen and Eddie Jr., highlighting Eddie Jr.'s struggles with blindness and his father's imprisonment.

Did Edward Kanieski Sr. kill Clara Bates as the crime lab evidence purported to show in 1952? Or did his prior record and evasiveness about frequenting the tavern make him an easy scapegoat?

Crimes of Politics

16

Anarchy in the Precinct
Milwaukee, 1917

Desk Sergeant Henry J. Deckert had never seen anything like it. Sure, he knew it was a bomb. But it wasn't the usual dynamite-and-fuse variety. This device obviously was a scientific construction. The problem was how to defuse it.

On Saturday, November 24, 1917, an Italian man known to Deckert only as Mazvinni had carried the bomb to Milwaukee's central police station, where Deckert had told him to deposit the device in the patrolman's squad room so he and other officers could examine it. The bomb had been found against a wall of the Italian Evangelical Church on Van Buren Street by church secretary Marie Richter.

Upstairs, second-shift detectives were completing their evening roll call. They were told about the bomb and asked to stop in the squad room to take a look at it and offer their opinions. A detective named Burns wandered into the squad room, took a look at the bomb and decided it should be placed in a pail of water. He went off to find the shift lieutenant to tell him that conclusion.

Two other detectives had been playing cards when the roll call interrupted their game. Afterward, two of the players, detectives John Hammes and John Shenar, left the room and stopped to answer a station telephone. Detective Fred Kaiser, who had beaten them at cards, called after Hammes and Shenar that they'd better practice so they could beat him the following day.

Deckert's speculation about the bomb ended abruptly when it exploded, blowing him to bits. The lethal device blasted the station house with smoke and flying bits of metal. Witnesses heard haunting cries of pain, then eerie silence. Kaiser was among eleven people killed but Hammes and Shenar, by sheer luck, escaped injury. The detective who had run off to find the lieutenant also survived.

"I think we were probably lucky," Shenar said afterward. "It was a good thing that telephone rang or we would not be here today."

Windows were shattered and the ceiling of the squad room was damaged. An alarm switchboard also received minor damage. Overall, property damage was estimated at less than $1,000. Firefighters rushed to the scene and worked long into the night, digging out bodies from debris under lantern light.

Edward Spindler, the alarm operator, was killed by a piece of metal. Detective Dave O'Brien was found face down in the center of the squad room, covered with debris. The mangled body of Detective Stephen Stecker was found in the squad room doorway. Other detectives who died in the blast were Charles Seehauer, Paul Weiler, Albert Templin and Frank Carwin.

Catherine Walker, who worked as an expert spot remover at Otto Pletsch Dye Co., apparently had paused in front of the station as she walked by. She also was killed in the blast along with an unidentified Italian man. Detectives Louis Hartman and Herman Bergin were injured.

"A chamber of horror, conceived by the most diabolical mind, could have been no more gruesome," the *Milwaukee Sentinel* reported.

Mrs. Fred Kaiser had just put her three children to bed when she got the news that her husband had died in the blast.

"It can't be true," she said. "He was home just an hour ago."

Her young daughter, Andrea, also was in disbelief. "Papa really isn't dead, is he?" she asked her grandmother.

O'Brien had remarried six weeks earlier after he had been a widower for twenty years. His new bride rushed to the hospital when she heard about the explosion, hoping to find him still alive.

A public funeral for all of the victims was suggested, similar to one held for Fire Chief James Farley and several firefighters killed in an acid disaster. But the detectives were of different faiths so they were buried separately.

A fund was set up for the widows and children. Widows would receive forty-five dollars a month each while children each would receive six dollars a month. Charley Metric, a popular Milwaukee boxer, offered to appear at a series of benefits to help raise money for the survivors.

With a thirst for revenge in their throats, members of the decimated detective squad immediately began an investigation. Sgt. Mike Mills, a bomb expert from the Chicago Police Department, was dispatched to

Milwaukee. After surveying the scene, he said the bomb was the most powerful he had ever seen.

A small vial had been removed from the bomb prior to the blast. The vial contained sulfuric acid that dripped on to a zinc plate, resulting in a chemical reaction and heat that ignited the black powder bomb.

Detectives didn't have to search very hard to find the motive. The target obviously was the Rev. August Giuliani, pastor the Italian Evangelical Church. Giuliani was scheduled to be a key witness against eleven rioters in a trial set to begin on November 28.

Two people had been killed and five wounded, including two detectives, in the September 9 Bay View riot at Bishop and Potter streets, which began when a band of anarchists came to disrupt a patriotic speech by Giuliani. The minister, who had emigrated from Italy six years earlier, had broken with the Roman Catholic Church.

His speech concerned the duty of immigrants to support the draft and serve, if necessary, in the U.S. effort in World War I, then raging in Europe. He had finished speaking and was leading the crowd in singing "America the Beautiful" when Mary Nardina, described as the queen of the anarchist gang, came down the street followed by a group of supporters. The anarchists sang their own words: "We fight against all tyranny; we fight against all citizens; we fight, we fight for anarchy."

"Wilson is a pig!" one anarchist shouted. "The American flag is a rag and this country is a jail!"

"You cowards," Nardina said, turning to her group of followers. "Why don't you get your guns to shoot? Who is going to be the first to shoot?"

Detective Albert Templin, later killed in the station explosion, began searching one of the gang members. Another gang member pulled a gun and shot and wounded Templin, instigating a full-fledged riot.

The riot was not unusual during a time of great political foment. President Woodrow Wilson declared war on Austria as German troops were advancing in Italy. In Russia, the Bolshevik revolution was under way.

The Bay View neighborhood seemed prone to unrest. Thirty-one years earlier, the National Guard had been called in to quell another riot and Robert Schilling had been arrested for inspiring a boycott but the charge was dismissed due to a hung jury.

Two days after the station blast, six suspects had been rounded up but detectives still were searching for the national leaders of the anarchist group, who had been in Milwaukee on the day of the riot. The U.S. Secret Service was called in to help with the investigation.

Milwaukee attorney Thomas Mohan reported receiving a death threat in a Black Hand, or Mafia, letter mailed from the Bay View Post

Office. "Prepare for death; we are watching you," the letter said.

Judge A.C. Backus delayed the trial of the Bay View rioters, but only for a couple of days. Attorney William Rubin, who represented ten of the eleven accused rioters, filed a motion for a change of venue due to the negative publicity surrounding the explosion. His motion was denied.

As the two-week trial of the Bay View rioters got under way, Rubin wrangled with District Attorney Zabel. Despite the threats on his life, Giuliani provided key testimony against the rioters and all were convicted on December 20 of assault with the intent to murder. An arsenal of weapons had been found in Nardina's home.

John LaDuca, national secretary of the Italian branch of the Socialist Party, was quietly taken into custody by federal authorities when he came to testify at the trial. LaDuca had been in Milwaukee on September 9 and gave a speech to the anarchists.

The Milwaukee station bombing was one of Wisconsin's worst tragedies but it paled in comparison to other events of the time, when explosions were not uncommon. In Halifax, Nova Scotia, two thousand people died, three thousand were injured and most the city was razed when a munitions ship exploded on December 7, 1917. No one was injured on December 18, when a dynamite bomb exploded at the California governor's mansion.

On December 5, a dynamite bomb was tossed into the Phi Kappa Sigma fraternity house at the University of Wisconsin-Madison. A quick-thinking fraternity member plunged the sputtering fuse in a pail of water and doused the threat, just as Detective Burns had suggested with the station bomb. But that solution probably wouldn't have worked with the more sophisticated Milwaukee device.

17

Teddy's Wounded Campaign
Milwaukee, 1912

Milwaukeean Arthur Bremer was thrust into the national spot-light in 1972 when he shot and crippled third-party presidential candidate George Wallace at a Maryland shopping center. Sixty years earlier, Milwaukee was the scene of another attempted political assassination with striking similarities to the 1972 incident.

The year 1912 was a time of turmoil for American presidential politics. Republican Howard Taft sought re-election and he was opposed by Democrat Woodrow Wilson. But a Third-Party movement also was afoot and Wisconsin played a key role. Wisconsin Sen. Robert "Fighting Bob" LaFollette made an early bid for the presidency on a progressive platform but his candidacy was overshadowed by a bigger name in American politics who yanked the progressive banner from LaFollette three months before the election — former President Theodore Roosevelt, who ran on the Bull Moose Party ticket.

Roosevelt, the fighting colonel who led his Rough Riders to victory on San Juan Hill — the crucial battle of the Spanish-American War — ascended to the presidency on September 14, 1901, when President William McKinley died eight days after receiving a gunshot wound from an assassin's bullet. During these times of John D. Rockefeller, holding companies and emerging corporate power, Rough Rider Teddy warred with Wall Street, using the federal government to restrain corporate excesses. Roosevelt was elected to his own term in 1904 and pledged not to seek a third term in 1908, supporting Taft instead.

After Taft's election, Roosevelt put politics aside and traveled to

Africa and Europe. But when he returned, he became concerned that Taft was weakening on some critical issues. Roosevelt's growing dissatisfaction with his successor peaked in 1912, when he challenged Taft for the Republican nomination. After losing that bid, Roosevelt accepted the nomination of the Progressive Party, shoving the lesser-known LaFollette aside. Teddy became the spoiler in the 1912 election, just as Wallace would try to become the third-party spoiler sixty years later.

LaFollette was angry that Roosevelt had usurped him as the Progressive Party nominee. He questioned Roosevelt's devotion to the progressive cause in articles LaFollette wrote for Wisconsin newspapers and the senator decried the political maneuvering used by Roosevelt supporters to build the colonel's candidacy. Republican loyalists also were outraged. They feared Roosevelt would siphon votes from Taft and make certain a Wilson victory. In fact, Wilson was elected by a landslide, winning thirty-six of forty-eight states.

It was in the midst of this political turmoil that Roosevelt made his final campaign swing in October. As Teddy traveled around the country by train, he was shadowed by a short, plump man with receding brown hair. John Schrank, a saloon keeper in New York City, had followed the former president's political career since Roosevelt's days as a New York police commissioner. Schrank was born in Erding, Bavaria, about two hours from Munich, and had come to the United States with his parents at age three. In the newspapers, Schrank had read how Teddy cried "Thief!" when Taft beat him for the Republican presidential nomination. The saloon keeper was convinced he would cry "thief" again if he lost the election. And that Roosevelt would raise such a stink that the nation would certainly be plunged into another civil war.

But Schrank also was haunted by a dream. The ghost of McKinley, Roosevelt's predecessor, appeared and told Schrank that the blood of his assassination was on Teddy's hands. The ghost told Schrank that Roosevelt had killed McKinley so Teddy could become president.

With responsibility for the nation's future weighing heavily on his shoulders, Schrank had no doubt about the patriotic thing to do. On September 21, he left the saloon with three hundred dollars and bought a gun. Then, he hurried to Charleston, South Carolina, hoping to catch up with Teddy's campaign entourage. Schrank left his personal items in Charleston and followed Roosevelt to Atlanta, Chattanooga, Evansville and Indianapolis, waiting for his chance to shoot the former president. But each time, he was foiled by schedule changes, being in the wrong place or other problems. In Chicago, for example, the saloon keeper hid in wait for Teddy's train but the train came in at a different station. The would-be assassin stalked the Chicago Coliseum, where Roosevelt was speaking, but the former president left by a different exit.

Former president Theodore Roosevelt, holding cane, at the Milwaukee train station with his entourage.

Schrank knew the next campaign stop would be in Milwaukee and this time he was determined to get his man. Traveling under the alias of Walter Ross, Schrank arrived in Milwaukee the day before the speech and got a room at the Argyle Lodging House on Third Street. He pored over newspapers to deduce Roosevelt's exact itinerary.

The next day, October 14, Roosevelt's campaign train slowly wound its way north from Chicago, with stops for speeches from the caboose at Kenosha and Racine. Teddy arrived in Milwaukee about 6:00 p.m., in plenty of time for his speech at the Gilpatrick Hotel, where he also planned to spend the night. The former president and his entourage originally planned to eat dinner on the train but instead dined at the hotel.

After dinner, Teddy put on a thick Army coat, stepped outside into the crisp fall air and greeted the crowd that mingled near his open car. His speech notes, about fifty pages, were wadded into a breast pocket of the coat. His spectacle case, metal covered with leather, was jammed into the same pocket.

As the colonel stepped into the car, a shot rang out. The bullet pierced the wad of speech notes and was deflected by the spectacle case. It clipped off a corner of the case and lodged two inches inside Roosevelt's chest, shattering a rib. The former president swayed slightly, then whispered to an aide:

"Shh! Not a word. They've pinked me. Don't say a word."

Roosevelt's bodyguard, Colonel Cecil Lyon, a fellow Rough Rider, leaped from the car at the sound of the shot, pulling out a gun to shoot the assailant. Elbert Martin, Teddy's stenographer and a Rhinelander native, jumped from the car onto the gunman's back and wrestled him to the ground.

"Lynch him! Lynch him!" the angry crowd shouted.

"Bring him to me," Roosevelt said. "Don't hurt him."

The assailant, of course, was Schrank. He had taken up a position outside the hotel earlier in the day where he knew he couldn't miss this time. Roosevelt questioned the saloon keeper briefly about his motive before Schrank was whisked to the hotel kitchen and held for police. Against the advice of his aides, Teddy demanded to go to the auditorium to deliver his speech. He was introduced by Harry F. Cochems, who told the shocked crowd about the shooting. The audience shuddered when Roosevelt was introduced, then cheered so loudly that the building shook.

"I shall ask you to be as quiet as possible," he began softly when the applause died down. "I've just been shot but it takes more than that to kill a Bull Moose."

An elderly woman in the front row could stand it no longer.

"Colonel Roosevelt, please," she interrupted, "go back and let the doctors dress your wound."

"Dear Madam," Roosevelt replied, "it is nice of you but I am not hurt. If you saw me on horseback, you would know that I have a pretty strong seat now."

Flashing his trademark grin, Teddy didn't look injured and it was hard for some in the audience to believe he had been shot. But then he faltered and a half dozen men rose from their seats, preparing to rush to his aid.

"Sit down, sit down," he said, then went on with his speech. For more than an hour, Roosevelt railed at his political opponents. He compared himself favorably to Wilson and blamed the political bosses for his defeat at the convention. He appealed to working men to support him and criticized LaFollette for deserting the progressive cause. At one dramatic moment, Teddy tore open his coat and showed the crowd two splotches of blood on his shirt. Toward the end of the speech, his voice grew weaker as the loss of blood began to take its toll on his stamina.

As Roosevelt was leaving the hall, a tire exploded on a car and the crowd rushed outside, fearing another assassination attempt. Finally, Teddy let the doctors examine him. The colonel's physician, Dr. S.L. Terrell, and Milwaukee Dr. R.G. Sayle reported to the press:

"The injury to Colonel Roosevelt is a superficial flesh wound below the right breast with no evidence of any injury to the lung. His condition is so good that the surgeons did not try to locate the bullet nor did they use a probe. An x-ray picture of the wound will be taken in due course to locate the bullet. The bullet probably is lodged somewhere in the chest wall because there is no wound and no sign of injury to the lung."

Roosevelt was taken by train to Mercy Hospital in Chicago, where doctors closely monitored his condition, standing by to operate in case of infection. In characteristic upbeat style, Teddy described his own condition as "bully." The next morning, he ate three eggs and toast for breakfast as get-well messages poured in from around the world.

Wisconsin State Journal file photo
Teddy Roosevelt

Meanwhile, Schrank paced nervously in his cell at the Milwaukee County Jail. He had failed McKinley's ghost and failed what he saw as a patriotic duty. He said he didn't care about Roosevelt's condition. Was he sorry for the act?

"No, I'd do it all over again if I had the chance," he said. A note in Schrank's pocket indicated he may have thought about suicide but the saloon keeper denied this.

"The reason I wrote that was because I fully expected to be killed by a mob. You know there's a chance of losing your life in a matter of this kind."

Milwaukee Police Sgt. Robert Flood tried to question the gunman but Schrank was not in a talkative mood.

"I did it because I was opposed to the third form (party)," he said. "Do not talk to me. I will not say any more until tomorrow. I want to sleep."

In his cell, Schrank made out a will, claiming the bullet in Teddy's chest as his own property and willing it to the New York Historical Society. From his hospital bed, Teddy, the keeper of the bullet, contested

Schrank's claim.

"Now that bullet belonged to Mr. Schrank when it was in his revolver and while it was on its way to me. But after it reached me, it was mine."

On November 12, Schrank pleaded guilty to shooting Roosevelt but still showed no remorse.

"I shot Roosevelt as a warning to other third-termers," he said. Some Republican loyalists defended Schrank and one described him as "the man who tried to assassinate the man who tried to assassinate the Republican Party."

After six days in the hospital, no infection appeared and Teddy was taken by train to his home at Oyster Bay on Long Island, New York. Democrat Wilson suspended most of his remaining campaign schedule in fairness to the wounded candidate. A week after Roosevelt's hospital release, Schrank was declared insane and sentenced to confinement in an asylum.

He had been twice haunted by McKinley's ghost. The apparition first appeared to him in a dream on the day McKinley died and told him that Roosevelt was the killer. In 1912, the ghost reappeared and begged Schrank not to let a murderer become president. Schrank had begun tracking Roosevelt on the eleventh anniversary of McKinley's death and he had shot the former president exactly a month later.

The .38-caliber bullet never was removed from Roosevelt's body and he carried it until his death seven years later in 1919. Schrank remained hospitalized for the rest of his life. In 1940, when Franklin Roosevelt sought his third presidential term, Schrank said he would shoot that Roosevelt too if he were free. The saloon keeper died September 15, 1943, exactly 42 years after McKinley's ghost first appeared to him.

18
Last-Ditch Violence
Marshfield, 1922

"For God's sake, come up here!" Those were the desperate words Ole Gilberts heard when he picked up the phone at the Klondike Corners General Store shortly before 2:00 p.m. December 27, 1922. He recognized the caller's voice as that of James Tarr, grandson of James and Clementine Chapman.

"What happened?" Gilberts asked but Tarr hung up too soon to offer any more information. Gilberts rushed to the Chapman farm, about a mile away.

When he arrived at the farmhouse, Gilberts saw Chapman lying on the threshold between the dining room and an adjoining bedroom. His left hand had been blown off and his leg was cut. Not far away, his wife was lying face down in a pool of blood. Tarr had been bruised above an eye by flying debris. The walls and ceiling in the dining room were peppered with holes from flying metal fragments and a large chunk of metal was wedged in the floor.

Gilberts called for an ambulance, then collected fragments of the bomb, large pieces of metal piping. He also gathered pieces of heavy gray wrapping paper and twine.

The Chapmans were rushed to St. Joseph Hospital in Marshfield, where Mrs. Chapman died a few hours later of severe breast and stomach injuries caused by the flying bomb fragments. Chapman, whose injuries were less serious, would survive.

Just a few hours earlier, Tarr had trudged to the end of the Chapman driveway to pick up the day's mail. He found a few late Christmas cards and a gray package about a foot long. When he got back to the house, the Chapmans were curious about the mysterious package. Was it a late Christmas gift? Who was it from and why was there no return address? Why did the address say "Marshfild" instead of "Marshfield?" Chapman sat down and placed the package on his knees. While his wife leaned anxiously over his shoulder, he used a pocket knife to cut the wrapping paper lengthwise. Then he cut through the twine and the package exploded.

Chapman had served twenty years on the Wood County Board, the last six as its chairman, and possible motives for the bombing soon focused on his political activity. Was it moonshiners who had sent the bomb in retaliation for his support of a $5,000 appropriation to clean up illegal stills? Or did the explosion have something to do with his support of a drainage ditch that wound through many of the farms in the southeastern part of the county? The ditch wasn't popular with some farmers and Chapman also served on the county drainage commission, which supervised the project.

Two months earlier, fire had destroyed a barn on the Martin Olm farm. Olm, another drainage commissioner and county board member, had circulated petitions favoring the project. The previous summer, dynamite demolished a large dredge used to dig the ditch in the town of Auburndale. Could the fire and explosions be connected?

Postal inspectors and local police officers went to work to find out. They found out mail carrier John Heath had delivered the package about noon and it had stayed in the mailbox until Tarr removed it three hours later. Mail carrier Eugene Fehrenbach recalled picking up the gray parcel the day after Christmas at the Knute Moen residence. But Moen wasn't considered a suspect. Police figured someone must have put the package in Moen's mailbox shortly before Fehrenbach came by.

The bomb was activated by a trigger, which went off when Chapman cut the twine around the wrapper. It was made of a six-inch piece of iron pipe encased in a block of wood. Fumes and black smoke in the house after the blast meant the iron pipe probably was stuffed with explosive picric acid, not dynamite. The county agricultural agent provided a list of farmers who received hundreds of pounds of picric acid for stump removal. The list included only one name within the boundaries of the drainage district — a large Swedish immigrant named John Magnuson.

Sheriff Walter Mueller went on the Saturday after the blast to arrest Magnuson at his farm, but the farmer's wife said her husband had gone to have an engine serviced. Magnuson lived about forty rods north of the Mill Creek Creamery and the drainage ditch ran through his property. His farm wasn't far from where the dredge had been blown up six months earlier. An expert mechanic, Magnuson operated a garage in Chicago before buying his eighty-acre farm in Wood County several years earlier.

But the most significant detail and the one that sent the sheriff knocking on his door was that Magnuson was bitterly opposed to the drainage project.

About 3:45 p.m that day, a Ford lurched down the icy road past the creamery. Mueller waved the car down and told the driver, Magnuson, that he was under arrest for the bombing. The sheriff agreed to let him return home for a change of clothes before going to jail. A search of the suspect's farm turned up pieces of iron pipe, wood shavings similar to the wooden block that encased the bomb and gray wrapping paper. Investigators also found three dozen packages of picric acid. Magnuson was held in the empty women's section of the jail and allowed no visitors.

Magnuson was born in Sweden and once claimed the British paid his way to the United States because he had served as a British spy during the Boer War in Africa. Later, however, he denied that tale. Detectives obtained samples of his handwriting and found similarities between his spelling of some words and the misspelling of Marshfield on the bomb package.

A huge crowd gathered January 4 at the Moose Hall in Marshfield for Magnuson's preliminary hearing. Brought into the hall under heavy guard, Magnuson appeared cool and confident that the murder charge wouldn't stick.

The first witness was Dr. W.G. Sexton of Marshfield, who had treated Mrs. Chapman at the hospital. Then came F.E. Sullivan, a Mill Creek farmer who had asked Magnuson to sign a petition he was circulating against the drainage district.

"I'll fight this on my own hook," Magnuson had told him. "I'll take my .44 and peck away."

Fred Krueger, another farmer, said Magnuson also told him that the drainage commissioners would stop their efforts only when they heard the "peck, peck, peck away of a rifle."

Snow fell heavily as throngs of farmers and Marshfield residents kept arriving at the Moose Hall. The *Marshfield Daily News* said it was the largest crowd ever assembled in the area. Spectators heard farmer Gregor Durst, Jr. testify that Magnuson told him drainage project officials should watch out or they would get their heads blown off. The testimony was enough to bind Magnuson over for trial. Bond of $5,000 later was set for him at Stevens Point.

His trial was scheduled for the March session of the Wood County Court at Wisconsin Rapids. These were the days of true circuit judges who served several communities, traveling from one to another to hear cases.

Magnuson's defense lawyer, C.E. Briere, blasted the state's evidence presented at the preliminary hearing as circumstantial, characterizing the hearing as "a vaudeville act." He pledged to find his own handwriting experts to counter the prosecution's analysts.

On January 9, a hay fire destroyed ten tons of the crop at the Gus Wunrow farm. Although Fire Chief E.E. Finney said the blaze probably was caused by spontaneous combustion, many didn't believe it. Magnuson's arrest had worked up people on both sides of the drainage ditch controversy to a fever pitch. Wunrow insisted the fire was arson in retaliation for his support of the ditch.

The trial got off to a rocky start on March 20. One juror, Clara Reidl of Wisconsin Rapids, was sidelined by an attack of appendicitis. Another juror also became ill. The first witnesses were Magnuson's older children, called by the state to testify about the gray wrapping paper. Former Marshfield Mayor George Campbell told the jury how the drainage project began under his administration. A.P. Vesper, a drainage commissioner, told how Magnuson once threatened to keep the dredge off his land as long as he could wield a gun.

The mastermind who put together the state's case was Theodore Brazeau, a special prosecutor from Wisconsin Rapids. Brazeau, a short but dynamic man, earned the nickname "the little giant of Wisconsin Rapids" for his prosecution of Magnuson. His style wasn't particularly flamboyant or overly dramatic but he managed to build a circumstantial case against Magnuson detail by detail.

Making his way slowly to the witness stand with a crutch in his remaining right hand, Chapman made a dramatic court appearance on March 22. He said Magnuson had told him the preceding year that he'd hired the best lawyer in Chicago to fight the drainage district and, if that failed, Magnuson pledged to use his guns. The farmer had visited Chapman's home to complain about his drainage project assessment. He came a second time to complain that some people were taking money to support the ditch. On that occasion, Chapman had asked Magnuson if he knew who blew up the dredge. Magnuson didn't answer. Instead, a sheepish look spread across the big Swede's face and he looked at the floor.

It wasn't the drama of Chapman's testimony, however, that won the case for Brazeau. Instead, it was the parade of experts assembled by the brilliant prosecutor. The case was tried about a quarter century before the Wisconsin Crime Lab was established, yet Brazeau took a novel scientific approach to the evidence that was nearly impossible for Magnuson's attorney to counter.

Professor John Sweneheart, a chemist with the University of Wisconsin's College of Agriculture, said the explosive in the bomb was either TNT or picric acid because of the fumes and black smoke. Arthur Koehler, another UW professor, testified that wood shavings found beneath a lathe on Magnuson's farm were white elm, the same kind of wood used to make the block that encased the bomb. E. David Fahlberg, a professor of engineering, said the steel in a part used to trip a gas engine on the suspect's farm was identical to steel in the bomb trigger. Under microscopic examination, he said, the two pieces matched in the thickness and size of minute crystals. J.H. Mathews, a UW chemistry professor, found similarities between the bomb's metal and pipe found on the farm.

Brazeau didn't stop with the professors. He also assembled three handwriting experts from Milwaukee, Chicago and New York. They agreed that samples of Magnuson's handwriting taken after the bombing matched the writing on the gray wrapper. Using charts and enlarged photographs of the writing samples, the experts also showed how the spelling of Marshfield on the wrapper was consistent with the way a person of Swedish heritage might pronounce the name.

The defense called its own handwriting expert, Wilbur W. Way of Milwaukee. He said the writing on the gray paper indicated it was written by someone more sensitive and artistic than Magnuson. Way also found differences in the way some individual letters were made. But Brazeau destroyed him on cross examination when Way admitted he didn't use a microscope for his analysis and that he'd only received the samples a few days before his testimony.

Magnuson took the stand in his own defense on March 25. He described how he came to the United States at age fourteen with two sisters and his stepfather. He later went to Africa with a load of mules and served in the British army during the Boer War, but denied he'd ever been a spy. He said his drainage district assessment of sixty dollars surprised him when other farmers were assessed twelve dollars to fifteen dollars each and the high assessment prompted his visit to Chapman. Magnuson also described his treatment after arrest. He said investigators sat him close to a radiator and questioned him all night. When he asked for a drink of water, the interrogators told him he had to confess before he could have a drink. He said the detectives also instructed him how to make certain letters in the handwriting samples and told him how to spell Marshfield. He said a postal inspector told him he'd be lynched and a detective had tried to hypnotize him.

Two farmers testified they'd seen strangers in a horse and buggy near the Moen mailbox the day the bomb was picked up. One farmer insisted the strangers, who may have mailed the bomb, spoke German. Emil Budtke, a farmer who lived a mile north of Magnuson, said the accused bomber had spent the week before Christmas helping him move his mother's house and wouldn't have had time to make a bomb. Magnuson's children agreed with Budtke that their father had no time to build the device.

Brazeau called eight police officers as rebuttal witnesses. They denied Magnuson was threatened or refused a drink of water during his interrogation. He wasn't told how to make his handwriting samples and there was no attempt to hypnotize him, they told the jury.

Brazeau's closing arguments lasted four-and-a-half hours. Consistent with his presentation of the state's evidence, the prosecutor was more methodical than dramatic, reviewing detail after meticulous detail. He didn't soar into flights of rhetoric but hammered away ploddingly at the twenty-one points that formed the basis of his case. When he finished, Brazeau strode abruptly to a corner of the courtroom and hugged his young son, who had watched his father's presentation.

On Good Friday, March 30, the season's first carload of picric acid arrived in Wood County for stump clearing. In 1923, the newspaper reported, the county was allocated 100,000 pounds of picric acid, three times the federal government's allotment of the previous year. The following day, the jury found Magnuson guilty of first-degree murder in the explosive death of Clementine Chapman.

When he heard the jury's verdict, the once-confident Magnuson collapsed in his chair, his large head and shoulders slumping to the table. He broke into incoherent moans and muttering as his huge body trembled and his head rolled from side to side. His reaction moved the jurors so much that two or three of the women turned tearful faces toward the judge. When Briere asked Judge B.B. Parks to poll the jury, Magnuson straightened up a little, hoping for a dissenting vote. But, by the fourth juror, he broke again into muttering as it became clear that the verdict was unanimous.

"What can I say?" Magnuson said later after regaining some of his composure. "I am convicted and they have got me but I can look you or any other man in the eye and say I am innocent of the crime. It was a frame-up from the beginning to the end with the postal inspectors living up to their reputation of never failing to get their man. You know as well as I do that it is always said that they get their man. If they haven't the evidence, they make it."

Magnuson sat immobile, under obviously intense mental and physical strain, as he was sentenced to life imprisonment at Waupun on April 4, 1923. Fearing suicide, jailers had been careful not to leave any eating utensils in the bomber's cell. The judge also ordered that Magnuson spend every December 27 in solitary confinement to reflect on his deed.

"Time will prove my innocence!" Magnuson told the court. He was wrong. In May 1925, the Wisconsin Supreme Court affirmed the guilty verdict in a unanimous decision.

19

An Amerikan Crime

Madison, 1970

"Okay, pigs, now listen and listen good," said the anonymous voice on the phone to a Madison police dispatcher. "There's a bomb in the Army Math Research Center, the university, set to go off in five minutes. Clear the building. Get everyone out. Warn the hospital. This is no bullshit, man."

The message was relayed to university police and four officers rushed to the campus building. Summer was winding down and the fall semester was about to begin. That night, August 24, 1970, Norbert Sutter, a night watchman, was making his rounds. Nothing seemed amiss. In the basement of Sterling Hall two floors below the math research center, three physics researchers were hard at work, even at the unlikely hour of 3:40 a.m. Paul Quinn, a post-doctoral researcher, reviewed experimental data in a lab down the hall from where twenty-eight-year-old David Schuster a researcher from South Africa, was working. Across the hall from Schuster, Robert Fassnacht, age thirty-two, was so engrossed in his work that he was oblivious to the late hour. He certainly wasn't aware of the 1967 Ford Falcon Deluxe station wagon parked outside, loaded with fifty-five-gallon drums containing a deadly mixture of fuel oil and nitrogen fertilizer.

Barely two minutes after the phone message to police, the station wagon exploded, causing more than $2.5 million damage to Sterling Hall and nearby buildings. Schuster was buried in rubble for three hours with a broken shoulder until searchers found him lying partially protected from falling debris under a blown-out door frame. Quin suffered cuts on his legs when he crawled through shattered glass to escape the building through a first-floor window. Sutter suffered multiple cuts and bruises in the blast. Fassnacht was killed, leaving a wife and three children, three-year-old Christopher and twin girls, one-year-old Heidi and Karen.

A half hour later, four men stopped for breakfast at a truck stop north of Madison. They cheered when they heard a newscast reporting no one had died in the blast they'd set. They figured it had been a successful action to paralyze the war effort, striking at an important military target. But their joy faded when they got back on the road. A bulletin came over the car radio that a body had been pulled from the wreckage.

"I was completely devastated," Karleton Armstrong said in a 1986 copyrighted story in the *Milwaukee Journal*. "All anyone could say was, 'Oh, my God!' for at least ten minutes. David started crying. I was numb from grief."

Police Chief Ken Heding of Belleville, about thirty miles south of Madison, said he and his wife were awakened by the blast as were several neighbors in the southern Dane County village. A Monona couple argued over whether it was thunder or an explosion and finally decided it was probably "those radical students raising hell again."

The anti-war movement had grown ugly. What began as peaceful demonstrations inspired by the civil rights movement had evolved into vandalism by the Weatherman faction in Chicago. Three months earlier, National Guard troops had shot and killed unarmed protestors at Kent State University in Ohio. Meanwhile, the war still raged in Vietnam.

Even many people who wanted an end to the war condemned the Sterling Hall violence while those who supported it used the blast to criticize the peace movement. In an editorial, The *Wisconsin State Journal* called for university officials to stop taking a neutral stance on student unrest:

"They've been playing with murder for years. Now, they've achieved it.... The blood is on the hands of anyone who has encouraged them, anyone who has talked recklessly of 'revolution,' anyone who has chided with mild disparagement the violence of extremists while hinting that the cause is right all the same."

While money began to pour into a memorial fund for Fassnacht's family, a Madison alternative newspaper, *Kaleidoscope*, published a statement from the bombers, who called themselves the New Year's Gang, also known as the Vanguard of the Revolution. On New Year's Eve of 1969, two of the men had taken a Cessna from a private airport and flown it over the Badger Army Ammunition Plant near Baraboo. They had dropped three mayonnaise jars filled with a homemade fertilizer and fuel oil mixture onto the plant but the jars failed to detonate. In the statement published after the Sterling Hall blast, the gang demanded immedi-

Wisconsin State Journal file photo
Robert Borchers surveys the damage after the blast.

ate release of three members of the Milwaukee Black Panther Party charged with attempted murder of a police officer. They also demanded abolition of the Reserve Officers Training Corps (ROTC) on the UW-Madison campus and an end to "male supremacist" women's hours on campus, a reference to curfews for freshman women living in dormitories.

Like other radical groups at the time, the bombers spelled "American" with a "k" instead of a "c":

"If these demands are not met by October 30," the statement said, "revolutionary measures of an intensity never before seen in this country will be taken by our cadres. Open warfare, kidnapping of important officials and even assassination will not be ruled out.

"The AMRC (Army Math Research Center), a think-tank of Amerikan militarism, was a fitting target for such revolutionary violence. As the major U.S. Army center for solving military mathematical problems, it bears full responsibility for Amerikan military genocide throughout the world.

"While hiding behind a facade of academic neutrality, the AMRC plays a vital role in doing the basic research necessary for the development of heavy artillery, conventional and nuclear weapons, biological weapons and much more.

"Today's explosion was the culmination of over a year's effort to remove AMRC's ominous presence from the Wisconsin campus. Previous efforts even to negotiate were met with indifference. Such is the response of imperialistic authority to public sentiment. Our actions, therefore, were deemed necessary, for with every passing day, the AMRC takes its toll in mutilated bodies.

"We see our achievement as more than just the destruction of one building. We see it as part of a worldwide struggle to defeat Amerikan imperialism."

Pieces of the Falcon van were found on top of an eight-story building three blocks away. Part of the engine was retrieved from the roof of Birge Hall a block away. Another piece was found in a swimming pool inside Lathrop Hall. The explosion also damaged an adjacent lab and smashed stained glass windows at area churches.

A week after the blast, Robert Borchers, Fassnacht's supervising professor, shook his head in disgust as he surveyed the debris inside the demolished nuclear physics laboratory.

"The future of the whole nuclear physics program here is not only a question of money but whether people are in fact willing to go in and rebuild the laboratory," he told a *Wisconsin State Journal* reporter. "Clearly, you can't just let the rubble lie because then they've won hands down. But on the other hand, if you get all blown up again in year, it's really futile.

"Lots of people have simply talked about getting out of academic life. I think that's a very real possibility."

But within a year, the nuclear physics lab was up and running again in the patched-up basement of Sterling Hall. And Borchers had decided to stay on.

Meanwhile, the FBI took over the bombing investigation and members of President Nixon's Commission on Campus Unrest came to Madison.

Mark Knops, editor of *Kaleidoscope*, was jailed under $15,000 cash bail in Elkhorn on contempt of court charges for failing to reveal information to a grand jury on an arson case in Whitewater. Police identified the Sterling Hall suspects as Karleton Armstrong, his brother Dwight, David Fine and Leo Burt. The four bombers drove to Ann Arbor, Michigan, and then to Toledo, Ohio, where they split up. Burt and Fine went their own way while the Armstrongs drove separately to New York City, where they reunited at a clandestine Times Square meeting on September 2. By subway, bus, foot and stolen car, the brothers headed north to Montreal, where they sought help from an organization for draft resisters and Army deserters. Karleton eventually settled in Toronto while Dwight moved to Vancouver.

At the funeral of Robert Fassnacht, Rabbi Manfred Swarsensky expressed the community's frustration and horror at the researcher's death.

"We have not come into this world to hurt, to hate, to hunt — but to love, to build and to preserve God's creation. Research wantonly interrupted can be resumed but a life sinfully destroyed can never be restored."

The Army, of course, refused to knuckle under to the bombers' demands and pledged to keep the research center on the Madison campus. Instead of igniting more protest, the bombing numbed other campus radicals.

"It had a leveling effect," Madison Mayor William Dyke said a year later. "I think it diminished the zeal of some of those who would use any means to achieve an end. It showed what can come of being unreasoning and unwilling. The people who did the bombing were unreasoning."

By the summer of 1971, a grand jury had convened to investigate the bombing. Among the witnesses called to testify were Donald Armstrong, father of Karleton and Dwight, and Malcom Sliter, a family friend arrested as a material witness to the incident. Madison Ald. Susan Kay Phillips drafted a proposed ordinance condemning the grand jury as "a tool to eliminate dissent."

The ordinance didn't pass but its supporters feared the grand jury would be used to compile a history of the radical movement in Madison and list those involved in it. By September 1971, Sterling Hall repairs were completed and the grand jury indicted the four suspects for first-degree murder. Karleton Armstrong also was indicted on three counts of arson for other incidents in 1969 and 1970 on the UW-Madison campus.

Despite several narrow escapes from police, the suspects remained at large. On the night of the bombing, their car was stopped by Sauk County deputies for speeding near Devil's Lake but there was no evidence at the time to link them to the bombing. A few days later, the Armstrong brothers were stopped in Little Falls, New York for driving a car with a loud muffler. They were released before Little Falls police learned they were wanted for the bombing. Fine and Burt were sighted September 5, 1970, at a YMCA hostel in Peterborough, Ontario.

In September, 1971, Dane County Sheriff Vernon Leslie and Madison Police Detective Charles Lulling rushed to Toronto to check out a tip the bombers might be there. They came back with two burglary suspects instead.

In February, 1972, Karleton Armstrong's luck ran out. He had grown a full beard and worked as a gear machine operator in a small suburban Toronto factory under the alias of David Weller. He told co-workers at the Toronto Gear Works Ltd. that he hoped to get a job on a tramp freighter so he could see the world and eventually land in Algeria. An attempt to get a Canadian passport probably tripped him up. An informant who tipped police to Armstrong's whereabouts later was given

Wisconsin State Journal file photos

Karleton Armstrong   Dwight Armstrong   David Fine

$12,000 from a UW-Madison reward fund. Armstrong fought extradition to Madison for thirteen months but finally was returned to Wisconsin on March 8, 1973.

Represented by renowned radical attorney William Kunstler, Armstrong confessed to the bombing. He said he was sorry about Fassnacht's death but that he had no misgivings about the bombing itself. He pleaded guilty to second-degree murder and arson.

"The acts with which I have been credited were undertaken with the purpose of crippling the efforts of the American government to wage an illegal, criminal and aggressive war against the Indo-Chinese people, to prevent further loss of life, devastation and suffering," he said. "These actions were intended as an affirmation of life and great precautions were taken to prevent injury to human life."

In October 1973, while his three accomplices remained on the run, Armstrong was sentenced to twenty-three years in prison. Two years later, Dwight Armstrong drifted south from Canada to San Francisco, where he lived with an acquaintance in a rooming house. He worked as a day laborer, sold Christmas trees and passed out handbills to earn money.

Later in the year, he moved south to San Diego, where it was warmer, finding a place to stay at Ocean Beach. He was arrested for stealing three pounds of cheese. Although Dwight Armstrong was on the list of the FBI's ten most-wanted fugitives, San Diego police unwittingly released him after he served three days of a thirty-day sentence for the cheese theft.

A few weeks later, however, David Fine was arrested by the FBI in San Rafael, an exclusive suburb twenty-two miles north of San Francisco. An anonymous caller led agents to a man using the name William James Lewes. Fine was attending Marin Community College as a part-time student studying biology and psychology. He rented a room in a family home, where he kept a cat named Camilla after Symbionese Liberation Army member Camilla Hall. The SLA was a radical group credited with a string of bank robberies in California and kidnapping newspaper heiress Patty Hearst.

In a San Francisco courtroom, Fine, sporting a mustache, long sideburns and a thin beard, told spectators: "Greetings to everyone that showed up." He then gave a clenched fist salute and shouted, "Power to the MPLA, too!" MPLA stood for the Movement for the Liberation of Angola. Unlike Karleton Armstrong, Fine waived his right to fight extradition to Wisconsin. A native of Wilmington, Delaware, Fine had transferred to the UW-Madison from the University of Delaware where he'd been active in the Students for a Democratic Society (SDS). In June 1976, he pleaded guilty to third-degree murder, conspiracy and flight to avoid prosecution and was sentenced to seven years in prison. Police tried to prove through voice prints that Fine was the caller who warned police of the bombing but Karleton Armstrong later revealed the caller actually had been his brother Dwight. At the time, analysis of some voice samples taken from Fine indicated a high probability that Fine was the caller, but police were blocked by U.S. District Judge Myron Gordon from obtaining more samples.

Wisconsin State Journal file photo
Leo Burt

In April 1977, two plainclothes officers approached a man known as Gary Mitchell in a Toronto restaurant. The man, sitting with a woman, was clean-shaven with short hair. He wore blue corduroy pants and a long-sleeved jersey shirt. The officers showed Mitchell FBI pictures of Dwight Armstrong.

"Are you Dwight Armstrong?" one asked.

"Yes," Mitchell replied.

The woman, identified only as Ann, was under surveillance before Armstrong came to meet her at the downtown restaurant. He had known her for three weeks. Armstrong had lived in Toronto for about six months and held a job as an apprentice printer. He had been hired by Corpus Publishers Services Ltd. after he'd placed an ad in the *Toronto Star* saying he wanted to learn the printing trade. A day before his arrest, his co-workers threw a lunchtime pizza and wine party for him because Armstrong said he planned to head for Vancouver or Calgary to make and sell jewelry on the street. Co-workers said the man they knew as Mitchell liked movies, science fiction, health food and long philosophical discussions about the meaning of life. In his small room at a middle-class rooming house, Armstrong had a hot plate and access to a refrigerator. He had lots of books and shared a telephone but made no long-distance calls. He spent evenings working on a correspondence course to finish high school through the Toronto Board of Education. Co-workers described him as more of a flower child than a bomb thrower.

Dwight's arrest ended more than six years of flight that included frequent bouts of hunger and constant fear of capture. According to a 1975 *Berkeley Barb* article later reprinted in the *Milwaukee Journal*, it had meant stepping from tie to tie along a little used railroad line between Coutts, Alberta, and Sweetwater, Montana with heavy snow blowing across his path. It meant holding up a night deposit man for $5,000 and staging other "rips" to survive.

"We got so hungry those first weeks, we stole bags of noodles and tomato soup to fill ourselves up," Dwight told the California newspaper. "And finally we went into a wealthy district and robbed a man walking in the street."

Armstrong pleaded no contest to a charge of second-degree murder and, on May 5, 1977, he was sentenced to seven years in prison. At Oxford Federal Prison in Adams County, Dwight had a perfect grade-point average in college courses. He was paroled in 1980 and got a wood-working job in Madison. Fine, who served his sentence at Morgantown, West Virginia, was released in August 1979.

Karleton Armstrong's twenty-three-year sentence later was reduced to fourteen years and he was freed in February 1980.

"The year 1970 was a real climactic year for the anti-war movement," Fine said on his release. "I think all of us sort of became a little desperate. In retrospect, maybe there was a lot of overreaction to that. It obviously didn't end the war in Vietnam."

Fine, known to his friends as "Buzzy" when he graduated in 1969 from the Friends School in Alatocas, Delaware, relocated to Oregon and studied law. In high school, his interests had been politics and journalism and he'd carried these interests to the UW-Madison, where he maintained a 3.7 grade-point average and worked on the *Daily Cardinal* student newspaper. He graduated from Oregon School of Law in May 1984 with above-average standing and settled in Eugene. Fine passed the bar exam but his role in the bombing prevented him from practicing law in Oregon. Bar examiners described him as a bright but self-centered person who should not practice law because he did not show remorse for his illegal activities. Later, Fine, who wrote the *Kaleidoscope* communiqué about the bombing, said he was convinced the incident was totally wrong.

After his release, Karleton Armstrong drove a cab in Madison and, for several years, operated a vending cart that often appeared on the Library Mail at the end of State Street, several blocks east of Sterling Hall. He had married a Canadian woman while he was on the run.

Dwight Armstrong continued his education at the UW-Madison after he was paroled, becoming a student judge who heard cases involving violation of student government rules. But by 1987, he was in trouble again, charged with six others for operating a clandestine drug laboratory near Bloomington, Indiana, where methamphetamine, a potent form of speed, was manufactured.

Armstrong spent several months on the run again until his capture in July 1987, at one of his old haunts — Vancouver, British Columbia. He was arrested on traffic charges in Canada and extradited to Indiana to face the drug charges. He was convicted in late 1988.

Of the four bombers, only Burt was successful at eluding authorities. He was spotted with Fine in Ontario shortly after the bombing and was seen again at a rally several years later in Norman, Oklahoma. But nothing has been heard about him since then. Burt came to the UW-Madison in 1966, attracted by the Big Ten sports program. He won awards in 1967 and 1968 as a member of the university's crew teams. He planned a journalism career, joining the *Daily Cardinal* and covering campus demonstrations.

"If there was a leader," Dwight Armstrong told the *Berkeley Barb* in 1975, "it had to be Leo Burt. He was the strongest of any of us politically. I remember when Karleton was arrested, they called him the 'mastermind.' Actually, Karl was the mechanic. He handled the explosives. I was a kind of worker."

In 1995, speculation arose that Leo Burt might be the Unabomber, who sent a series of mail bombs to prominent businessmen over seventeen years. Tom Bates, a *Portland Oregonian* reporter author of *Rads,* a book on the case, said the Unabomber's rambling writings revealed that Burt was the culprit. Karleton Armstrong, however, disagreed and he apparently was proven right when Ted Kaczynski was arrested and charged as the Unabomber. "I think Leo would probably come in from the cold if a reasonable deal was cut," Armstrong said at the time.

Perhaps Burt drifted overseas to Algeria, where Karleton Armstrong planned to go. Cuba or Nicaragua are other possibilities. Now in his fifties, Burt may be working a respectable job under an assumed name somewhere in this country or Canada, keeping his true identity and involvement in the bombing long ago to himself.

20

Idzi's Reign of Terror
Milwaukee, 1935

On a cool fall evening, October 26, 1935, Detective Maurice Kavanaugh stood in front of the Shorewood Police Station. It was almost 7:30 p.m. in the Milwaukee suburb and the daytime bustle had faded into the stillness of another routine night. Suddenly Kavanaugh was knocked to the ground by the force of an explosion so powerful that it knocked a large hole in the brick foundation of the village hall, broke an outside chandelier, splintered a tall, white column at the entrance, seared young pine trees and shrubbery and shattered windows and cracked plaster at nearby homes. Residents scurried into the street while firefighters and police raced from the station a few feet north of the village hall. Glass littered the pavement.

The quiet fall evening was shattered by the sudden sounds of sirens wailing, people screaming and footsteps crunching on a carpet of broken glass. Nobody knew exactly what happened until a fire truck rolled out and turned a spotlight on the gaping hole in the side of the building.

No one was injured in the blast. Claude Barth, a janitor, had left the building six hours earlier, leaving a rear door unlocked so a Works Projects Administration (WPA) foreman working in the basement could get out. When WPA foreman Oscar Vestren left about a half hour later, he locked the door.

The odor from the blast told experts that it was dynamite. A natural gas explosion would have blown out more windows while gunpowder would have blown a hole in the ground. Vestren later estimated about five sticks of dynamite were used and he deduced the explosion probably was the work of an amateur. Scraps of paper indicated the dynamite had been concealed in newspaper. Village officials decided to convene a special board meeting to make some sense out of the mysterious bombing. Did someone have a grudge against the village?

On Sunday night, it became clear that the Shorewood bombing was part of a larger campaign of terrorism. Within a few minutes of each other, blasts damaged two Milwaukee branches of the First Wisconsin National Bank. A small gray car was spotted fleeing the scene shortly before one of the explosions and six Milwaukee police officers were assigned to track down the perpetrator, thought to be a crank with some kind of fancied grievance against society. At 6:40 p.m., the first blast tore a large hole in the rear wall of the bank branch at 3602 Villard Avenue, shattering windows and damaging the building's interior. A half hour later, the second explosion at the bank's East Side office on North Farwell Street damaged eight cars and endangered nearby theater-goers. At the Villard branch, dynamite had been placed on a window sill. At the Farwell office, the explosive had been placed in an empty gasoline tank. In both explosions, the bank vaults weren't threatened and it was apparent that robbery wasn't the motive.

Fear began to grip the city. Police officers were assigned to guard other bank branches. Investigators also found the source of the dynamite. Three weeks earlier, thieves had broken into a shed at Estabrook Park, stealing one-hundred-fifty pounds of dynamite, four-hundred-fifty fuse caps and two hundred feet of fuse line from Public Works Administration supplies. The thieves had waited to strike at midnight when two employees guarding the shed went to lunch. They had vaulted a four-foot fence and pried open a lock on the shed. Bits of fuse found at the bank branches were similar to the stolen fuse.

The city prepared for a continuation of the siege on Monday night, when guards were posted at all public buildings. There were no further bombings but the first of several contacts from the bomber was found on a fire alarm box at East Park Place and North Farwell Street. The package contained several dynamite fuses and a card which said: "There are no serial numbers. Be careful. The price will go up." The bomber then asked for $100,000 in various specified denominations. Guards maintained their vigil on Tuesday and Wednesday nights at downtown buildings and bank branches but the city was quiet. Detectives interviewed a man who in 1930 threatened to blow up a downtown bank but determined he wasn't involved in the latest bombings.

On Halloween night (Thursday), the mad bomber struck again, this time at the very heart of law and order. The targets were two police stations on the west and north sides. At one station, damage was estimated at $1,500 and the blast damaged police radio testing equipment but failed to knock police communications off the air. The explosions tore holes in the station walls, wrecked cars, smashed windows and chipped plaster in neighboring buildings.

Once again, the bombings were accompanied by a circus of swarming people and emergency vehicles. Three false fire alarms were set near the stations shortly before each blast, sending fire trucks honking and wailing into the streets and adding to the confusion. The bombings were eleven minutes and one and a quarter miles apart. The first occurred at 6:47 p.m. at the 5th Precinct Station; the second was at the 3rd Precinct Station. At each station, the dynamite was placed on a window ledge overlooking alleys. At the North Side Station, the blast ripped out a steel window casement, sending it sailing sixty feet across the room. Forty-two window panes were shattered in the police garage. Officer Carl Fritzke barely escaped injury, walking away from a coffeepot near the window moments before the blast. Detectives writing reports upstairs were lifted three inches out of their chairs. Nearby homes looked as if they'd been struck by a minor earthquake.

Although no one had been killed or injured in any of the explosions, the city was in a panic. The *Milwaukee Journal* reported: "Police headquarters and the seven precinct stations were armed camps Thursday night. For the first time in the memory of anyone, citizens were challenged before they could set foot into the grounds surrounding the precinct stations. At headquarters, where scores of bluecoats and detectives called in for extra duty sat waiting for the next call, everyone entering the safety building was compelled to identify himself and explain his errand. Each door was guarded by a detective and an officer in uniform."

The City Council scheduled a special meeting to consider a resolution condemning the bombings and calling for swift capture of the perpetrator.

Police Chief J.G. Laubenheimer called the bombings "the work of a maniac."

In a seething November 1 editorial, the *Milwaukee Sentinel* charged that the bombings were inspired by communists: "Milwaukee has been challenged by a dangerous gang of Reds — Reds whether they belong to the Communist Party or not. Dynamitings such as have occurred must be classified as the work of anarchists and Milwaukee must arouse itself to the fact that it is in a battle with a dangerous and underhanded enemy. Professional agitators and political opportunists have been breeding communists and anarchists faster than we thought. Call them what you may, but only a Red would bomb a police station."

The newspaper made much of reports that a car with a spotlight and siren — perhaps a stolen police car — was spotted fleeing the scene of one bombing. In blaring headlines, the *Sentinel* announced:

MILWAUKEE IN A STATE OF SIEGE!

Another communication from the bomber came on Friday. This time, a note was sent to police Capt. Robert Sandow of the Mineral Street Station. The note read simply: "You're next, no fooling." The note was scrawled on a soiled piece of cheap writing paper and had been mailed Thursday. Earlier, another note typed almost illegibly on a typewriter stolen from the Center Street School demanded $125,000 from police Capt. Frank J. Prohaska to stop the bombings.

In an attempt to close in on the terrorist, police raided several pool-rooms in the city, catching forty-five people in their net. But the bomber still eluded them.

A man entered City Hall Friday afternoon with a package under his arm. He fumbled with string wrapped around the package, then shoved it under a steam radiator. But City Comptroller William Wendt, who was strolling through the lobby with his wife, saw the man and shouted to a nearby news vendor to see what he was up to. When the vendor turned, the man grabbed the package and fled from the building. Wendt reported the incident to police. Newspapers speculated the bomber apparently was an amateur who used fuses, which were seldom used by professionals because they were too dangerous. Experienced bombers were said to use more reliable electronic detonation systems.

Tension was thick in the city as 6:00 p.m. approached on Saturday. Hundreds of residents tuned their radios to police frequencies to make sure they wouldn't miss reports of the next bombing. Police guarded public buildings and other officers cruised the streets in squad cars. Every entrance to the safety building was guarded by an officer stationed inside the door. Some people nervously suggested betting pools on where the mad bomber would strike next. But by 7:30 p.m., the tension eased and people returned to the streets, continuing on their way to the theaters or work. There would be no bombings that night.

On Sunday afternoon, sixteen-year-old Paul Chovenec, known to his friends by the nickname "Shrimp," left his home at 1744 S. 17th Street. He had borrowed a quarter from his father to see a movie. About the same time, shortly after 2:00 p.m., a squad car with two detectives pulled up next to a garage at 2121 S. Mitchell Street. The detectives had parked outside the same garage a week earlier after neighbors pointed it out as a place where stolen loot might be kept. The detectives stopped their car outside the garage. This time, they were investigating a car theft. Maybe the stolen car was inside. But they didn't have a warrant so they drove on.

A half hour later, the garage was gone. It was leveled by a blast far more powerful than those that had damaged the police stations, the bank branches and the Shorewood Village Hall. This explosion had the force of thirty-five to forty sticks of dynamite. And this time the blast was fatal. Patricia Myinarek, age nine, was in her home adjoining the garage when one wall of the home was shorn off. She died when her skull was crushed, either by falling debris or when she was flung against a wall. Every window on the block was shattered as well as some several blocks away. Thousands of spectators flocked to the scene, where they stood among the wreckage in a steady drizzle and listened to the eerie booming of a fog horn.

It was the mad bomber's most powerful explosion yet. Not only had he outdone himself but he also had done himself in. Twenty-year-old Idzi Rutkowski, whom police identified as the mad bomber, was blown to bits. His head was found against the door of another garage. A leg was found at the Alexander Mitchell School, five hundred feet away. When police found two spinal sections, they realized that Idzi's sidekick, Chovonec, also had died in the blast. Bits of clothing and a piece of scalp with brown hair attached to it had to be Chovonec's remains because Rukowski had black hair. Eleven people who lived close to the garage, including Patricia's mother and younger brother, were injured.

In Idzi's room, police found a typewriter and books on gasoline engines. They found a relief map of South America he'd helped his older sister make for a school project. There were trade school textbooks and, most important, a book of instructions on how to set off dynamite. His parents were Polish immigrants who spoke little English. Through an interpreter, Idzi's mother said he hadn't been the same since he was age seven, when another boy knocked him unconscious with a rock. Idzi had been treated for the injury at a hospital but, five years later, he began suffering fainting spells and holding his mouth open in an odd gaping way. His mother said Idzi had good mechanical skills, fixing the plumbing and her electric iron. He also helped her beat the rugs when they needed cleaning.

"If Idzi could have found a job, this never would have happened," she said.

"For two years, he looked at the factories. He got up early and went looking. At breakfast time, he came back and said 'No help wanted,' the signs read. Then he would go back to bed. He was going to be an engineer. He was graduated from the technical school and went to night school. But his father could not send him to college. Twice he had jobs as a mechanic and he brought me his paychecks."

The year before the bombings, Idzi had gone to a Civilian Conservation Corps camp about two-hundred seventy miles from Milwaukee in hopes of joining the corps but he was rejected because of his bad teeth. His teeth also kept him out of the Navy. While at the CCC camp, Idzi had been fascinated by the use of dynamite in public works projects and watched the blasting for hours.

His visit to the camp may have prompted the dynamite theft but not the bombings. Those were spurred by his vendetta against the police for frequently arresting him. Police Chief Laubenheimer described his theory of Idzi's motive: "He was a worthless character, idle most of the time. He was undoubtedly the confirmed criminal type as shown by his record of arrests as a juvenile. Although he was treated more leniently than he deserved, he developed hatred of the police and law enforcement agencies that amounted to a mania. It was this, I believe, that prompted his bombings of the police station and his personal note to Capt. Robert Sandow. His bombings of the 3rd and 5th precinct stations were done entirely in revenge for his numerous arrests."

Rutkowski — muscular, athletic and an avid swimmer — dominated his sidekick, slight and wiry "Shrimp" Chovenec, leading the teenager into a life of crime. The two boys became good friends when their families lived next door to each other for three years. Idzi and Paul would capture stray cats, cut off their tails and stick pins in them. Chovenec got into a brush with the law for stealing cigarettes. An acquaintance of Rutkowski, sixteen-year-old Alice Kabling, told police she had been threatened by Rutkowski's pals when she discovered the group might be involved in car theft. Chovenec had spent a year in a boys' home after several shoplifting incidents.

From her hospital bed, Patricia's mother told the *Milwaukee Journal* about the irony of her daughter's death: "He (Rutkowski) swore and used bad language. He swore around the garage so much that I couldn't stand it. I used to shoo the children away when he was around because I didn't want them to learn the vile, obscene talk that he was always using. And now Patricia, the one I most wanted to protect from his foul language, is dead."

Both Rutkowski and Chovonec were buried in the same coffin because it was impossible to separate their bodies. Nobody else was implicated in the bombings. In fact, police discovered that Rutkowski would stand and block the garage door with his body when his friends came to see him so they wouldn't find out about the explosives inside. Stolen jewelry was found in the garage debris along with scorched fragments of pornographic prose.

The series of bombings was the worst in Milwaukee since the explosion on November 24, 1917, in the city's central police station killed eleven people. (See Chapter 16.)

After Idzi's final explosion, police discovered he kept a notebook of his press clippings. Perhaps he had read the news story a few days earlier that the mad bomber was using antiquated fuses, because Idzi had been trying to professionalize his operation, experimenting with an electrical detonation system using an alarm clock and storage battery when the dynamite in the garage exploded accidentally. The *Milwaukee Sentinel* reported he had been hard at work on a "super bomb."

But the *Sentinel's* editorial writers, who had been so positive the bombings were the work of communist terrorists, finally conceded they had been the handiwork of "a single, warped intelligence." They said Idzi "cherished the same hatred of law and order and organized society that (characterizes) the preachers of violent communism." The *Milwaukee Journal* simply reported that Idzi was an enthusiastic supporter of President Franklin Roosevelt, telling his family that "the president is the best man we can get."

21

The Siege of Cameron Dam
Thornapple River, 1904

In mid-April 1904, loggers were poised to raise the gates on the Cameron Dam so hundreds of thousands of logs could flow downstream.

"Don't raise those gates!" John F. Dietz shouted at them. When they ignored him, he fired a single shot that whizzed close to one of the men. They stopped.

"Nobody else come close to my dam!" he warned. The single shot ignited a six-year battle between Dietz and the lumber barons. His struggle captured the public's fascination and marked the twilight of the Wisconsin frontier.

Dietz had a rather simple gripe. He believed he should be paid for the three years he spent watching the dam for the Chippewa Lumber & Boom Co. of Chippewa Falls. But the lumber company claimed Dietz was only hired for a couple weeks during the spring lumber drive.

Although the dispute was simple, its resolution was not. Dietz battled the lumber company for six years and his struggle became symbolic of a poor farmer's fight against the rich lumber barons. He single-handedly stopped a log drive by the Midwest's biggest lumber combine. He spurned several attempts to arrest him, often sending lawmen in hasty retreat. Dietz was the last of the Wisconsin frontiersmen.

During the early years of this century, the lumber business in Wisconsin was controlled by two powerful men. Edward Hines, who owned several Great Lakes barges and a large Chicago lumber business, teamed up with Frederick Weyerhaeuser to log the dense forests of northern Wisconsin.

Dietz was born in 1861. His father, a German immigrant, fought on the Union side in the Civil War and afterward, moved to Wisconsin, settling in Barron County. The Dietz family became known as "Winchester" farmers, quick to defend their property with a rifle.

In 1882, Dietz married Hattie Young, whom he called "Tatsy," and the young couple started a family. But young Dietz didn't care for farming and, by 1899, he decided to go into the real estate business with his brother. The business, however, didn't go well, although Dietz was able to acquire some property along the Thornapple River near the Cameron Dam.

In April 1901, he was approached by John Mulligan, a foreman with Chippewa Lumber & Boom. Mulligan offered Dietz a salary of two dollars a day if he would keep an eye on the company's Price Dam on the Brunet River, Dietz moved his family into a shack near the dam. In 1902, he was paid seventy-two dollars for thirty-six days of work watching the dam. Dietz claimed he had earned more. The lumber company claimed Dietz had been hired only to watch the dam during the spring drive.

In February 1904, Dietz went to see Mulligan about the additional wages. A brawl ensued and Dietz claimed he was attacked with fists and a stick by Mulligan and one of his workers.

Dietz decided to fight back. He moved his wife and six children to the Cameron Dam on the Thornapple River and, from April 10-15, 1904, he blocked the dam, holding up the lumber drive. An estimated six-and-a-half million feet of timber was jammed into the flowage above the dam. The blockade clearly hurt the lumber company but it took several months for them to do something about it. In July and again in November, representatives were sent to the Dietz homestead to reach a settlement.

But the situation already was becoming more complicated. After the incident with Mulligan, it seems Mulligan swore out a complaint against Dietz and an arrest warrant was issued. The sheriff, however, was reluctant to serve the warrant.

Another complication was that Dietz learned a portion of the Cameron Dam, originally built by Thomas Leavitt and sometimes called the Leavitt Dam, was on his land. He posted a "No Trespassing" sign and told lumber company representatives a fair settlement would be payment to him of ten cents per thousand for logs sluiced through the co-owned dam.

Two weeks after Dietz first blocked the dam, the lumber company won a court judgment for $84.12 in damages. But the judgment ne-

The Dietz family and friends at the farm.

glected to mention who was supposed to pay the damages.

"I won't be taken alive!" Dietz told Deputy Fred Clark, who came to serve the warrant on May 3. Two more deputies were sent out five days later but ran into an ambush Dietz had set up behind a knoll. One shot grazed a deputy's hat. The following day, a group of loggers were shot at by a sniper while they were eating dinner. A bullet broke the left arm of one logger. Dietz later wrote a poem describing the loggers scrambling for cover behind pea sacks.

By October 1904, a judge found Sheriff Peterson in contempt for failing to serve the warrant on Dietz. Peterson was sentenced to pay a one-hundred-fifty dollar fine and serve thirty days in jail. Instead, he was defeated in that fall's election by James Gylland. When another deputy tried to serve the warrant in November, Dietz grabbed it out of his hands and threatened him. The deputy picked up the warrant and fled back to Hayward.

Sawyer County officials concluded they might need some help in bringing Dietz to justice. The county board passed a resolution authorizing the expenditure of five hundred dollars, clearly a reward, to bring in the difficult farmer.

Early the following year, the lumber company got tired of trying to deal with local officials and got a federal court injunction that prohibited Dietz from interfering with the log drives. The injunction assessed damages at $20,000.

In early April 1905, three men came to the Dietz homestead, claiming to be interesting in buying land. One of them returned later with a paper for Dietz. But Dietz ordered him off his property and, when the man didn't comply, the farmer hit him and physically kicked him out of the house. Dietz picked up a rifle and threatened to shoot the man but his wife stopped him. The men were Herman Jonas of Madison, Charles Callaghan of Hayward and Henry Conlin of Bayfield, acting under authority of U.S. Marshal Charles Lewiston.

With several failed attempts to snare Dietz, U.S. Marshal William Appleby decided to go a step further. He rounded up a posse of twenty-five men, including eleven Chicago detectives. On May 22, Appleby, Lewiston and the posse set up camp near Cameron Dam. Appleby sent a neighbor, Charles O'Hare, to the Dietz home as a peace envoy. Dietz refused and the posse departed without him, leaving the federal warrants with Sheriff Gylland.

On July 3, 1905, Gylland went to the Dietz homestead carrying a subpoena for Dietz to appear a the trial of his accomplice in the knoll ambush. Dietz hid behind the barn and Gylland failed to serve the subpoena.

Justice continued to move at a snail's pace. The following April (1906), the determined U.S. marshals tried again to serve their warrants on Dietz. The farmer confronted Deputy Marshal William Pugh and Conlin outside his home. Dietz raised a rifle and ordered them to halt. Pugh set down his papers on a pile of lumber. When the men were gone, Dietz jabbed a pitchfork into the papers and tossed them in the river.

By this time, authorities had made ten attempts to arrest Dietz but failed each time. The case was gaining some notoriety and newspapers debated the pros and cons. Some editorialized that the state militia should be sent in to bring the scoundrel to justice; others argued that the poor, crusading farmer should be left alone. Gylland tried to round up another posse but none of the locals would join. He went to Milwaukee and recruited a group of men, dressing them in National Guard uniforms to strike fear into Dietz.

When Gylland and his new posse sneaked up on the Dietz family, son Clarence was standing with a pitchfork in a load of hay. Daughter Myra was driving a team of horses while Dietz and his wife were in the barn loft, stomping down the hay. Hattie Dietz looked outside and saw a cow perk up its ears, as if at something in the bushes down by the river. She alerted the family. Dietz and his son grabbed their rifles.

"Get out of here, you sons of bitches!" Dietz shouted, then he started firing into the bushes, wounding one of the men, John Rogich, in the neck. Several men fled back to the lumber camp. Rogich picked up his gun and fired, creasing young Clarence's skull. Son Leslie and Dietz hunted down Rogich and shot him in the hip and heel.

Gylland ran to help Rogich but got stuck in the mud as a pair of bullets whizzed past his ear. Dietz and his sons retreated and Gylland was able to rescue Rogich. Swarms of deer flies and mosquitoes attacked Rogich's wounds. Miraculously, he survived by submerging himself in the water. Clarence Dietz carried a scar on his head from the gun battle for the rest of his life.

The shootout at Cameron Dam fueled Dietz's popularity and enhanced the growing legend around him. A postcard featured "the cow that served as a watchdog for Dietz." The Milwaukee Journal sponsored a poll on what should be done with the renegade farmer. Most readers said he should be left alone.

Logs continued to jam the flowage above the dam until a portion of the dam was washed away in 1906. More than a million logs were strewn everywhere, many on the Dietz property. By June 1907, officials of the lumber company had had enough and decided to settle with Dietz. W.E. Moses was sent out as a representative of Frederick Weyerhaeuser. Dietz was paid $1,717 in back wages, although Dietz claimed the company owed him $8,000 by this time.

"For four long years, myself and my family have been the targets of blackmail and bullets of the land pirates and timber wolves," he said. Dietz was allowed to keep the logs that wound up on his land. A.E. Roese, editor of the *Osceola Sun*, also came to the farmer's aid, paying his property taxes for 1907. For awhile, Roese arranged clandestine shipments of flour, sugar, coffee and other staples so family members wouldn't have to risk coming into nearby Winter to buy necessities.

The lumber company settlement appeared to end the dispute. Dietz and his family began making regular visits to Winter for supplies, making the pipeline arranged by Roese unnecessary. For more than three years, law enforcement officials made no further efforts to arrest Dietz.

But the warrants remained on the books and local officials were as determined as ever to bring Dietz to justice. In 1907, the Sawyer County Board upped the ante to $1,000 for anyone who could bring in the fugitive.

An ironic aspect to the entire controversy was that Dietz demanded that the town board provide a teacher for his children because his homestead didn't lie within an existing school district. Despite the attempts to arrest Dietz, the town officials complied and Ethel Young, who taught during the 1905-06 school year, began the first of a succession of teachers provided to the family. In 1908, one of the Dietz children, Stanley, age eight, died of pneumonia.

In 1909, on one of the family's visits to Winter, Dietz approached Dick Phelan, owner of the local hotel, and taunted him.

"Woof! Woof!" he called to Phelan. "Ain't you afraid of me?"

Wisconsin Historical Society

John Dietz in jail, 1910.

"Why don't you give yourself up?" Phelan suggested.

"No sirree! I'll never give myself up. They'll have to come and get me."

On September 6, 1910, Dietz and his son, Clarence, went to Winter for supplies. Clarence approached Charles O'Hare, a town board member, about whether the town would assign a teacher that fall for the younger Dietz children. A fight ensued and Bert Horel, another town board member, hit John Dietz in the neck. He responding by pulling out his rifle and shooting Horel in the shoulder. The incident rekindled the ire of local officials, who agreed someone must put an end to the renegade farmer's unlawful acts.

Later that month, Sheriff Mike Madden recruited Fred Thorbahn, a Radisson shopkeeper, and Ray Van Alstine to help him arrest Dietz. Madden decided to wait for Dietz to come to Winter on one of the family's supply runs. On Saturday, September 21, the three men lay in ambush for the family's wagon. As luck would have it, Dietz stayed home that day for an interview with Floyd P. Gibbons, a Minneapolis reporter. He sent Clarence, then twenty-three, Myra, then twenty-one, and Leslie, then twenty, to town instead.

Thinking Dietz might be hiding, Madden and his men ambushed the wagon anyway. The trigger-happy Thorbahn and Van Alstine began firing. During the ensuing gunfight, Clarence was shot in the arm and Myra was hit in the stomach.

"I didn't tell them to shoot!" Madden shouted, running out of the woods. Leslie escaped but the other two Dietz children were handcuffed and arrested. Myra Dietz was rushed in a railroad baggage car to St. Joseph's Hospital in Ashland for treatment of her serious wounds. Although she survived, the incident ignited the Dietz controversy all over again. The *St. Paul Dispatch* editorialized that the botched arrest attempt was "a travesty of law and order." Wisconsin Gov. Davidson received ten thousand letters about the case, most of them supporting Dietz.

In the face of public outcry, the governor sent Attorney General Frank Gilbert to meet Dietz. The farmer met Gilbert's entourage on the banks of the Thornapple River and raised his hat.

"Can you see any horns on my head?" he asked.

Gilbert conferred with Dietz and left a letter from the governor on the kitchen table but Dietz may never have opened it. The next day, the attorney general came back. He offered to drop all charges except for the shooting of Horel. Dietz refused the offer. He said he also wanted all civil actions dropped and clear title to his land. Meanwhile, Clarence languished in jail at Hayward for his role in the Horel incident.

Fog shrouded the banks of the Thornapple on October 8, 1910, when Sheriff Madden once again summoned his deputies. This time, they were assisted by a posse of neighbors grown weary of the renegade farmer's defiance of the law. The posse surrounded the homestead and Thorbahn passed a note to Dietz.

"John Dietz," the note began. "You had better surrender. It will be for the best for yourself and your family. You will be treated right and get a square deal. There is no way for you to win any other way."

The note was answered by gunfire and the battle of Cameron Dam began that day in earnest. Hattie Dietz and her children took cover on the floor as the lawmen sprayed the house with fire. More than eighty rounds were blasted into the house. Dietz ran to the barn, hoping to deflect their shots away from his family. One posse member, Oscar Harp, was fatally wounded in the mouth. Harp, who had taken cover behind a pile of lumber, was the first and only casualty of the six-year Dietz siege.

After six hours of fighting, Dietz ran back to the house about 3:00 p.m., hoping to bandage his wounded left hand. Mrs. Dietz persuaded her husband to surrender and Dietz came out. As Thorbahn placed handcuffs on him, Dietz said that was unnecessary.

"Oh, you don't need to put those on me," he said. "I give up. You have got my word. We surrender."

Thorbahn collected the thousand-dollar reward and probably split it with Van Alstine. His Radisson shop burned to the ground a few days after the arrest and Thorbahn moved to Montana, where he opened a dry goods store.

Floyd Gibbons, the aggressive Minneapolis reporter who had interviewed Dietz the day his children were ambushed, cut a telephone wire at the Hotel Winter, hoping to get a leg up on the competition. But Gibbons was taken into custody and brought to Hayward to appear before a judge for the offense. He posted bail and rushed back to Cameron Dam but missed all the action. Gibbons left the Minneapolis paper and moved to the *Chicago Tribune*.

The Dietz trial began May 2, 1911, in Milwaukee. Dietz, who appeared a hero to many defending his property, became an object of pity when he insisted on defending himself in court. The *Minneapolis Tribune* described his efforts as "pathetic." His best moment was getting Van Alstine to admit that Harp could have been killed by friendly fire from posse members. Dietz also tried to raise a key issue during his cross-examination of Attorney General Gilbert.

"Is there not a law on the state book saying that a man's home is his castle, that a man has a right to defend it at the cost of his life?"

"No," Gilbert responded. "There is no such law on the state books."

Dietz was found guilty of murdering Oscar Harp and sentenced to life in prison. In 1913, a silent film titled "The Battle of Cameron Dam" was made. The Dietz family moved to Mayville to be closer to their incarcerated patriarch. In 1914, the sentence was commuted to twenty-five years and, on May 12, 1921, Gov. John Blaine pardoned Dietz for all his crimes. Without the pardon, he would have been released anyway the following year.

Dietz went on the lecture circuit, doing five shows a day at the Miller Theater in Milwaukee. But his family's support for him had dwindled during the years in prison and the incarceration also had taken a toll on his health. Dietz died May 8, 1924, at age 73.

In his 1974 book, *The Battle of Cameron Dam*, Malcolm Rosholt writes about the significance of the Dietz case as a symbol of transition to the new century.

"(These were) the closing days of the American frontier," he writes. "In Wisconsin, the frontier closed on the banks of the Thornapple River."

On July 4, 1970, the village of Winter celebrated Dietz Pioneer Days. Leading the parade were Myra Dietz and her brother, John Jr.

22

A Dose of His Own Medicine
Darlington, 1985

Judge Daniel McDonald screamed and cried as he was dragged forcibly into the Darlington courtroom. When District Attorney Jerry Lynch came through the door, McDonald bolted out of his chair and lunged at him.

"You son of a bitch!" McDonald shouted. "Get him out of here!"

McDonald's brother, Patrick, who served as his attorney, reached out to restrain him. Then McDonald collapsed in his chair, brushing back his fiery red hair and burying his face in his arms folded on the table. Later, he angrily interrupted the proceedings again to profess his innocence.

"I was not down at that office or anywhere near that office! I don't know who did this or why. But I have a pretty good guess why. And I have a pretty good guess who. For God's sake! I can't stay in jail! I've got to get out!"

But he didn't get out. Visiting Green County Judge Franz Brand ordered Lafayette County Judge Daniel McDonald held on $500,000 cash bail as the accused judge choked back sobs and protested he didn't murder Darlington attorney James Klein.

So, from the other side of the bench where he'd ruled on cases for fourteen years, McDonald was ordered jailed that day in the same cell where the tough-sentencing judge had sent many a lawbreaker.

With his shock of red hair neatly combed and a fiery temperament to match, Daniel Patrick McDonald began his public service career in 1968 in a campaign for district attorney. He was age twenty-six then, a hometown boy, raised on a farm near Darlington and presented himself as a vigorous alternative to incumbent John Schleifer, age thirty-nine, of Benton. Unlike McDonald, Schleifer was an outsider, hailing from Milwaukee, but had served seven years as district attorney. McDonald, a Democrat, faced an uphill battle in a Republican county, especially in a year of assassinations, campus protests and Richard Nixon. McDonald was fresh out of the armed services, back from Vietnam, and he'd opened a law practice in Darlington a few months after his discharge. He graduated in 1960 from Darlington High School and earned a bachelor's degree in business administration four years later from Marquette University. In 1966, he graduated from Marquette University Law School and then entered the military. He married the former Catherine Cosgriff and the couple later would have two sons.

McDonald blasted Schleifer for not being available even though the position was part-time. McDonald said the demands on the office were increasing and the district attorney needed to spend more time on the job in all areas of the county. McDonald's youthful charisma and his energetic farm-to-farm campaign swept him into office and he won re-election two years later.

When Lafayette County Judge Joseph Collins died in early 1971, Gov. Patrick Lucey appointed McDonald to fill the unexpired term. A year later, McDonald was elected to the judge's post by the narrow margin of one-hundred forty votes over Ervin Johnson, another former district attorney. Over the next dozen years, McDonald stayed on the bench, building a reputation for tough sentencing.

In December 1976, he dismissed a perjury charge against a Monticello police officer and delivered a stinging rebuke to the prosecutor who brought the charge. The officer, Scott A. Cairy, was charged with perjury for testimony he gave against two men. He had accused the men of striking him when he stopped their car. McDonald, as a visiting judge in Green County, didn't see the case the same way as District Attorney James R. Beer. He scolded Beer for bringing frivolous charges against Cairy, an officer merely trying to do his sworn duty.

McDonald's reputation as a relentless law-and-order judge was enhanced in July 1978, when he refused to reduce a sixty-day jail sentence he imposed against an Argyle girl convicted of telephoning a bomb threat to Argyle High School.

Claire Schmidt, age seventeen, who pleaded guilty to the charge, already had served twenty-four days of the sentence when her court-appointed attorney, former Madison mayor William Dyke, asked McDonald to show compassion and allow the girl to serve the rest of her term on probation. But McDonald refused, saying the Wisconsin Legislature apparently considered telephone bomb threats a serious crime because, a

Wisconsin State Journal file photo

Judge Daniel McDonald, center, sobs and rests his hand on his brother Patrick's shoulder as he is led into his own courtroom to face charges of first-degree murder.

month earlier, lawmakers had elevated the offense to felony status. He also said Dyke, who happened to be the law partner of McDonald's election opponent Ervin Johnson, had failed to produce any new evidence that merited a lighter sentence.

"It is inappropriate for a sentencing court to make a change in an imposed sentence unless new factors are made known," the judge said. "A trial court should not reduce a sentence on reflection alone, or simply because it has thought the matter over and had second thoughts. It must base modification on the facts brought to its attention."

Dyke argued in vain that the rights of the public had been protected and that "the public is very well aware of the fact that bomb threats will not be tolerated in this jurisdiction."

McDonald not only ruled against him, but the judge also fired Dyke as the girl's public defender, saying she could afford a private attorney because she held a $2.65 per hour job at a Yellowstone Lake restaurant.

In 1984, the Lafayette County district attorney worked out a plea bargain with a man arrested for selling marijuana. The prosecutor agreed to drop two of four counts for delivery of marijuana in exchange for a guilty plea. The district attorney also recommended the man, Dick Wahl, be sentenced to no more than five years in prison. But McDonald scuttled the plan, sentencing Wahl to consecutive terms of four years on each of the two charges. That decision later was overturned by the state Court of Appeals, which ruled that McDonald used a "mechanistic approach" in setting the sentence.

By early 1985, McDonald, the once-young, fresh-faced attorney, had become middle-aged. At forty-two, his hair remained bright red but lines had begun to set in his face. And he faced the toughest election battle of his career against William Johnston of Darlington, also forty-two. Johnston waged a merciless campaign against McDonald, criticizing the judge for refusing to release defendants on signature bond.

"In our county, we have farm economy problems and a lot of people have trouble making bail," Johnston told the *Wisconsin State Journal*. "I'm not talking about Son of Sam cases. I'm just suggesting common sense and discretion."

Because of his tough reputation, McDonald was not a favorite of local attorneys. Many filed substitution requests when they drew him as a judge. Johnston said some of the requests arose out of fear by attorneys that he wouldn't conduct an unbiased trial.

McDonald struck back against his opponent, claiming Johnston was conducting a negative, untruthful campaign. The judge defended his tendency to ask questions of his own during court proceedings and admitted that he didn't favor signature bonds.

"There are times when it's necessary for a judge to ask questions. Some of these poor people don't understand what's going on and don't have a lawyer. Even when a lawyer is present, it is sometimes necessary to ask a question to clarify something.

"I don't like signature bonds, that's true. But I certainly don't set high bail when it isn't warranted. Often I release a defendant with no bail."

McDonald accused Johnston and "some of his lawyer friends" of filing indiscriminate substitution requests against him to artificially inflate the number of substitutions so it could be used against him politically.

In the April election, Johnston succeeded in turning McDonald out of office. The tough-sentencing judge took the defeat hard, brooding about it for weeks and blaming other Lafayette County officials and attorneys. McDonald leveled his harshest criticism at District Attorney Jerry Lynch, whom the judge often had rebuked from the bench. Close associates noticed McDonald grew quiet and pensive after the election and became slipshod about his court calendar.

On Saturday, June 22, Johnston, who hadn't yet taken office, had some errands to run. He drove out to the county dump and later stopped by the Darlington post office. McDonald, who'd been seen earlier driving repeatedly past Johnston's law office, followed his election nemesis to the dump. Later, McDonald was spotted sitting in his car parked on Darlington's main street, where he could watch traffic coming into town. After the post office stop, Johnston crossed the street to his law office. As he fumbled with the keys to the office door, he looked through the glass and saw two men struggling inside. He recognized one of them as his law partner, James Klein. The other was McDonald. He heard Klein screaming, then saw Klein backed against the door. Johnston watched helplessly from outside as McDonald lunged with a knife at Klein's chest.

Dan Leahy, age twenty-two, a Darlington-area pig farmer, was working on his stalled truck across the street when he heard Johnston yell for help. Leahy ran to the front door of the law office and peered inside. He saw a man with orange hair stab another man in the back.

Twenty-seven-year-old Loren Sheldon, a Viroqua welder, was in town that day to attend a wedding. Sheldon was on the sidewalk near the law office when he saw Johnston run back across the street, shouting, "Get the police! Get an ambulance!" Sheldon saw Leahy kick the door and ran over to help. When the two men got inside, they saw McDonald holding a knife and kneeling over Klein on the floor. The judge was breathing hard and his knees wobbled as he tried to get up.

"Please help me," McDonald murmured.

"Give me the knife," Sheldon said but McDonald backed down a rear hallway and warned Sheldon not to follow because he had a gun.

The judge didn't try to cover his trail. Investigators found his bloodstained clothing strewn around the countryside outside Darlington. They arrested McDonald later that day at his home and brought him into his own courtroom that night for the dramatic initial appearance before Judge Brand on the murder charge.

By the time of McDonald's second court appearance a few days later, the courtroom cast of characters had changed. Milwaukee County Judge Janine Geske replaced Brand and Assistant Attorney General Michael Zaleski was appointed special prosecutor instead of Lynch. McDonald hired attorney William Hayes of Beloit, replacing his brother Patrick.

The accused judge was calmer when he entered the courtroom this time, stopping to chat with his wife and to shake a relative's hand. Instead of the green jail jumpsuit he wore at the first hearing, he was attired in a black business suit. Hayes argued that McDonald should be freed on signature bond, something the accused judge never would have allowed, while Zaleski cited McDonald's conduct at the first hearing and asked that he be held without bail.

Geske denied bail. And on July 8, the Wisconsin Supreme Court ordered a halt to McDonald's judicial salary although he still had three weeks left of his term.

On July 18, McDonald looked despondent with his head resting on his hands as he pleaded innocent and innocent by reason of insanity to the murder charge. The insanity plea surprised some courtroom observers who knew the accused judge. "I didn't think his ego would let him plead insane," one said. Lafayette County Sheriff Vernus Olson refused any special privileges for the jailed judge. McDonald ate the same food as other inmates and was subject to the same visitation rules. But he began losing weight in jail and he was transferred July 30 from his cell to University Hospital in Madison for treatment of malnutrition. He had lost nearly twenty pounds and was partially dehydrated. McDonald said his jailers had been starving him and his attorney announced he would file a motion to have McDonald transferred to another jail, along with a motion to declare the judge indigent so he would receive assistance in paying attorney and psychiatric fees. The defense attorney also requested a substitute judge and Milwaukee County Circuit Judge Ralph Adam Fine was assigned the case.

Wisconsin State Journal file photo

William Hayes, McDonald's attorney, cross-examines a witness while McDonald, center, and his brother Patrick watch the testimony.

Four county bar associations in southwestern Wisconsin established a memorial fund for Klein's widow and two children. Meanwhile, McDonald turned his full attention to preparing his defense, consulting law books and conferring often with his brother and Hayes. He was denied a public defender after the court ruled he was not indigent. Despite an emotional plea that he wasn't properly read his legal rights at the time of his arrest, McDonald failed to convince Fine to suppress evidence compiled by detectives during an early interview.

On August 2, onlookers were solemn in the ornate Lafayette County courtroom as William Johnston was sworn in as judge. In his speech, Johnston praised his slain law partner as a "humanist who devoted his life to helping and caring about people."

McDonald's first-degree murder trial began in Milwaukee during early September. Darlington police Chief Jim Tuescher testified about the blood-smeared law office he inspected on the day of the murder and described the body of Klein, stabbed eight times, he found lying on the floor. Johnston, Leahy and Sheldon told the jury about the struggle they saw between the two men in the office. Blood-stained clothing — a blue shirt and black pants the accused judge was known to wear almost daily — were introduced as evidence.

After a week of testimony, the state rested its case and the defense abruptly changed tactics. McDonald took the stand and, in dramatic testimony, he admitted striking Klein with a knife but claimed he had done it in self-defense.

The accused judge said he went into the law office after Klein invited him to chat. When McDonald made some comments about Johnston, Klein asked him to leave. But when he tried to go, McDonald said Klein blocked his path, holding out an arm to stop him and grabbing him in a hammerlock from behind. As the pair wrestled to the floor, McDonald said he picked up a flat steel bar and swung it at Klein.

"I fell down on all fours to the carpet, put my head down to regain my senses. I thought I was going to pass out. I knew if I passed out I probably would never get out of that office except on a stretcher."

McDonald said he saw a knife in Klein's hand as he tried to get to the rear door where his car was parked.

"I said, 'Jim, my car is out back in the parking lot. I want to go to my car. Please go back in your office and let me by.'"

McDonald said he dropped to his knees as Klein moved toward him with the knife. When the knife dropped from Klein's hand, McDonald said he picked it up.

"All I remember was I was swinging this knife back and forth and then Jim put his arms up and let out an animal-type roar and just charged at me and then everything went haywire."

In a frail voice, McDonald's wife, Cathy, testified that her husband didn't own a gun or knife and never even hunted or fished.

"Dan couldn't do something like that," she said of the murder.

But the jury wasn't convinced and, on September 14, the former tough-sentencing judge was found guilty of first-degree murder. McDonald trembled as the verdict was read while his wife bit her lip to hold back tears.

Psychiatrists debated McDonald's sanity during the second phase of the trial. Two psychiatrists said the former judge was dissociated from reality when he stabbed Klein. A colleague said it was clear that McDonald was aware of the crime because he heard a gurgling or roaring sound as the dying lawyer lunged at him. Hayes, McDonald's attorney, said his client opposed the insanity plea.

"He has given indications he would rather stand convicted as a criminal than be declared insane. To him, that is less degrading. That's just his personality." jurors gave him his wish. They deliberated less than an hour and ruled that McDonald was sane when he murdered Klein. Jurors said if he had been insane, McDonald wouldn't have recalled so many details about the stabbing.

Throughout the trial, the red-haired, hot-tempered former judge had restrained himself. But now he grew angry at the jury's verdict. Asked by Judge Fine if he had anything to say, McDonald stood up and spoke loudly.

"Yes I do. What has happened in this courtroom during the past weeks should be compared to Nazi Germany in the 1940s, not America in the 1980s. Throughout the trial, I have looked at that picture of the lady of peace on the wall behind you. I think you should take that picture down and put up one of Adolph Hitler — it would be more representative of you and this court than of what is found in America. You've got a job to do, go ahead and do it."

At McDonald's cue, Fine gave him the mandatory life sentence and the convicted judge mumbled, "They were not a jury of my peers."

Fine ignored McDonald's remarks as he passed sentence:

"You have taken the life of a young attorney in the prime of his career. You have not only destroyed his family by your actions but your own family. You have also deeply hurt the people of Lafayette County who held you in high honor."

Lynch, the Lafayette County district attorney, said the McDonald trial cost the county more than $25,000 including witness fees of $9,500 plus the cost of the Milwaukee jury and psychiatrists.

McDonald arrived at the Dodge Correctional Institution at Waupun on September 23. To the convicted judge, it was a hostile environment where he'd sent many convicted criminals. But McDonald chose to share a cell with another inmate rather than opting for solitary confinement. He ate his meals in the inmate cafeteria with the other prisoners.

"We try not to call him judge," said Ken Sondalle, a deputy warden. McDonald filed another indigent claim, asking the state to pay for his appeal. Despite opposition by a legislator and Zaleski, this time McDonald was declared indigent, entitling him to representation by a public defender. About the same time, a $5.6 million wrongful death claim by Klein's widow, Barbara, was denied by the state.

Wisconsin State Journal file photo

Judge Ralph Adam Fine

Eric Schulenburg of the public defender's appellate division said McDonald met all legal criteria for indigency. State Sen. Mordecai Lee, a Democrat from Milwaukee, wrote to the public defender's office suggesting steps to prevent defendants from being able to shed their assets to qualify for a public defender. That elicited an angry reply from McDonald, who criticized Lee for "taking great delight in running back and forth over a downed man." Gary Gates, secretary of the Department of Employee Trust Funds, estimated McDonald probably earned between $600,000 and $650,000 during his sixteen-year government career and could draw more than $50,000 from his retirement account.

In early March, 1986, McDonald was visited in prison by his former priest, the Rev. Robert Gille. McDonald told Gille he expected to die soon of a heart attack but didn't elaborate. A few days later, on March 10, the high-spirited judge was dead. He had committed suicide by taking an overdose of stress medicine prescribed by prison officials. Toxicology tests revealed 800 milligrams or the equivalent of 16 tablets of Doxepin in McDonald's stomach.

Dr. R. Robert Huntington, III of Madison, who supervised Klein's autopsy, also completed the autopsy on his killer. Prison officials later found out that McDonald apparently stole some of the drug from an unlocked nurse's room at the prison.

But even his death couldn't stop the feisty judge's legal efforts. His attorney filed a motion to vacate McDonald's murder conviction because the former judge died before he was able to appeal the case. On May 5,

Judge Fine denied the motion and upheld the conviction. Fine said if the conviction were set aside, it could not be used as evidence in civil suits against McDonald's estate that might be filed by Klein's family. That would allow McDonald to profit by his own wrong, Fine reasoned. The Appeals Court affirmed Fine's decision in March 1987. Fine later waged two unsuccessful campaigns for a seat on the state Supreme Court.

Despite McDonald's courtroom theatrics, it was Fine who ultimately had the last word. In ruling against his attorney's effort to set aside the conviction, Fine accused McDonald of "trying to win his case from the grave when he was unable to do so before a jury of his peers and chose not to do so in the appellate courts."

Crimes of
Greed

23
Shootout at Little Bohemia
Mercer, 1934

When Chicago mobsters of the Prohibition Era wanted to cool their smoking guns and relax, they escaped to Wisconsin. Al Capone had a 370-acre hideaway about thirty miles south of Hayward. Joe Saltis, another Chicago area gangster, settled in Sawyer County. Other hoodlums came to Wisconsin when Chicago began cleaning house for the 1933 Century of Progress exposition.

So, it wasn't unusual that John Dillinger and his gang should look to Wisconsin for a place to hide when federal agents were hot on their trail in April 1934. Unlike Capone and Saltis, however, Dillinger found little relaxation.

Perhaps the most famous outlaw in U.S. history, Dillinger's criminal rampage actually spanned no more than eleven months. Born and raised in Indianapolis, he was sentenced to prison in 1924 for slugging and robbing a Mooresville, Indiana storekeeper. He made friends in prison and returned to crime when he was paroled in June 1933. Upon his release, Dillinger went on a rampage of bank robberies. His background as a high school baseball star left him with an uncanny ability to vault easily over bank counters. Despite his tremendous notoriety, he was credited personally with just one murder and eleven bank robberies that netted $318,000. But he captured the public's imagination as something of a Robin Hood figure, often refusing to take the personal money of elderly customers.

An accomplice was George "Baby Face" Nelson, whose diminutive, blond appearance and high-pitched voice belied a brutal nature. Nelson, whose real name was Lester Gillis, often entered a bank shooting first and then asking for money. Carl Sifakis writes in the *Encyclopedia of Crime* that Nelson was addicted to violence like Bonnie and Clyde, but even Bonnie and Clyde tempered their ruthlessness at the sight of gray-haired victims.

"Nelson was vulnerable to no such sentimentalism, as demonstrated by his approach to bank robbery, which was to come through the door shooting and then simply force the lucky survivors to hand over the loot."

In early 1934, Dillinger was captured in Tucson, Arizona and returned to Crown Point, Indiana to stand trial on charges of bank robbery and murder. The outlaw sought the best attorney available and settled on Louis Piquette, who was born and raised in Platteville. Piquette reluctantly agreed to represent the outlaw. When his client was brought into the courtroom, four men with machine guns surrounded Dillinger and Piquette loudly objected.

"To try this man now, in this atmosphere of hatred and pointed guns, is sheer murder. If this is to be nothing but a mock trial, why cause the state to go to the expense? Why not shoot him down against a wall and have it over with? Even Christ had a fairer trial than this."

Piquette's objection was moot because the trial never took place. On March 3, Dillinger made a dramatic escape from the Crown Point jail to begin his final rampage. Fingers pointed to Piquette as the man who arranged the escape. The attorney later revealed he met his outlaw client in Chicago a few hours after the escape and reproved Dillinger sharply for his actions. Piquette urged him to surrender at a local police station because, he said, ultimate capture was inevitable. But the outlaw ignored his attorney's advice and stayed on the run.

By late April 1934, Dillinger, Nelson and several other gang members, including Tommy Carroll and John Hamilton, had taken refuge from federal agents in a two-story resort house known as Little Bohemia on Spider Lake near Mercer. The long house with log siding on the first floor was back in the woods about four hundred yards off the main highway. The lodge's proprietor was Emil Wanatka, a former Chicago nightclub owner and intimate of Windy City bootleggers, and the lodge was named after a Racine restaurant. For protection, the gangsters mounted a machine gun on a second-floor porch.

Dillinger fled to Little Bohemia after visiting his sister in Sault Ste. Marie, Michigan. The gang immediately began staking out several area banks and decided the bank at nearby Ironwood, Michigan offered the best chance for a successful holdup. It was not Dillinger's first visit to Wisconsin. On November 20, 1933, the gang stole $27,000 in cash and $11,000 in bonds and securities during a holdup at the American Bank and Trust Company of Racine. Dillinger's girlfriend was Evelyn "Billie" Frechette, also a Wisconsin native. She was a Menomonie Indian who

Wisconsin State Journal file photo

John Dillinger clowns with prosecutor Robert Estill in the jail at Crown Point, Indiana a few weeks before his escape.

grew up in Neopit but left the reservation at age thirteen, although she came back for annual visits. She had been waiting for Dillinger when several gang members busted him out of an Ohio jail and shot the sheriff to death.

In his book, *Gangster Holidays,* Wisconsin writer Tom Hollatz quotes newspaper accounts from resort owner Wanatka about the Dillinger gang's stay at Little Bohemia:

"Once Dillinger and his crowd were settled, we couldn't complain about them even though we were virtually held prisoners. They were pleasant enough to all of us. They acted like any other guests do at a summer hotel. The only difference was that the men always carried guns. When they played poker, they put their weapons on the table. Dillinger invited me to play with them. They weren't cheapskates. It was a real game. Those boys had money."

After a tip that Dillinger was holed up at Little Bohemia, about fifty FBI agents and local police officers converged on the resort shortly after dark, preparing for a surprise attack. As they were taking their positions, the agents spotted three men walk out of the resort, get into a car and begin driving through the trees toward the highway.

"Stop!" officers shouted to the driver but he kept moving down the roadway.

The agents opened fire, shooting a fusillade of bullets at the them. Officers sprayed the car from front to back with machine guns until it crashed into a tree. It looked like the criminal career of the notorious Dillinger finally had come to an ignoble end.

But when the firing stopped and the smoke cleared, the agents realized their terrible mistake. They had shot the wrong men. The driver, Eugene Boiseneau, a Civilian Conservation Corps worker from Mellen, was killed. Wounded were John Morris, another CCC worker, and John Hoffman, a city employee of Ironwood, Michigan. Besides blasting away at innocent people, the authorities also had tipped off the outlaws to their presence.

"The radio was playing in the car and then something hit me," Hoffman said when he was pulled from the wreckage. "I didn't know anything was wrong before that."

The police hastily regrouped but it was too late. Even before the flurry of gunshots, the outlaws had been alerted to the agents by barking dogs and Dillinger, Hamilton and Carroll fled the resort on foot during the confusion surrounding the shooting. They ran to a nearby resort, where they pounded on the cottage door of Robert Johnson, a Manitowish carpenter. After knocking and hollering for several minutes, the outlaws finally awoke Johnson.

"What do you want?" Johnson shouted through the door.

"The resort owner, Mrs. Mitchell, is sick," they yelled back to Johnson. "We need you to get a doctor."

Johnson went outside, where he was confronted by three gunmen. They forced him into his car and fled the area on side roads until about midnight, when they threw him out of the car near Antigo.

Meanwhile, Nelson heard the gunfire that killed Boiseneau and began firing from inside the resort, driving back the police and killing FBI agent J.C. Newman. The officers regrouped and staged another assault on the resort about 2:30 a.m. The police raiders blasted doors and windows with rifle fire and buckshot but Nelson continued to hold them at bay.

"Machine guns flamed on both sides and several raiders fell as bullets ricocheted through the dark forest," the United Press reported.

Nelson tried to slip away from the resort and was hiding behind a police car when agents spotted him. The gunman immediately opened fire, killing FBI agent W. Carter Baum and wounding Carl Christianson, a former Racine carpenter who had been appointed Spider Lake constable earlier in the month.

Nelson managed to get the car started and roared down the roadway and away on the main highway. Police officers were unable to follow him. When the car got a flat tire, he abandoned it about twenty miles east of Mercer and ran into the woods.

A third and final assault on Little Bohemia began at dawn and this time the resort fell without resistance. Police fired tear gas canisters into the building and three young women emerged, coughing and rubbing their eyes. An arsenal of weapons was confiscated, including three machine guns, five pistols, two automatic revolvers and an automatic rifle.

The women gave their names as Marian Marr, Rose Ancker and Ann Southern — the same name as a movie actress. Police figured the names were fictitious because one used the name of a movie star. Marr said she had just married one of the gangsters. But she spent her honeymoon with her two female companions locked in the Dane County jail in Madison where federal agents put all three women through grueling interrogation to learn gang secrets.

Willard R. Smith of the United Press reported:

"The only part of her trousseau which the bride has with her in jail here is the lounging pajamas in which she was attired when she and her feminine companions surrendered at dawn Monday after officers had riddled their hideout with bullets and filled it with tear gas. Another was in a pajama outfit and the third wore a jacket, riding breeches and boots.

"The girls missed the companionship of Rex, a tiny Boston bull pup which one had taken with her when she walked out of Little Bohemia's gas-filled interior. Knowing that she could not keep it in jail, its mistress gave the dog to Mrs. D.A. McGregor, wife of the Vilas County undersheriff."

The arrival of the women in Dane County caught Sheriff Fred T. Finn by surprise. In return for the sheriff's hospitality to the women, federal agents gave him a memento of the shoot-out — an authentic John Dillinger cigar. Finn said he wouldn't smoke it until he made sure there wasn't a bomb inside.

The women were arraigned on federal charges of concealing a fugitive and they were held on fifty thousand dollars bail apiece. The bail amount dwarfed the maximum penalty upon conviction of the charge, which was a year in prison or a $1,000 fine.

Federal agents stalked Dillinger and Nelson through snow-covered pine forests and small cities of northwestern Wisconsin. A splattered brown sedan had stopped for gas in Park Falls and the occupants matched descriptions of the gangsters. A Packard sedan stolen from the resort was found fifteen miles away at the end of a lumber road near Hurley. Northern Wisconsin residents were outraged and terrified at the Little Bohemia siege and the mistaken FBI shootings. A petition was circulated in the Mercer area calling for the firing of renowned federal lawman Melvin

Purvis, who masterminded the bungled raid.

"In isolated farm houses, housewives bolted their doors, although Dillinger always had shown an eccentric consideration for noncombatants in his war with the law," Smith wrote. "Lonely country stores were closed and the whole countryside watched their roads apprehensively.

"A score of brawny, brave lumberjacks, armed only with double-bitted axes and contemptuously unafraid of the city gangsters' machine guns, left Hurley today to join in patrolling the roads leading to the Canadian border."

In Madison, where the gang's women were held, police motorcycle squads guarded the city's banks and a point car loaded with shotguns and bulletproof vests was kept ready at headquarters. Near Portage, officers and vigilantes watched Highway 51 for southbound cars driven by the Dillinger gang. Three men were taken into custody at a Madison hotel after they received a large sum of money by telegraph and a telephone call from a caller who said, "Ted has been bumped off." But the men turned out to be in the sugar business and Ted, a truck driver, was not bumped off but beaten by hijackers who stole his truck in Waukesha County.

There was much speculation about why the Little Bohemia raid had failed so miserably. Pat Roche, a noted crime investigator, said the federal agents were not properly trained for the confrontation with the outlaws. Albert G. Feeney, Indiana director of public safety, blamed the agents for not cooperating with local authorities. Michigan state police complained they weren't informed Dillinger had been in their state. U.S. Attorney General Homer S. Cummings blamed inadequate equipment and a shortage of federal agents. If the agents had had an armored car at Little Bohemia, he said, they could have driven right up to the resort.

Dillinger fled to St. Paul, Minnesota, where police set a trap for him. An army of thousands of law enforcement officers with "shoot to kill" orders was mobilized in the Twin Cities to search for the outlaw and his gang. After several narrow escapes from police cruisers, the gang used the local expertise of Minnesotan Tommy Carroll and slipped across a little-used Mississippi River bridge into Wisconsin, then headed south on back roads. Dillinger had been wounded in a St. Paul shoot-out a month earlier and the city health officer, Dr. N.G. Mortensen, was suspended for failing to report an attempt by the outlaw to get medical help.

After escaping the latest police net, Dillinger was sighted almost simultaneously in Milwaukee, Indiana, New York and Ohio. A special detail of National Guard troops was sent to his father's Mooresville, Indiana home in case the outlaw turned up there. The FBI gathered its most expert machine gunners and sent them to the Midwest in hopes of a final confrontation with Dillinger.

Other rumors abounded: that Dillinger was holed up in Chicago nursing a severe wound or that notorious outlaws Bonnie and Clyde were speeding toward Dillinger's hideaway to join forces with him.

Actually, Dillinger was headed back to Chicago and spent three days and nights hiding out in the old Raisbeck mine at Jenkinsville, near Platteville. It wasn't clear what role Piquette played in arranging the mine hideout but there was talk the Platteville attorney had a special agreement with Dillinger that, in exchange for the safe hideout, the outlaw wouldn't rob any local banks.

Meanwhile, near Lac du Flambeau, Nelson burst into an Indian family's home brandishing three guns. He held Ollie Catfish, a Chippewa, and his family captive for three days, depleting their food supply before he escaped in another stolen car. Catfish said Nelson, who "talked more like a baby than a man," didn't sleep but kept constant watch on the family. After three days, Nelson and Catfish walked seven miles along a trail toward Lac Du Flambeau.

When a car came along, Nelson stopped it and yanked out the ignition wires. He then stopped a larger car driven by Al Snow, a Native American police officer. Snow didn't have a gun and Nelson forced him and another man out of the car, got in with Catfish and drove to Highway 70. There he left Catfish and continued west. Nelson, who apparently had developed some sort of camaraderie with his captive, left a gun for Catfish to protect himself. After the ordeal, Catfish was honored with a leading position in a local parade.

Nelson surfaced again in Pine City, Minnesota, between the Twin Cities and Superior, where he stole a car and then headed north toward Duluth. When a deputy tried to stop the car near Solon Springs for a routine check, Nelson shattered the squad car windshield with a gun blast. Nelson later was spotted near Dayton in Green County. District Attorney Randall J. Elmer said he was driving on a rural road when an approaching car slowed and the driver shined a spotlight on him. Elmer recognized the driver as Nelson and the license number roughly matched a car bought by Nelson earlier in the day at Marshfield.

A week after the Little Bohemia shoot-out, the rumors of the whereabouts of Dillinger and his gang ended when Nelson rejoined Dillinger for a confrontation with several police officers in Bellwood, a Chicago suburb. The outlaws humiliated the officers, disarming them and knocking one unconscious.

But time was running out on the criminal careers of Dillinger and Nelson.

On June 23, Dillinger's thirty-first birthday, he was named the FBI's Public Enemy Number One. After plastic surgery in which he nearly died on the operating table, Dillinger laid low in Chicago, assuming a fake identity. On July 22, he was betrayed by the famous woman in red,

Anna Sage, and shot to death by federal agents outside the Biograph Theater.

The day after his death, at least one plaster death mask of the famous outlaw's face was made in the Cook County Morgue. One such mask was made by Ken Coffman, formerly of Chicago, who lived in Oregon, Wisconsin, before his death in 1983. That mask later was sold by his widow, Mariette Van Den Steene-Coffman. Coffman also had masks of Pretty Boy Floyd and Bruno Hauptmann. Criminologists of the 1930s believed that every criminal's face had a good side and a bad side and that death masks could help identify criminal facial characteristics.

The *Encyclopedia of Crime* describes a later scene when federal agents Sam Crowley and Herman E. Hollis came upon Nelson, his wife, Helen, and outlaw Paul Chase on November 27, 1934, after the outlaws' car stalled near Barrington, Illinois.

A shoot-out erupted and construction workers nearby hit the dirt. Crowley rolled into a ditch while Hollis hid behind a car. After a few minutes, Nelson brazenly stood up and walked toward the agents, his machine gun blazing.

"I'm going down there and get those sons of bitches!" he yelled over the gunfire. After taking several bullets from the agents, Nelson walked to the ditch and fired a burst at Crowley, cutting him down. The outlaw chased Hollis to a tree and then shot the agent fatally in the head. But the wounds were severe for Nelson. His nude body was found the next day, dumped along a roadside about twenty miles away.

Ninety-four-year-old Harold J. Graham of Racine, one of the Dillinger gang's last-surviving victims, died in 1994. Graham was wounded sixty years earlier during the American Bank & Trust Company holdup on November 20, 1933. A bullet hit Graham in the right elbow, then passed through his belt and into his right side and back.

Graham, who worked forty-five years at the Racine bank, kept the leather belt with its single bullet hole for the rest of his left. In his later years, he also collected other Dillinger memorabilia.

24

Big Spenders from the Windy City

Lake Delton, 1961

When Illinoisans spend a lot of money at local tourist attractions, it usually doesn't faze anybody in Wisconsin Dells or Lake Delton. Tourism, after all, is what keeps these two towns along the Wisconsin River afloat. Visitors are welcomed each summer to empty their wallets riding the "ducks," munching pretzels in the downtown Dells or boating on Lake Delton.

But there was something strange about three Chicago-area men who took a forty-five-dollar-a-day suite at a Lake Delton hotel on August 4, 1961, and began spending lavish amounts of money at area nightspots. Lake Delton Police Chief Robert E. Kohl and Sauk County Traffic Officer James C. Jantz decided to investigate. Jantz was an Illinois native himself who'd moved to Baraboo in 1950 and graduated from Baraboo High School, where he starred in basketball. Kohl, who had served as Lake Delton chief for seven years, had a reputation as a strict but fair cop, known for sensible out-of-court penalties like making one group of youths upright seventeen outhouses they'd pushed over on Halloween.

The officers decided to stop the high-powered 1960 Oldsmobile driven by the Chicago trio so the men could be questioned. On August 21, Jantz and Kohl caught up with the Oldsmobile in front of the Lake Delton city hall. They noticed the car's front and rear license plates didn't match. The two officers got out of their squad car and started walking toward the Oldsmobile. At the very least, they'd be able to bust the Chicago men for improper plates and there was likely to be more.

Suddenly a shot rang out and Kohl fell to the pavement. Jantz ran to take cover behind his squad car as the Chicago men burst out of their car with their guns blazing. Bullets whizzed over the roof of the squad car, slamming into Jantz three times. One bullet pierced his skull, another lodged in his lung and a third grazed his left cheek. The three men scooped up the guns dropped by Kohl and Jantz, then scrambled back behind their car.

"For God's sake, stay back!" Kohl shouted at Deputy Fred Bayer, who'd pulled up across the street. Bayer dived under his car as bullets ricocheted around him. He fired at the men.

"Come on, let's get the hell out of here!" one gunman yelled. The three got back in the Oldsmobile and sped away.

The entire gun battle lasted about thirty seconds and thirty shots were fired, according to eyewitness James Agan of Madison, who was vacationing at Lake Delton. Jantz died at the scene, leaving a pregnant wife and five-month-old son. Kohl suffered bullet wounds in the lung, liver and spleen but recovered at Madison's University Hospital.

Angered that the brazen trio of gunmen had dared to cut down one of their own, police quickly set up roadblocks to snare the cop-killers. But the suspects turned around to avoid one roadblock and sped toward Baraboo at speeds clocked at 114 m.p.h. by Columbia County Officer Wayne Johnson in hot pursuit. They made another screeching U-turn to evade a roadblock on Highway 12 north of New Lisbon. The car careened into a ditch and one gunman, Richard Nickl, age twenty-two, of Prospect Heights, Illinois, was thrown from the speeding car and quickly

Wisconsin State Journal photo by Carolyn Pflasterer

Lake Delton Police Chief Fred Bayer in 1989 on Wisconsin Dells Parkway near the scene of the 1961 shooting.

captured. He had been shot in one leg and fractured the other leg when he hit the ditch. Sauk County Deputy Mike Spencer kept on the tail of the Oldsmobile, firing a twelve-gauge shotgun at the rear of the car before it crashed near Lyndon Station. The two other gunmen, William J. Welter, age twenty-three, of Franklin Park, Illinois, and Lawrence J. Nutley, age twenty-seven, of Chicago, fled the wrecked car into a field.

When they heard about the brutal murder of a fellow officer, hundreds of police officers from throughout southern Wisconsin poured into the area to Dells Parkway near Judson Street, where the shootout occurred, to search for the two remaining suspects. More than five hundred people joined the manhunt. David Niemann of the Dane County Sheriff's Department brought his tracking dog, Hector. Bloodhounds also were brought to the scene from La Crosse. Four truckloads of National Guardsmen from the Dells-Mauston area helped the police man roadblocks.

It became clear where the trio had gotten their cash and why they'd shot at the officers. Nickl and Welter were awaiting trial for a twenty-five thousand dollar fur robbery in McHenry, Illinois and Nutley was a long-time companion.

"They're not the outdoors type," said Chicago Police Lt. Richard Lewis, who came to the Dells to help track them down. "They're the kind who are used to their steaks medium-rare."

A Wisconsin Dells woman watched Tuesday morning as a man limped up the driveway toward her small tavern to ask if he could buy a couple bottles of pop. He puffed out a wad of bills to pay for the pop and gulped it down. When he left, the woman called the sheriff. A half hour later, officers came upon the limping man in dense underbrush north of the Dells and captured him easily. It was Nutley. Two down and one to go.

Welter eluded authorities for nearly a week. Police hitched a loudspeaker to a low-flying plane, asking Welter to surrender and offering to treat his wounds. Bloodhounds picked up his trail and finally led police to him, hiding in a swamp near Lyndon Station. He put up little resistance, suffering from a broken kneecap, insect bites and exposure.

The three suspects were bound over for trial October 5 and held in the Dane County Jail, which provided what police considered the best available security for the outlaws. Welter's father said he didn't believe his son was involved in the shootout.

"In my opinion, it hasn't been established that my son is definitely up there," he said. "He started running around with some wrong guys a few months ago. But we are going to stick by him. We'll do what we can for him. If the authorities feel it would help if I would go up there, I would be willing to do what I can."

Nickl's father wasn't as generous to his son, who had a wife and three children.

"I've lost my son; I've washed my hands of him," said Richard Nickl Sr., a dog breeder. "Rich was my only son. I wanted him to have this place (a two-story brick house and kennels). But I've lost my son; I don't have one anymore."

On Christmas night, Welter and Nutley jammed layers of paper in the lock bolt opening of the door jambs of their cells so the bolts would click shut when closed but could be reopened easily without a key. After the cell doors were closed for the night, Nutley took a piece of waxed string and slid it beneath the bolt between the door and the jamb. He curled the string around the loosely set bolt and yanked it from the opening, then swung open the cell door. Welter opened his cell the same way.

The two men hid in a shower room across the corridor from their cells, armed with a blackjack fashioned from pieces of soap wrapped tightly in socks. When jailer Howard Pinger found Nutley's cell door ajar on his 2:00 a.m. rounds, the two men leaped from the shower and grabbed Pinger from behind, beating him with the sock sap and wrestling him to the floor. They told him to call his partner, jailer Bill Keys, but Keys already was on his way to investigate.

Pinger gave this account of the escape attempt to Undersheriff Jack Leslie:

"I was making the rounds of the maximum security section when I noticed Nutley's door ajar about two-and-a-half or three inches. I went to call Bill Keys but I never got that far. At the shower, Welter came jumping over and swung something and hit me and from the back I was jumped by Nutley. The three of us went down in the shower. Welter had me around the neck and Nutley was hitting me with a sock sap made of soap, pieces of soap. They told me to call Bill Keys.

"I said, 'Release the grip on my neck so I can call him,' but I did not call him and in between Bill came to investigate. What happened to Bill I didn't know at the time but one released me so I got a chance to get a punch underneath at Welter and I got up on my feet. By that time, Nutley came back and started sapping me again and they tried to put me into cellblock E. I kicked the door closed and the three of us struggled and went down on the floor again.

"Then Welter says, 'I will kill you if you don't get in that cell!' So I told him 'Over my dead body will you get out of here!' They kept on sapping me so I thought I ought to faint a sapping, which I did. They hit me and I pretended to relax like I was passed out. They jumped up and got the set of keys which I thought was mine but they were Bill Keys' keys. Then they slammed the door to the maximum security by the hall and Bill was just coming out at the same time and we kept hollering to Lucy Johnson (jail matron). I kept hollering, 'Matron, jail break!'"

Wisconsin State Journal file photo

William Welter, left, appealed his conviction, claiming the media made a circus of the trial.

When Keys arrived, Nutley and Welter overpowered him. They grabbed a set of keys and slammed the door shut to maximum security, then headed for the control room. Matron Johnson heard the struggle and pushed a button that stopped all elevators from descending and summoned Madison police. Nutley and Welter got through the last three doors and stood outside the elevators, just a ride down away from freedom.

They frantically pushed the buttons, trying to summon an elevator. When the elevator didn't arrive, Nutley clawed at the ceiling, trying to remove the tiles while Welter crawled into a trap door in the elevator shaft.

An elevator door opened and Madison Officer August Pieper emerged. Welter rushed him and tried to grab his pistol. They struggled but it was a standoff and neither was strong enough to gain control of the gun. The minutes ticked by and other officers were on their way but would they get there in time?

"Stop fighting," Nutley finally told Welter. "Where can we go from here?"

At that moment, other officers burst into the elevator lobby and the two men surrendered. They were searched and returned to their cells. Pinger and Keys were treated for cuts and bruises.

"We should have killed the old guy and we would have made it," Nutley was quoted as saying about Pinger after the capture. Welter told police he tried the break "because I wanted to expend a little energy." Nickl didn't participate. His leg still was in a cast from the fall out of the escape car and he was kept in another part of the jail.

At their seven-week murder trial in early 1962, each of the three suspects denied firing at Jantz and Kohl. They said the only shots fired were by police, although ballistics tests determined six other guns were involved in the shootout. Police found a .38-caliber revolver that probably killed Jantz and wounded Kohl but no fingerprints were on it so they couldn't determine which of the trio had fired the weapon. That gun was found near Nickl when he was thrown from the getaway car. A loaded .38-caliber revolver and a loaded .25-caliber revolver were found beside the Oldsmobile when it crashed near Lyndon Station.

The three were convicted and sentenced to life imprisonment for the murder plus 30 years each for wounding Kohl. Welter mounted several legal challenges to the verdict, claiming excessive news coverage had made a circus of the trial and jury selection was improper. In 1970, the Wisconsin Supreme Court ruled Welter had received a fair trail.

In 1971, Nutley was brought from Waupun to Madison's University Hospital for treatment of an ailing knee. He ran from his unarmed prison guard at the hospital front desk but the guard, Sgt. Wayne Mohr, caught Nutley outside the rear emergency entrance on Linden Avenue.

Nickl, who had stayed out of the aborted jail break, ultimately was luckier than his two accomplices in gaining his freedom. On July 25, 1974, Nickl was being held at the Fox Lake Correctional Farm when he slipped away from an Alcoholics Anonymous meeting at the First Presbyterian Church in Horicon, nine months before he was scheduled for a parole hearing.

Nutley was paroled in 1983. Welter also was paroled in the mid-1980s after completing his sentence at the Oakhill Correctional Institution near Oregon.

In October 1989, a twist of fate landed Nickl back in prison after he had eluded authorities for fifteen years. He was captured in Phoenix using the alias Michael Conners and selling devices that unscramble cable television signals. A routine fingerprint check unmasked Conners as Richard Nickl.

Nickl, then fifty-five, pleaded guilty in Las Vegas to charges of making and selling the pirating devices, then was returned to Wisconsin and sentenced to up to three years in prison in addition to the life sentence he was serving when he escaped.

25

A Prince of Fine Fellows

Milwaukee, 1905

A warm spring rain fell on the day of the auction, the kind that turns the air into a stale sea of oppressive humidity. It was May 25, 1905, one of those days when the least exertion breaks out the sweat on your skin, making your clothes feel like a wet dishrag. Despite the weather, people jammed the spacious house at 657 Astor Street on Milwaukee's East Side just to look at the expensive rugs and opulent furniture. Some came to bid, even if it was just for a cut-glass finger bowl. A woman wearing a scanty shawl tiptoed through the rooms with a small boy clinging to her skirts, peering into bureau drawers and china closets. Another woman dressed in an expensive shirtwaist suit ran her fingers through the curtains while a young mother next to her with a baby in her arms picked up objects of bric-a-brac. The odor of wet clothing and umbrellas in the pressed-together crowd grew so strong that a man pushed his way to the front door, gasping for fresh air.

"Isn't it sad?" a woman said of the family who lived there. She turned away from her companion and picked up a candelabrum. "I'm going to have this if I have to stay here 'til night."

Through the front window, faces pressed against the glass as some stood on the porch for hours staring inside, where starched and ironed collars wilted as perspiration poured in rivulets from the bidders.

"Now, please don't break my ribs," said auctioneer James C. Wall, wiping a handkerchief across his forehead and motioning the crowd back. Across the room, a woman staggered slightly and then slowly collapsed to the floor.

"Open a window there!" Wall shouted. "A woman's fainting."

It was said the crush of people in the house that day was as great as those who jammed the Grand Avenue Bridge to see Prince Henry. The crowd admired glassware and a 102-piece blue porcelain dinner set. They saw dozens of fine tables of mahogany, rosewood, Japanese lacquer and French walnut. In the dining room, an antique Persian rug, twenty feet by twelve feet, was valued at $1,200. Paintings for sale included one entitled "Poultry Yard" and another by G. Tredupp called "Midnight in Holland." Handsomely upholstered chairs in richly colored tapestries graced the dining and living rooms. Pillows were everywhere, of velour, silk and satin. Near a piece of bronze Japanese pottery was a hand-carved settee of Flemish oak with a matching bookcase.

Despite the elegance of the furnishings for sale, some prominent Milwaukeeans were conspicuously absent. "It was tacitly agreed that it wouldn't be good form to go to an auction in a house where they'd been to dinner," wrote reporter Jean Airlie of the event in the *Milwaukee Journal.*

A month earlier, the Astor Street house had been the domain of Frank Bigelow, the longtime president of the First National Bank of Milwaukee, and his family, including his wife, Anne, a son and two daughters, one single and one married. The year before, Bigelow served as national president of the American Bankers' Association and presided at the organization's New York convention. But now he was disgraced and ruined, soon to be sentenced to ten years in prison. He was accused of diverting one-and-a-half million of the bank's assets to his own use in one of the largest embezzlement schemes of the century.

But even the one-and-a-half million wasn't the whole story. Frank Bigelow owed about $400,000 to other banks and $275,000 to individual creditors when he declared bankruptcy a few weeks before the auction. A year later, claims against Bigelow had climbed to over $3 million, a huge debt at a time when men's suits could be bought at Hahn Brothers for less than twenty-five dollars and women's shoes sold for a dollar and forty-five cents a pair.

It was a time when fortunes were won and lost, when great corporations formed and disbanded. Speculators poured money into gold mines, oil wells and other strike-it-rich ventures. It was the age of the entrepreneur, when newspaper advertisements heralded the cures of Stuart's Tablets for dyspepsia, Swamp Root for weak kidneys or Newton's Herpicide. Russia was locked in a war on land and sea with Japan and, in Wisconsin, state Senator Barney A. Eaton professed his innocence of bribery charges from the floor of the Legislature.

There was a spring in his step as Frank Bigelow, age fifty-seven, walked to work each day at the bank, looking dapper in his salt-and-pepper colored suit, fedora hat and overcoat. He was a proud corporate leader of the newly-dawned 20th Century.

He was constantly in motion, borrowing money from one place and investing it in another, wheeling, dealing, his head filled with financial schemes. His pockets were his files, where he stuffed dividend checks, stock certificates, grocery lists and other scraps of paper. For the most part, his mind kept the only record of the intricate details of his financial transactions. He was characterized as a man of untiring zeal, so busy that his conversations often consisted of curt, direct replies due to a shortage of time, it was said, rather than a lack of intelligence. When a fellow investor once asked him about dividends due on a mining property, Bigelow pulled a wad of paper from his pocket and gave the man a crumpled dividend check dated two years earlier.

Consistent with their social status, the Bigelows donated about twenty thousand dollars a year to Milwaukee charities, including the Bigelow Day Nursery and the Francis Swallow Kindergarten. They were patrons of the arts and the theater as well as supporters of civic projects like the Milwaukee street railway.

It wasn't clear when Bigelow began using other people's money but he invested a thousand dollars for a widow in 1890. Among his early creditors was another widow, Caroline E. James, who said he owed her fifty thousand dollars in 1894, eleven years before the scandal broke. A memorandum written by Bigelow promised to repay Mrs. James by 1900 with bank, railroad and American Express stock along with thirty thousand dollars in cash. She only got fifty shares of American Express stock.

The unsteady financial empire came tumbling down with a crash that reverberated throughout the nation on April 24, 1905, although the bank's board of directors had learned of Bigelow's massive theft two days earlier. But it wasn't until that Monday that they stripped him of the presidency and posted a statement at the bank in an attempt to act quickly and head off financial disaster:

"While the directors of the bank can say no word of assurance so far as the personal aspect of this unfortunate case goes, they feel it is their duty as citizens of Milwaukee and persons directly interested to assure the public that the First National Bank of Milwaukee is in an absolutely solvent condition. We make this statement because there is a possibility that many people may thoughtlessly confound what is a personal matter with the standing of the bank, which is one of the great financial institutions of the Northwest."

The statement was signed by the bank's directors minus Bigelow, including E. Mariner, George P. Miller, C. F. Pfister, John I. Beggs, J. H. Van Dyke Jr. and Fred Vogel Jr., who soon would be named president to replace Bigelow.

Another notice posted in the bank listed assets at $1.6 million. In those days before federal deposit insurance, about six hundred thousand dollars of that amount had been put up by the directors themselves to cover Bigelow's embezzlement. Bigelow signed over six hundred thousand dollars in life insurance policies and put up three hundred thousand dollars of his own assets while his brother, William, pledged one hundred thousand dollars.

The usually cool and confident Bigelow looked greatly agitated when he appeared at the bank that Monday morning. He didn't bother removing his hat or overcoat as he shuffled papers on his desk and spoke occasionally to bank clerks. He also issued his own statement about the scandal: "I have no excuses to make. I do not care to speak of motives, which I had and had no right to have. The big men among the board of directors of the bank have come forward in a way that should give absolute confidence to the community and they are deserving of the highest praise. There are no better men in any community and no stronger men financially. The bank will be better and stronger than ever. My family has been kept in ignorance of the conditions and their method of living is not to be laid open against them."

Milwaukee Historical Society

Frank Bigelow

Bigelow took the high road of confronting the controversy head-on, but his accomplice did not. Henry Goll, the bank's cashier, had actually entered the false figures in the bank's books at Bigelow's direction to cover up the missing funds. Goll, a widower, greatly admired Bigelow and even named his son after his boss. When the scandal broke, Goll vanished. Bank officials from other cities rushed to Milwaukee for consultations with First National directors. The directors wired Washington, D.C., and requested a federal bank examiner be dispatched to Milwaukee as soon as possible.

Despite strong efforts to head off a panic by depositors, a run on the bank began early the following day. A line of worried depositors had formed by 6:30 a.m., even though the bank wouldn't open for another three-and-a-half hours. Some had waited all night. Speculators worked the crowd, buying bank books at cut rates from many frightened bank customers. By the time the bank opened, the line stretched for several blocks. When the first few depositors inside were offered their money without any problem, some left without withdrawing it.

Outside, bank director Beggs circulated along the line, trying to assure everyone that the bank had enough money to guarantee their assets. At one point, he stopped and pointed to two elderly women who clutched their bank books.

"These poor women who are waiting in line for their money will receive it without any restrictions with regard to the time they shall ask for it," he said.

In a demonstration of support, the Boston Store sent someone over to the bank with a bag of currency to deposit. Other downtown Milwaukee businesses also rallied. Surrounded by a contingent of armed police officers and detectives, Mayor David Stuart Rose strode down Wisconsin Avenue with five hundred thousand dollars in cash and gold carried in canvas bags. The money was part of an emergency shipment from Chicago and other Milwaukee banks. The mayor paused to address the crowd.

"Everything I have on earth is deposited in this bank and is going to stay here because I know there is no danger of anyone else losing a cent."

As noon approached, Beggs suggested serving coffee and sandwiches to the crowd but then suddenly seized a new tactic. He told the depositors the bank would impose its thirty-day rule on withdrawals because it didn't have the cash on hand to pay all of them.

"The bank hasn't millions of dollars lying around to pay you people all at once," he said. At that point, many depositors went home, convinced the bank would stay in business. Within a few days, First National had amassed eleven million dollars in guaranteed assets.

But not everybody supported the struggling bank. The Milwaukee Chamber of Commerce initially voted to keep its seventeen-thousand-dollar account but later rescinded the action. The state withdrew two hundred thousand dollars, claiming the money was needed to protect its payroll in case there were runs on other Milwaukee banks. Gov. Robert M. LaFollette was persuaded to leave the state's remaining $540,000 on deposit.

"Come on in, Tom," Bigelow warmly greeted U.S. Marshal Tom Reid, who came to the banker's home to arrest him. "Yes, and read the warrant."

As tears welled in his wife's eyes, Bigelow listened to Reid say that the bank president was charged with defrauding a financial institution in excess of $100,000. Bigelow kissed his wet-eyed wife good-bye and said he preferred to walk to the courthouse, where he promptly was released on $25,000 bail put up by his son-in-law and a physician friend.

The next day, a hush fell over everyone inside the bank as Bigelow stopped by to check his mail. Clerks counting money stopped with hands upraised. The only sound was the persistent clicking of the ticker. Bigelow continued his rapid pace, now conducting the business of his bankruptcy. When they had gotten over the shock, those inside the bank that day grabbed his shoulder or shook his hand in signs of support. Despite the magnitude of his crime, Bigelow's business associates sought to excuse him somehow. Some blamed his son, Gordon, who, they said, had lost his father's money through his wild speculation in wheat. Bigelow embezzled the bank's money trying to cover his son's debts, so the story went. The massive theft didn't diminish the respect younger business-men had for Bigelow. He had, after all, helped many of them get started and taught them the mechanics of financial wheeling and dealing.

No matter what his crime, to them, Bigelow remained "a prince of fine fellows."

The unfortunate Goll did not fare as well. He fled to Chicago, slipping from hotel to hotel and registering under the alias of A. B. Smith of New York. He had seen Bigelow's demise coming a year earlier and destroyed negatives of his own picture, hoping it would make it tougher for police to trace him. The bank offered a thousand dollar reward for Goll's capture. When he was caught on May 3, Goll looked like he hadn't slept, shaved or bathed in a week. His collar was rumpled and he wore light-gray baggy trousers rolled up on the bottom. His eyes were bloodshot and his black coat was wrinkled and dusty. His hair was cropped short and his face was covered by overgrown whiskers, the start of a beard he apparently hoped would serve as a disguise. Goll had $28 in his pocket, a copy of *The Hunchback of Notre Dame* by Victor Hugo, a pair of glasses, a linen collar wrapped in newspaper and a toothbrush. Unlike his men-tor, Goll couldn't raise his $15,000 bail. His daughter, Elizabeth, age six, and his son, Frank, age eight, weren't told about their father's plight. As his condition indicated, Goll said he never received a penny of the bank's money.

Meanwhile, Bigelow's problems were escalating. The American Bankers' Association expunged his name from the organization's list of former presidents. *The Wall Street Journal* revealed the deposed president had offered to invest First National funds in New York banks to secure personal loans for himself. The story that Bigelow had lost money by bad investments in wheat futures prompted Milwaukee ministers to rail against him in their sermons.

"The man who speculates in grain is full brother to the thief!" preached the Rev. P. H. Kellen of the Pilgrim Congregational Church. At St. Paul's Church, the Bigelow pew was conspicuously empty as the family avoided embarrassing public contact.

Bigelow, it turned out, had long been regarded as an unsafe risk by New York banks and, in 1904, one bank pressured him to pay off an outstanding personal loan. In the wake of the scandal, he was forced to resign from the executive committee of Northwestern Mutual Life Insurance Co., where he also served on the finance committee. He soon was kicked off the boards of Milwaukee-Downer College and Allis Chalmers Co. He was replaced by Beggs as president of the National Electric Co., a bank subsidiary.

Two rough-looking strangers began shadowing Bigelow on his rounds. Some speculated they were hired by the bank to make sure he didn't leave town. As the weeks passed, the scandal began to wear on him. His gait slowed and his dapper appearance seemed to fade. His face often looked strained and older, sometimes as if he had been weeping. Bigelow's son was forced to take a job as a clerk at a Chicago grain brokerage firm and other family members also thought about looking for work. The nursery, kindergarten and other family-supported charities had to scramble for survival.

In mid-May, a little tin box found in a bank vault finally shed some light on the mystery of where much of the money had gone. When the box was pried open, a packet of stock certificates raised hopes that Bigelow had some hidden assets. The deposed president had been a speculator in every gold mine he could lay his hands on. But "NG" was stamped on each certificate, including seventy-five thousand shares of Mephisto Mining Co., five hundred shares of Berner Oil Co. and four-hundred thirty-four shares of United Rice Mines Co. "NG" stood for "no good on earth."

Bigelow pleaded guilty to embezzlement and was taken by train to the federal prison at Fort Leavenworth, Kansas, to begin serving his 10-year sentence. But the wealthy banker's manicured hands never touched hard labor. He served as a timekeeper at the prison while also counting the time until his own release.

Exactly a year after the scandal broke, Bigelow was brought back to Milwaukee to testify at Goll's trial. The former cashier was indicted on about fifty counts of entering false figures, misappropriating funds and embezzlement.

During his eleven-day visit, Bigelow continued to receive VIP treatment. He stayed with his family in Milwaukee instead of under guard and was allowed to freely roam the city, although he didn't take advantage of the privilege.

Testimony at Goll's trial exposed an intricate scheme of check-kiting used to cover Bigelow's debts and to permit him to pocket a fortune in other people's money. Scores of erasures were found in the bank's records where figures had been altered and courtroom spectators broke into uproarious laughter when bookkeeper James C. Bird, who wasn't charged in the case, suggested maybe the erasures were made to get rid of ink spots.

Assistant District Attorney T. Henning summed up the state's case, maintaining that Goll wasn't such a dupe of Bigelow as he appeared: "We have to deal here with a very complicated system. You are not dealing in this instance with a fool, but with the ablest banker, in my judgment, in the whole state of Wisconsin. . . . He understands the system from A to Z and he has learned it from the bottom up, starting as a messenger boy.

"In the olden days, men used to organize into bands to commit highway robbery but here you stood an equal show. Later, we have had bank robbers who, at the peril of their own lives, broke into and robbed banks and strongboxes. These men, I say, were heroes compared with he modern banker who, without risk to himself, holding a position of confidence and trust, uses that position to rob you of your savings."

Goll's attorney, William Rubin, argued that his client was no more guilty than other bank employees still on their jobs. Bigelow's testimony that he gave the orders in the embezzlement scheme apparently influenced the jury because Goll was acquitted of embezzlement charges. But he was convicted of nineteen counts of entering false figures and misappropriating funds. Unlike Bigelow, the former cashier also was treated as a common criminal and whisked off immediately to jail. He received the same ten-year prison sentence as Bigelow and soon joined his former boss at Fort Leavenworth.

The Bigelows had managed to shield some personal property, including a grand piano and extensive library, from the auction block but the rest was sold that rainy, humid day in the house where they had practiced their elegant lifestyle. The auction raised five thousand dollars, a pittance of the amount Bigelow had stolen.

"By Saturday morning," wrote Jean Airlie, "the house which two months ago was one of the social centers of the East Side and over which no shadow of unhappiness seemed to hover will be desolated; the cherished furnishings, the gifts of happy family anniversaries will grace other houses and be owned by strangers."

26

A Hit Man Strikes
Madison, 1983

James Hudson went to work that Friday morning as usual although there was very little usual about it. The day before, Hudson had filed for divorce. It almost had been as if a cloud of sadness over a failing three-year marriage enveloped the red-frame, ranch-style house for weeks. The couple's arguments had escalated to the stage of physical violence.

It was a sadness not unknown to Hudson, for Carolyn was his third wife. His first wife died of leukemia and he had been divorced from his second wife. He and Carolyn had no children together but she had three children from a previous marriage to Richard Wheeler.

Despite the emotional tension or perhaps as a respite from it, James Hudson, a Madison police officer, left his home on the city's far East Side that Friday, October 14, 1983, and went to work. He sat through briefing and went out in his squad car. At 6:56 a.m., he was dispatched to a routine call a couple miles east of the state Capitol.

After James Hudson left for work that morning, the Hudson household slowly awakened. Carolyn Hudson and children began their usual tasks — showers, toothbrush, makeup — of getting ready for the day. Seventeen-year-old Mischelle, Jacquelyne, age fourteen, and Robert, age seven, got ready for school.

Shortly before 7:00 a.m., while her husband was getting dispatched to the call on Oak Street, Carolyn Hudson heard a noise at the unlocked front door. As she walked to the door, she was confronted by a gunman she didn't know. While Mischelle looked on, the gunman fired four shots at Carolyn Hudson, then fled.

James Hudson handled his first call of the morning quickly, then received another assignment from the dispatcher. On the way to the second address, another call came over the radio that snapped his attention. It was the report of a shooting, but that wasn't all. Hudson recognized the address as his own.

Joey Hecht figured he had planned this murder down to the smallest details. Hecht would be the triggerman and his sidekick, Drew Slickman, the getaway driver. Hecht didn't share many details of the crime with Slickman, who had learned not to ask too many questions of his more intelligent friend. Slickman knew Joey was up to something — perhaps a burglary — but he wasn't sure what it was.

In a rental car, they cruised through the Buckeye Road neighborhood the day before, plotting out their escape route. They watched the Hudson house, learning the family's morning routine. They had come to Madison three days before the slaying with Hecht's girlfriend, Melany Brant. The trio spent two nights at the plush Edgewater Hotel and their final night at the Exel Inn.

Sitting outside the Hudson home in the rental car with the engine running, Slickman heard the shots and watched as Hecht ran out the door, pursued by a teenage girl, and jumped in the passenger side. At this

Wisconsin State Journal file photo

Joey Hecht

point, he obviously realized this was something more serious than a simple burglary. But Slickman didn't question Joey about what happened. He just followed the instructions he had been given for the escape.

Despite Hecht's intricate planning, police were waiting for Slickman when he returned the rental car to the Dane County Regional Airport. Jacquelyne Hudson, who chased Hecht out of the house, had written the license number of the getaway car.

Police put the pressure on Slickman, demanding to know the identity of his accomplice. He finally gave in, identifying Joey Hecht and adding that Hecht and Melany Brant were on their way to Milwaukee on a Badger bus. When Hecht went to pick up his luggage at the Milwaukee bus terminal, police were there to take him into custody. Melany was held as a material witness.

At first, Joey Hecht refused to admit his true identity. In San Antonio, Texas, where he had lived until shortly before the murder, he went by the alias of Bobby Brunson. He shared an apartment there with Slickman and Brant in an eight-unit building often occupied by students at nearby Trinity University. The building was sandwiched between stately, older homes of the Monte Vista historic district.

A neighbor remembered Hecht, a.k.a. Brunson, as a man big on get-rich schemes.

"He was always coming up with some big scheme to wind up a millionaire," the neighbor said. "Every time I saw him, he had another scheme lined up."

It was at his San Antonio apartment where Hecht received two envelopes addressed to "Resident." Inside were pictures of Carolyn Hudson and a typewritten note. The envelopes also contained ninety-three hundred-dollar bills.

"He had a wild tale about trying to meet somebody at a place where they had pre-Columbian artifacts," the neighbor said. "He told me he'd just gotten back from Guatemala, actually Belize. He talked about bringing pre-Columbian artifacts back."

Hit cases like the Carolyn Hudson murder often are difficult to solve because, when a stranger does the killing, the motive is money and difficult to track. Whoever hires the killer generally has an ironclad alibi. This case, however, had been different. Within eight hours of the murder, Slickman and Hecht were in custody. And police investigators had a pretty good idea who hired them.

Richard Wheeler, an over-the-road trucker, was out on the West Coast when his ex-wife was murdered. But Carolyn Hudson, probably in anticipation of her break-up with James, was pressuring Wheeler to increase the amount he paid in child support. Carolyn Hudson had seen an attorney the past summer about getting Wheeler to increase his $350-a-month payment and getting him to pay some dental bills for the children.

James Hudson recalled a conversation his wife had about four months earlier with Wheeler. After a brief conversation, Carolyn Hudson slammed down the phone.

"That son-of-a-bitch threatened to kill me!" she said.

Madison detectives John Cloutier and James Grann were assigned to the case from the beginning. Cloutier was a detective of the old school with an investigator's wisdom that comes only from working the streets. Grann, a younger detective, was nicknamed "J. Edgar," a reference to long-time FBI chief J. Edgar Hoover, for his hard work and no-nonsense

Wisconsin State Journal archives

approach. Within hours of the murder, the two detectives began to amass mounds of evidence they hoped would tie Wheeler to the killing.

Like pack rats, the two detectives began collecting everything they could lay their hands on that might have a bearing on the murder,

Melany Brant testifies against her boyfriend. even seemingly insignificant data. Grann, for example, got a complete meteorological record of the day of the murder, including time of sunrise and sunset, temperatures, sky conditions and wind velocity.

Early in the investigation, Hudson also was viewed as a prime suspect. Five days after the murder, Grann dreaded an interview he had to conduct with his fellow officer. Less than an hour before the interview, two other Madison detectives, Mary Otterson and Keith Hackett, called from Texas, where they had been questioning acquaintances and gathering evidence on Hecht and Slickman. They also had reviewed telephone records, discovering calls from Hecht's apartment to the Wheeler's Lodi residence. It was the first link between the hitmen and their benefactor but it wasn't enough to put him behind bars.

Subpoenas were issued for bank and postal records. A San Antonio post office box was found rented to Melany Brant. Hecht bragged shortly after his arrest that he had been involved in fifteen contract killings ,

Wisconsin State Journal archives

Richard Wheeler   **James Stromner**

many of them by mail order.

"A lot of it was kind of blowing smoke, although parts of it turned out to be true," Cloutier said.

Phone companies in Wisconsin, Illinois, Florida and Texas checked millions of calls against twenty names supplied by the detectives.

A district attorney special investigator, William Drenkhahn, was assigned to work with the Madison detectives on the case. They discovered a middleman helped arrange the contact between Hecht and Wheeler. He was James Stomner, owner of the La Petite Beauty Salon in Wisconsin Dells.

The case ultimately involved millions of records, at least a thousand interviews and 2,500 pages of police reports. After ten months, Drenkhahn and the two detectives persuaded deputy district attorney Stephen Bablitch they had enough evidence to arrest Wheeler and Stomner. The two men were arrested on August 10, 1984, along with Wheeler's wife, Jaqueline, later found innocent.

Slickman pleaded innocent to a charge of first-degree murder, then made a deal with prosecutors to plead no contest to a lesser charge. He was sentenced to two years in prison. He said it came as a complete surprise that Hecht planned to murder Carolyn Hudson.

"I had no idea of his intentions or what he was involved in at all," he told the court. "When I found myself under arrest for murder, it destroyed the last vestige of self-respect I had."

Prosecutor Stephen Bablitch said Slickman probably didn't know Hecht had killed Carolyn Hudson when he turned in the rental car and allowed the clerk to stall him until police arrived. It seems unlikely that Slickman didn't have some suspicions, but his cooperation with police helped persuade them to overlook that aspect of the case.

With the evidence weighted against him, Joey Hecht pleaded guilty to first-degree murder and received a sentence of life plus fifty-three years. The sentence included convictions for armed burglary and being a felon in possession of a firearm. It wouldn't be the last time, however, that the world would hear of him.

With Slickman and Hecht safely tucked away, prosecutors turned their full attention to Wheeler and Stomner. A three-week trial began in April 1985.

Wheeler claimed he wanted to scare his ex-wife perhaps by blowing up her car, but denied he plotted to kill her. Stomner's attorney, Raymond Gross of Clearwater, Florida, rejected overtures from prosecutors that his client plead to a lesser charge. Gross believed his client was innocent.

A jury deliberated six hours before finding the two men guilty of conspiracy to commit first-degree murder. Although both received life sentences, Judge Mark Frankel indicated he believed Stomner was the lesser culprit.

"It may be that he did not fully appreciate the potential criminal implications of his involvement," the judge said.

Six months after the convictions, Joey Hecht was taken from Waupun Correctional Institution to University Hospital in Madison for treatment of a feigned illness. Outside the hospital, he produced a gun, overpowered a guard and took a man and his young son hostage. Hecht forced the man, Earl Reiner, to drive him away from the hospital but, unfortunately for Hecht, Reiner's pickup truck was almost out of gas.

When Reiner stopped for gas, Hecht got out, demanded that Reiner "wait here and don't move." But Reiner grabbed his son and rushed to a cleaners to call police. Officers rushed to the scene and surrounded Hecht on the Glenway Golf Course on Madison's West Side. He fired a shot at them before surrendering.

A year later, prison guards found a .22-caliber bullet concealed in a typewriter in Hecht's cell. But Hecht used his typewriter for more than just hiding bullets. By December 1987, the contract killer had turned jailhouse lawyer, winning a state appeals court decision that allowed him greater access to law books in prison.

The appeals court overturned a decision by Dane County Circuit Judge Daniel Moeser that Hecht should abide by prison rules limiting inmates to just two law books a day.

Hecht's sudden inspiration to study the law came from a need to defend himself against the Madison escape charges which, appeals Judge Paul Gartzke said constituted a "special need for access to legal materials."

The brutal murder of his wife took a heavy emotional toll on police officer James Hudson. He left the department and, several years later, engaged in a standoff with police when he holed up in his house with a gun, threatening to kill himself. The standoff ultimately ended peacefully but Hudson could not shake the tragic memory of his wife's violent death.

27

The Keating Gang

Menomonie, 1931

Bank robberies have been a notorious part of Wisconsin's criminal history. In recent years, many robberies have been committed by perpetrators who were mentally unbalanced or addicted to drugs. It takes a certain amount of moxie or irrationality to know that you'll be photographed by bank cameras and probably identified within a short period of time.

Latter-day robbers try disguises to fool the cameras or schemes that prove ingenious for a while. One of the more enterprising robbers of the 1980s would fly into Milwaukee's Mitchell Field and rent a car. He would drive out to a small town, rob the bank, return the car and fly back to his home in California. Inevitably he was caught, like most contemporary bank bandits.

It wasn't always the case, however, that a bank robber was likely to be captured. During the Depression years, banks seemed a source of easy money for roving gangs. The most famous of these was the John Dillinger gang. Dillinger stirred the public's fancy with his Robin Hood antics, often vaulting bank counters and showing special consideration for customers. Dillinger robbed only a few Wisconsin banks and his most famous exploits in the state concerned the shootout at Little Bohemia, where several innocent people were killed or wounded by FBI bullets.

Francis Keating wasn't such a gentleman bandit. In fact, his gang's holdup of the Kraft State Bank in Menomonie in 1931 was among the bloodiest in the Wisconsin history.

Keating was a Chicago hoodlum sentenced to twenty-five years in

Leavenworth Prison for a mail robbery that netted $135,000. He and his sidekick, Tommy Holden, escaped in February 1930, using stolen trustee passes supplied to them by none other than George "Machine Gun" Kelly, who would later join the Dillinger gang and play a crucial role in the Little Bohemia shootout.

Chicago was crawling with gangs so Keating and Holden decided to seek their fortune, quite literally, in the Twin Cities. They selected their gang members carefully, seeking the craziest partners in crime they could find.

The most prominent member may have been Alvin "Creepy" Karpis, later captured by J. Edgar Hoover in New Orleans. After a few years with the Keating-Holden gang, Karpis went on to found his own outfit with Freddie Barker, another Keating-Holden robber, and Freddie's mother, known as Ma Barker. Another notorious member included Frank "Jelly" Nash, later gunned down in Kansas City.

None of these characters were along on October 20, 1931, when the Keating-Holden gang descended on the Kraft State Bank shortly after it opened. Two bandits entered the bank while a third stood guard outside with a sub-machine gun, liberally firing up and down the street to keep away anyone who sought to interfere.

The two gunman inside ordered ten bank employees and four customers to lie on the floor while they scooped up all the available cash in the tellers' cages. After cleaning out the cash drawers, the bandits demanded more money from owner William F. Kraft. When he said there wasn't any more money, one of the cold-blooded robbers fired at Kraft's son with a .45-caliber revolver, wounding him in the shoulder. The bandits grabbed a female bank teller, hoping to use her as a shield so they could reach their getaway car.

Outside, a crowd began to gather despite the gunman's efforts to keep them away. In the excitement, the teller escaped but James Kraft, the owner's son, was forced into a getaway car. As the bandits drove off with a haul of about seven thousand dollars, Ed Kinkle, a Menomonie resident, fired at the fleeing auto. One of his bullets went through the rear window.

Kinkle said later he must have scored a direct hit on one of the bandits because he heard someone yell, "Ouch!" In fact, Kinkle's shot probably killed robber Frank Webber of Minneapolis, whose body was thrown from the car about eight miles from Menomonie. Webber, age thirty-three, was a Wisconsin native who served time at a Salt Lake City prison for bank robbery. As retribution for killing one of their gang, the gunmen murdered nineteen-year-old James Kraft and also flung his body out of the car on the road to Wheeler.

Vernon Townsend, a bank guard, also fired at the getaway car from the roof of the building. Townsend watched the entire robbery from his station above the teller cages but claimed he was under strict orders not to shoot inside the bank. He sounded the burglar alarm, then crawled to the roof. One of his shots hit the car's gas tank.

The gunmen headed north, through Wheeler, Boyceville, Prairie Farm and on toward Clear Lake. When word of James Kraft's murder reached Menomonie, hundreds of angry citizens grabbed guns and took off in pursuit of the killers.

Margaret King reported spotting the gunmen near her family's farm north of Menomonie: "I was hunting in the woods near home when I saw three men in a car parked along the road. I thought they were hunters and one of them had been shot because the other two were bandaging him. I kept out of sight but I noticed that the windshield of the car was broken and that there were bullet holes in it."

The King farm had no phone and hadn't heard of the robbery when Margaret spotted the men.

The brutal robbers pressed on, zigzagging across northern Wisconsin. A third body was found near Shell Lake. He was identified as Preston Harmon of Texas. He served time in a Texas prison for holding up a poker game and also was at Leavenworth with Francis Keating for robbing the post office at Davenport, Iowa. Buckshot lodged in Harmon's body indicated the gun fight outside the Kraft State Bank wasn't his first. A machine gun and two pistols believed used in the robbery were found near Harmon's body.

An airplane was brought in from Eau Claire to search the woodlands. Circling over the isolated lake shores, the plane found no sign of the bandits. On the ground, posses from six counties armed with rifles, shotguns and pitchforks kept watch along main highways. The citizen army found the abandoned getaway car about six miles east of Webster. Bullets had shattered its rear window and blood was found on the back seat.

Sheriff Ike Harmon, no relation to the dead bandit, reported his deputies were near collapse after working long hours to track the bandits. The trail led back into Minnesota as the bandits were spotted crossing the border near Markman and heading for Sandstone.

As part of the investigation, detectives questioned Babe White, a Chicago man who called himself "the human fly." White was seized and handcuffed in Portage, in front of a crowd of several hundred spectators gathered to watch him scale the Raulf Hotel.

White, who had climbed the Marion Hotel in Menomonie the night before the robbery, was seen shaking hands with Frank Webber before the performance. But White said he wasn't acquainted with Webber.

"I thought that man was a Swedish singer, one of a show troupe whose act at a Menomonie theater was to have been announced by me during my ascent," White said.

The Kraft robbery was only the beginning of the Keating-Holden gang's reign of terror. Keating quickly recruited new members to replace the dead men and the gang was linked to robberies at Colfax, Cumberland and Duluth, Minnesota. Investigators gave up the search for the Kraft bandits after three weeks.

Unlike Dillinger and many other bank robbers of the era, Keating and Holden didn't die in a flash of gunfire. They were arrested by FBI agents on July 7, 1932, along with accomplice Harvey Bailey, while playing golf at the Old Mission Golf Course in Kansas City, Missouri.

The agents didn't realize that a fourth golfer was part of the group. Frank "Jelly" Nash was such a terrible golfer and trailed so far behind his three comrades that he avoided capture. The capture ended the criminal careers of Keating and Holden, who spent the rest of their lives in prison.

But Nash wouldn't always be so lucky. Less than a year later, he died during a shootout with federal agents in what was known as the Kansas City Massacre. Besides Nash, four agents were killed and two were wounded. The shootout on June 17, 1933, occurred in an attempt to free Nash, who had been captured in Hot Springs, Arkansas and was being transferred to Kansas City. Among the gangster machine-gunners was the legendary "Pretty Boy" Floyd.

28

Death in a Paper Vat
Green Bay, 1992

The pungent stench of the paper mills greets drivers along the stretch of highway between Appleton and Green Bay. But the smell is more than just an unpleasant odor. It is also the smell of money for paper is an industry critical to Wisconsin's economy and mill workers are paid well, earning annual salaries of seventy-two thousand dollars a year or more.

Paper pulp is blended in huge vats two stories tall and holding tens of thousands of gallons of the ooze. The James River Corporation paper mill is one of these mills — producing paper, providing jobs and spewing the smell of money.

One mill worker, Thomas Monfils, was one of those blue-collar guys who likes to fix things. He helped his aunt, Erma Klaus, remodel her Green Bay home.

"Anything I wanted done, I asked Tom and I got it," she said.

But when Monfils tried to fix something he viewed as wrong at work, he ran afoul of his fellow workers and paid with his life.

The thirty-five-year-old Monfils had worked ten years at the James River mill. He was a union member who lived in Ashwaubenon with his wife, Susan, and their two children, ages nine and eleven. Like many other paper mill workers, he believed in the solidarity of the union.

But something in November 1992 caused him to break that solidarity. When Keith Kutska made plans to steal electrical cord from the mill, Monfils felt he had to report the matter to police. He dialed 911 and anonymously told a dispatcher of Kutska's plan.

Paper mill security guards confronted Kutska and demanded to search his duffle bag. When he refused to let them search, he was suspended for five days. Monfils was terrified that there would be retribution. He feared that Kutska would discover who turned him in. Monfils called police Lieutenant Kenneth LaTour and said he was worried that "someday in the middle of the night I don't show up at home... I would hate to have (Kutska) take me out first."

LaTour assured him that the tape of the 911 call would never be released: "I don't believe it is a matter of public record. I don't believe that stuff can be released to the general public. I'm not a hundred percent sure of that."

Angry at the suspension, Kutska wanted to find out who the snitch was. Using Wisconsin's Open Records Law, Kutska demanded and got a tape of the anonymous 911 call.

He brought the tape to work, where he played it over and over again for his co-workers. Perhaps he also had played it for some of them the night before over beers. Each time the men heard the tape, their collective anger grew that one of their own would turn against them. They also recognized the voice as Monfils. Among those who listened to the tape were Dale Basten, Michael Johnson, Michael Piaskowski, Rey Moore and Michael Hirn.

When Monfils came to work for his 7:30 a.m. shift on Saturday, November 21, he was confronted by at least three of his co-workers.

"How could you do that?" they demanded. "We know it was you." "How could you rat on one of your union brothers?" "You know what happens to rats?"

Monfils may have tried to deny that he had placed the call. But it was no good. His co-workers clearly recognized his voice and they had turned into an enraged mob. A punch was thrown, followed by a few well-placed kicks. Monfils collapsed unconscious to the floor when one of the men hit him over the head with a wrench.

Realizing Monfils was badly hurt, the men grew afraid they would get in trouble for the beating and possibly jeopardize their high-paying jobs. They tied a 40-pound weight to Monfils' neck and threw him in a paper vat. Monfils was still alive when he went into the vat but quickly sunk to the bottom beneath tens of thousands of gallons of the oozing white paper pulp. At the bottom, his body was caught in a blender and mutilated.

When he didn't return from work that day, Susan Monfils reported her husband missing. When the liquid pulp was drained from the vat on Sunday, the body was found. Police soon learned that Monfils had an argument with several co-workers immediately after coming to work that day.

"I am totally convinced there is no foul play," said Marlin Charles, president of Local 327 of the United Paperworkers International Union. "I feel very convinced that the three individuals who talked to him have nothing to do with it."

Charles described the issue that prompted the argument as "minuscule," over unproven theft allegations: "Tom got along good in the plant. He was just as good a union member as the rest of us."

Monfils' mother, Joan, said her son "was dedicated to James River and had a very tight family unit with lots of quality time and love. Everything was with the family, his wife and children."

The vat was open at the top and surrounded by a wall. Jim Taylor, deputy chief of detectives, didn't believe that Monfils had slipped and fallen into the vat. Suicide was a possibility but the argument with his co-workers made the death suspicious. What Taylor knew, however, and didn't reveal was that Monfils went into the vat with a weight tied around his neck with a former employee's five-foot jump rope.

An autopsy two weeks later confirmed that the death was due to strangulation, not from suffocation in the liquid paper pulp. Taylor said Monfils clearly had been murdered. Monfils died of asphyxiation due to "ligature strangulation," according to Brown County Coroner Genie Williams.

Finding the killers would not be as difficult as proving they did it. Police interviewed more than a hundred people. Many of those questioned were among the 1,300 employees of the James River plant. Three workers who had confronted Monfils the morning he disappeared were suspended without pay.

Erma Klaus said she wasn't surprised at the revelation that her nephew was murdered. She said she knew the man who she relied upon to fix things around her home would never kill himself.

A year later, no one had been charged with the murder. But Joan Monfils, the mother of the dead man, testified before a legislative committee that her son had been murdered because someone misinterpreted the Open Records Law.

"He didn't deserve what he got," she told members of the State Senate Judiciary and Insurance Committee. "If the tape had not been turned over, he'd still be alive. Tom asked to remain anonymous. Someone in the city attorney's office said the tape should be released."

Representative Rosemary Hinkfuss, Green Bay Democrat, introduced a bill that would allow police to withhold records if they are part of an investigation or juvenile case. The bill was opposed by newspapers and the Wisconsin Freedom of Information Council. But the bill was enacted into law.

"This bill will give protection to a person who gives information to a law enforcement agency about a crime that has been or will be committed," Hinkfuss said.

Two years after the murder, police had spent eighty six thousand dollars in overtime pay on the Monfils case. An interview room crammed with investigative files was dubbed the "Thomas Monfils room."

Joan Monfils had grown tired of waiting for police and prosecutors to charge mill workers with her son's murder. She filed a civil lawsuit against eight of Monfils' co-workers, accusing them of causing his death. She pleaded with mill workers to come forward:

"If they didn't intend to do it, if it happened by accident, just pick up a phone to call and say, 'Mrs. Monfils, things got out of hand.' I'd understand."

Erma Klaus wore a white ribbon each day as a symbol that her nephew's murder wasn't settled. She too wanted answers. Monfils father, Ed, age sixty-four, was more patient. He said the family wanted investigators to "do it right."

District Attorney John Zakowski said he wanted to make sure there was a solid case before charging anyone with the murder: "We know, on the second anniversary, it's understandable if some people are wondering why it's taking so long. The worst thing to do would be to run to court when you're not ready and you don't have everything."

What prosecutors and police had was a major problem finding witnesses and piecing together enough physical evidence for a case. They had convened a grand jury investigation and repeatedly questioned mill workers. The suspects were suspended from their jobs and grilled during unemployment hearings. But a wall of silence shrouded the men involved in the Monfils murder and no one was ready to squeal on a union brother. Unlike Monfils, who had courageously reported a theft, no one would report a murder.

Finally, frustrated investigators got a break. In May 1994, David Wiener was sentenced to ten years in prison for the shooting death of his brother, Timothy, six months earlier. Wiener claimed he shot his brother because he broke into his home in Allouez. Wiener was a former mill worker at James River and he was willing to testify in exchange for consideration of a reduced sentence on his murder conviction.

Wiener told detectives he had seen Basten and Johnson carrying something heavy toward the vat where Monfils body was found on the morning he disappeared. Wiener said he didn't remember that important piece of evidence until six months after the murder, when he was drunk at a wedding reception.

The trial lasted five weeks and a jury of nine women and three men was brought in from Racine County because extensive publicity about the case in Brown County could jeopardize the men's rights to a fair trial.

On October 28, 1995 — nearly three years after Monfils was killed

— a packed courtroom watched as a jury of nine women and three men convicted six mill workers of the murder. The verdict came after ten hours of deliberations. Besides Kutska, other convicted were Hirn, Moore, Piaskowski, Johnson and Basten. The jury deliberated ten hours before returning the verdict.

The men displayed little emotion and some left the courtroom almost nonchalantly with their hands in their pockets. But relatives of the convicted killers were outraged by the verdict. Moore's wife and another relative, Kathy Miller, were ejected from the courtroom for their outbursts when the verdict was announced.

"All he did was go up to Tom and say, 'why did you do that?'" she said. "And they sentenced him to prison for life... I've never seen him raise his voice. He never got in a fight."

Johnson's daughter, Dawn, blamed the police: "The police disclosed a tape that they shouldn't have. So as a scapegoat, they blamed it on six men to take the blame off their errors and they succeeded."

Bonnie Vervaeren, Johnson's sister, said the men were innocent: "They're just ruining our lives, that's what they're doing."

In his opening arguments, prosecutor Larry Lasee admitted his case was based on circumstantial evidence and he lacked hard proof that any of the men committed the murder. He couldn't show the jury where Monfils was attacked.

Each defendant testified that he wasn't involved in the murder. The mill's union brotherhood was unshaken but the jury believed the men were guilty anyway.

After his testimony, Wiener, the snitch who implicated the killers, had his prison term reduced from ten to eight years by Brown County Judge Peter Naze. He was paroled on August 25, 1997. Wiener said he had been threatened and assaulted in prison due to his testimony. Joan Monfils civil case against the six men convicted of killing her husband also went to trial during the summer of 1997.

In 1996, a Outagamie County sheriff's dispatcher was found innocent of violating the Monfils Law that protects the identity of police informants. But Shawn Treiber agreed to give up her job in exchange for about $20,000. Treiber had been placed on paid leave for giving the name of an informer to a Hortonville police officer.

The six mill workers were given mandatory life prison terms. Earliest parole eligibility for Kutska was set at twenty years, when he will be age sixty-four. Basten was given an earliest parole date of seventeen years, when he will be seventy-years old. Three workers, Hirn, the youngest of the workers at age thirty-one, Moore, age forty-nine, and Johnson, age forty-seven, each received earliest parole eligibility dates of fifteen years. Piaskowski must serve at least thirteen years in prison before he is eligible for parole.

"This signals the ending of the first chapter of a book whose ending has not yet been written," said Judge James Bayorgeon when he handed down the sentences.

For Joan Monfils and Erma Klaus, the end may never come. "Our intentions are now to begin going on with our lives," Joan Monfils said after the sentencing. "Tom would have wanted that."

29

Their Calling Card
Burlington, 1962

The early 1960s were a rough time for Wisconsin law enforcement officers. During an eight-month period, four officers were murdered in confrontations with suspects.

In June 1961, Waukesha Detective George Schmidling was shot to death after fatally wounding two of three burglary suspects he was taking in for questioning. In August 1961, Wisconsin Dells officer James Jantz was killed in shootout with three suspects from the Chicago area.

During the fall of the same year, Patrolman Nick Klaske of Fond du Lac was fatally wounded as he closed in on two men burglarizing a gas station.

The following February 5, a Monday, Burlington Sgt. Anthony Eilers was on routine patrol shortly before 3:30 a.m. when he spotted a car dragging its tail pipe near highways W and 11. Eilers, a big man, wasn't afraid of making a traffic stop without calling for backup. At six feet three inches and weighing 218 pounds, he could handle most other men.

"He's strong as an ox," said fellow officer Edward Wismefsky. "I would have hated to tangle with him."

Eilers, age thirty-eight, had served five years on the Burlington force and received his sergeant's stripes a month earlier. He had served five years in the Army, serving in the South Pacific during World War II, where he was wounded and awarded a Purple Heart. He had worked as a roofer before becoming a cop. He was an avid hunter and fisherman who also coached a Pony League baseball team.

Although he liked the extra money and responsibility of the sergeant's job, Eilers didn't like the night hours. He didn't like being away from his wife, Dorothy, and their children, John, age ten, and Jean, age eight. But it never occurred to Eilers that there could be any danger in pulling over a car with a minor equipment violation. In this case, however, that confidence would be a fatal mistake.

Inside the old car were Wilson "Sonny" Brook and his seventeen-year-old brother, Max. Brook, about five inches shorter than Eilers and lighter, didn't appear threatening to the strong cop. What Eilers didn't know, however, was that the two men were returning to South Milwaukee from a burglary in Janesville, where they had taken $970 from a school safe.

Sonny Brook pulled the car off the road. Eilers stopped his squad behind Brook's car. Brook rolled down his window. The sergeant flicked on his powerful silver flashlight to light his way on the dark roadway. As he approached the other car, he noticed the car's rear license plate was dangling by a single screw.

"What'd I do, officer?" Brook asked Eilers.

"That tailpipe back there," the sergeant responded. "That's a violation." Sonny Brook nervously drummed his fingers on the steering wheel. Eilers shined his flashlight over at Max Brook, sitting on the passenger side. He swept the light into the rear seat and it was there he spotted the cash from the Janesville burglary. "But I guess that's not all," he said. "It looks like we've got something more serious."

Brook's nervousness turned to anger as Eilers motioned with the flashlight, ordering him out of the car. He had been paroled two months earlier from prison after confessing in 1959 to burglaries of six schools. At the time of his parole, he had served two years of a five-year term. After his release, Brook had gotten a day job at the Guardian Container Corporation in Sturdevant. At night, however, he obviously hadn't given up his old habits.

As he got out of the car, Brook knew that he didn't want to go back to prison. He grabbed for the sergeant's flashlight and a life-and-death struggle began. Catching the burly officer by surprise, Brook was able to overpower him. He beat Eilers with the heavy flashlight, until the officer sunk to his knees. Then, Brook grabbed the sergeant's .38-caliber service revolver and shot him five times.

Dr. Myron Schuster would say after the autopsy that Eilers was beaten so badly that, at first, it was difficult to tell that he also had been shot. Bullet wounds were found in his lower back, head, upper right cheek, neck, right shoulder and right side.

But Brook wasn't satisfied with the brutal murder. Now, he wanted to conceal the crime. The brothers loaded the sergeant's body into the squad and drove the two cars to a quarry, where they hoped to push the squad off a cliff into the deep water. With their own car, they rammed the quarry gate several times but failed to break it open. Brook couldn't turn off the flashing squad lights and he feared the lights and noise might alert neighbors so they left the body in the squad near the quarry gate and fled. The squad's motor was still running when Eilers' body was found several hours later. The quarry was just a block from Eilers' home, where his children slept soundly, unaware of their father's terrible fate.

When Eilers failed to make his routine check-in with headquarters at 3:30 a.m., an all-points-bulletin was issued. But the squad and the officer's body weren't found until more than two hours later, when bus driver William Boy spotted the squad with the motor running. He lived about 100 feet north of the quarry gate and was leaving for work. Boy had heard nothing of the scuffle two hours earlier.

"My dog didn't even bark," he said. The dog was a German shepherd that slept outside.

When officers Freddie Peklo and Richard Lichtenwalner arrived at the quarry gate, they found Eilers' mangled body. His watch, rings and four dollars in cash weren't taken. However, what was missing were the new sergeant's stripes from his sleeve, the flashlight, his service revolver and his hat.

When the Brook brothers got to their parents' home after the murder, they went to the basement. They hid the money and Brook washed the blood off his hands and shoes. Then, he burned his clothes and Eilers' hat. Earlier, he had thrown the gun into a snowbank along the highway near Sturdevant.

If he had been able to crash the quarry gate and get the squad into the water, Brook might have pulled off a perfect crime. The squad may not have been found for quite awhile and he might have been able to continue his night burglaries. But Brook made another mistake. He had left a calling card that led police right to him.

When the news of Eilers murder became public, Bruce Kettenberger recalled that he'd noticed the officer pull over a car early that morning on Highway 11 near Highway W.

When officers searched the area, they found the sergeant's coat in a pool of blood behind a snowbank about fifteen feet off the highway. They also found a license plate.

That rear plate on Brook's car, dangling precariously by a single screw, had come off as the brothers rushed to cover up their crime. It left police the clue they needed to track down the vicious killer. In his desperate effort to turn off the squad's revolving light, Sonny Brook yanked it off the roof and stomped on it while sitting in the driver's seat. His foot hit the accelerator and the squad rear-ended his car parked a few feet ahead. The impact knocked off the plate.

Police traced the car to Brook's father, Woodrow, who lived in South Milwaukee. The elder Brook said his two sons had borrowed it on Sunday night. The car was found in a parking lot at the Bucyrus-Erie plant in South Milwaukee, where the elder Brook worked. The car's rear plate was missing and blood was found on the seat.

After Brook was arrested, he cooperated with police. He confessed to the crime and helped them find the gun. Despite his cooperation, he received a life sentence for the brutal murder. Max Brook told police his brother "went crazy" for some reason and attacked Eilers.

Brook's mother said a childhood injury caused her son to turn to crime. "He fell out of a tree and hurt his back when he was little. He was about fifteen when it happened. After that, his first mischievous acts started."

She said her son was in good spirits that Sunday night before venturing out with his brother to Janesville. The family hosted a party at their home: "Sonny had been dancing and cutting up. We'd all had such a good time. I suppose I'll always remember that party."

Brook was paroled after fourteen years but, by 1982, he was back in prison. Even after the long stint in prison, he couldn't give up the burglary habit. In prison, he enjoyed tinkering, sometimes building wall clocks from kits. He also studied Spanish.

In 1985, he was serving a ten-year sentence and, then in his midforties, he hoped for parole. He had been transferred to the minimum-security Winnebago Correctional Institution and appeared to be doing well. But Eilers' partner, Roy Knollmueller, still had vivid memories of the 1962 crime. He organized a letter-writing campaign to keep Brook behind bars. At an April parole hearing, Brook lost his temper, threatening to "get Eilers' partner" if he got out. The threat helped persuade the Parole Board to reject his request.

On September 19, 1988, Brook found his own way out of prison. While running some morning errands, he drove away in a prison pickup truck and never returned. The truck was found nine days later in Madison.

After Brook's escape, the Wisconsin Department of Corrections removed all but three of the twenty-five lifers from minimum-security prisons and changed the inmate classification system. Corrections officials claimed the move had nothing to do with the escape and that the changes already were in the works when Brook left.

He vanished for about a year, heading west and finding a construction job in Nevada. He might have succeeded in eluding authorities if his case hadn't been profiled several times on "America's Most Wanted." A telephone tip led authorities to North Las Vegas, where Brook was found plastering a ceiling. He was taken into custody without a struggle. He had been working under the alias of David Giselbach.

"He tried to disguise his appearance," said Tom Nicodemus, an FBI spokesman in Las Vegas. "He dyed his hair, grew a small mustache and changed his hairstyle."

Brook's fate as a career criminal was sealed that cold winter morning on a Burlington highway. Perhaps he would have given up his burglary habit if it weren't for the murder. Or, perhaps his criminal tendencies ultimately would have led him to kill someone else.

30

Supernatural Questions
Middleton, 1947

The snow was beginning to fall heavily outside as the wind whipped it into small drifts. Inside the Madison railroad station, Carl Carlson checked his watch. It was almost 10:00 p.m. and the train carrying his sister-in-law to Madison was late. There was no way they'd make the last bus to Badger Village near Baraboo.

Carlson was a medical student at the UW-Madison. Born and raised in Superior, he had served a six-year stint in the Navy during World War II. He had married his wife, Carol, a year earlier and he thought tonight would be the first chance for her sister to see their six-week-old daughter, Carla. The next day they planned to watch the Wisconsin Badger football team play Michigan.

A winter storm was closing in on southern Wisconsin although the snow and bitter winds were a little early in the season. It was November 14, 1947, still more than a month before the official beginning of winter.

As the snow began to pile up on the ground outside, Carlson couldn't help thinking about a conversation he'd had earlier in the day with Edna Taylor, a graduate student in English. He told her he was tired of studying medicine. It was too concrete and didn't excite him anymore. He wanted to change his studies to an area that was more philosophical and intellectually less confining.

As he'd walked from class with Taylor, the conversation turned to life after death. Carlson told her he was an atheist.

"When you're dead, you're dead," he said, adding that science would prove someday that man has no immortal soul. But she argued that in-

Wisconsin State Journal archives

Carol and Carl Carlson in their wedding photo.

justice could only be explained by the existence of the soul.

"If man has no soul, if there is nothing after death, then how can there be hope for any ultimate justice in a world in which the forces of evil can strike down the good and the innocent?" she asked him.

After she had dinner that night and while Carlson awaited his sister-in-law's train, Taylor still was thinking about their conversation. She grabbed a book on religion from a shelf in her living room and set it aside to give to him later.

When the train finally arrived, they had missed the last bus, so Carlson and his sister-in-law, a nineteen-year-old University of Michigan student, trudged through the storm to University Avenue and Park Street, where Carlson stuck out his thumb to hitch a ride.

They were picked up by two young men, Buford Sennett and Robert Winslow. The Plymouth that Winslow was driving that night had been stolen from a water superintendent in Galena, Illinois. It had been repainted black and Sennett had put plates on it issued to a car his father had sold. Carlson and his sister-in-law got into the back seat.

After driving through Middleton, Sennett suggested they change seats so he could lie down in back. Carlson and his sister-in-law squeezed into the front seat next to Winslow. The Plymouth turned north on Highway 12 and headed toward Sauk City.

Carlson stared at Winslow. He couldn't help noticing the driver's beady eyes that glimmered and darted around in the dim light.

Near Springfield Corners, Sennett suddenly pulled out a revolver and fired two shots into the back of Carlson's head and one in his ribs. Carlson's body toppled on to his sister-in-law, spurting blood all over her clothes. The woman was stunned, too hysterical to scream. She was forced into the back seat, where Sennett and Winslow repeatedly raped her while they took turns driving.

Carlson's body lay in the front seat, propped against the passenger door. Winslow fired a fourth shot into the body.

"We've got a bullet left for you," he told the terrified woman.

Sennett later revealed his motive for the brutal slaying: "I didn't like the way he was looking at Bob."

Sennett, age twenty-two, was so intelligent that he graduated early from high school. His father worked for the Richland County Highway Department. But Sennett was sentenced to the Green Bay Reformatory in 1943 for the burglary of a Grant County school. He escaped from a prison farm on April 3, 1945, but was captured the following day near his Richland Center home after he had stolen cars in DePere, Oshkosh and Baraboo. He was paroled December 7, 1946, and had been released from parole ten days earlier.

"He had served three years, he was a boy of high intelligence and we thought he should be given a chance on parole," a state parole employee later explained to the *Wisconsin State Journal*. "In some cases, too much institution can do more damage than good. We thought that was the case with him."

While serving time at Green Bay, Sennett became friends with Winslow, a grade school dropout who was convicted of car theft. Winslow, the son of an Owen farm family, was sentenced to prison on June 16, 1943, for a one-to-three-year term. He escaped and was transferred to Waupun Correctional Institution for a year after his capture. He had been released about a year earlier, on November 5, 1946.

Sennett later was described by a prosecutor as "the brains and financier of the pair." During the previous summer, Winslow had lived at Sennett's family home and both worked part-time at a bowling alley. Sennett also worked at a lumber company but on the night he murdered Carlson, he hadn't shown up for work in a week.

As a bitter wind whipped snow across highways and knocked down power lines, the men drove, crisscrossing Columbia, Sauk, Richland, Vernon and Grant counties. At one point, they pulled the car to the side of the road and stuffed Carlson's body in the trunk. Near Blue River, they parked at a bridge and weighted the body with chains and a rock. Winslow went through Carlson's pockets, removing thirty cents and a watch before dropping the body into the Wisconsin River.

After they had finished raping her, the two men forced the woman to lie down in the back seat so she wouldn't be seen. During the drive, she heard them talk about a farm or place up north. Finally, after hours of driving, they pulled off on a rural road near Richland Center and slept for about four hours, taking turns holding the woman so she wouldn't escape. At daybreak, they drove back to Blue River to see if the body had surfaced. It hadn't.

Sennett and Winslow stopped again about 7:00 a.m. at a Pine River bridge about a mile from Richland Center. Winslow held the woman in a culvert while Sennett drove home to change clothes. He took off his blood-stained black and white plaid jacket, pants and shirt. His mother fixed him some cheese sandwiches and he told her that he and a friend were headed for an abandoned farm near Owen.

When he pulled into a Richland Center gas station, an attendant noticed the heavy snow caked on the car and remarked that Sennett must have been out all night.

"You don't know the half of it," Sennett replied. The attendant filled the car's tank and a five-gallon can.

Sennett picked up Winslow and the woman, then drove north on Highway 80 from Richland Center. But the car stalled on an ice-covered hill. When he tried to back slowly down the hill, the car skidded into a ditch. Winslow got out and started across the road to get a piece of fence wire to repair the car's tire chains.

As he slammed the door, the woman watched him stick the gun in his pocket. She quietly opened the back door but Sennett heard the click and whirled around in the driver's seat.

"If you make a break, you're the first one that'll get knocked off," he hissed at her. But he was too late. She jumped screaming from the car, then ran to other cars stalled on the hill. The driver of a car with Iowa plates thought she was drunk. A milk truck driver took one look at the blood splattered on her clothes and refused help. Then she ran to a car driven by William Harris, a Richland Center stone mason, who had his wife and two children with him.

"They killed my brother!' she screamed to Harris. 'They're gonna kill me!"

Sennett got out of the car about thirty feet away and walked half-way toward the woman.

"She's crazy," he told Harris, "Don't believe her."

But Harris recognized Sennett. He told the woman to get in his car

Wisconsin State Journal archives

Convicted killers Buford Sennett and Robert Winslow. Behind them are Leo P. Lownik, Richland County district attorney, and William J. Coyne, Dane County district attorney.

and "cool off." Sennett walked nonchalantly across the road to help Winslow with the fence wire.

Harris quietly got out of his car. He walked slowly up to the Plymouth, grabbed the ignition keys and threw them in a snowbank. Then he returned to his car and tried once more to negotiate the icy hill. When Winslow and Sennett saw the keys were gone and the woman was in the other car, they fled up the highway on foot.

Harris finally got his car over the hill and drove the woman to authorities in Hillsboro. Because of the storm, it was four hours before Vernon County Sheriff Morris Moon could notify other police agencies that the woman was safe. A rifle, shotgun and a pair of brown oxford shoes were found in the abandoned Plymouth.

Police also suspected Sennett and Winslow of slugging a Madison cab driver in a gravel quarry near Cottage Grove three hours before Carlson and his sister-in-law hitched the ride. The two men also were linked to three Richland Center home burglaries in which a .22-caliber rifle and a small amount of cash were taken.

With her baby wrapped in a pink blanket, Carlson's wife came to the Dane County jail seeking information about her missing husband, but sheriff's deputies would not tell her immediately about the murder. She thought her sister was in Methodist Hospital with injuries from a traffic accident. Police still were tracking down Carlson, hoping he was alive. They called his parents in Superior and, when all leads failed, they finally told his wife of her husband's fate.

Meanwhile, Sennett and Winslow fled up the highway to the Donald Laska farm, where they asked Mrs. Laska for a car. She offered to get her husband from the field so he could pull their car from the ditch with his tractor but they refused the offer and ran from the house. The two men walked until almost midnight, then stole a car from a farmer near Yuba, about 17 miles north of Richland Center. Their feet nearly froze from trudging through the heavy snow.

They spent the night in an abandoned school near Yuba, then drove north to Westby. They spent Sunday night in another school and swapped the car for a Studebaker. They drove on to Owen, where Winslow's brother-in-law, George Schultz, refused to take them in and notified police of their whereabouts.

Anthony Pomputis was milking cows Monday morning on his family's farm near Longwood when Winslow walked into the barn.

"I was glad to see Bob," Pomputis said later. "Hardly anybody around here knew about that murder and rape business down toward Madison and our family sure didn't know Bob was mixed up with it."

Winslow said he and a friend were in a jam and needed a hot car repainted in the barn. Pomputis went inside the house and talked to his parents. The two fugitives shared a bottle of whiskey with Pomputis' father and he agreed to let them stay.

But by 7 a.m., police officers searching the area on Schultz's tip showed up at the farm. Pomputis quietly told them that the killers were hiding in the barn. Then, he went out to the barn and told Winslow the police just wanted to talk to him about a minor traffic accident. More than two hundred police officers converged on the Clark County farm.

"Bob and his friend never threatened us, although they showed us their gun," Pomputis wrote later in a special article for the *Wisconsin State Journal*. "I don't think any of us were afraid of them. We just wanted to stay out of trouble."

Pomputis and his brother, Al, told the two fugitives they'd go to the store to buy cigarettes and paint for disguising the stolen Studebaker. On the way, they met a police roadblock. A deputy was sent to pick up the paint and the Pomputis brothers returned to the house.

"The officers told us to get our folks away from the house at all costs because there was almost sure to be shooting," Pomputis said. "We made up a story about my sister, Julia Twait, being sick and having to take the folks over there. But we didn't have to use it because Bob and Sennett weren't in sight when we got home."

Sennett and Winslow nervously kept going back and forth between the house and the barn. Pomputis hid his rifle, shotgun and ammunition so the two men couldn't use them, then took his parents to the police roadblock. When the family was safely out of the house, police used a bullhorn to ask the fugitives to surrender:

"Buford, this is Leo P. Lownik, district attorney of Richland County. You are surrounded by law enforcement officers of Clark County and several surrounding counties and we advise you to come out with your hands upraised or you will be shot."

Nothing happened. There was no sound from inside. As the minutes ticked by, police prepared to storm the house. The only sound was a plane circling overhead.

Finally, Sennett emerged.

"He was meek, dirty and tired," wrote *State Journal* reporter June Dieckmann. "His faded plaid jacket and hunting cap were covered with hay seed. He made no resistance to the officers' search, which revealed he was not carrying any weapons in his pockets."

Winslow came out a few minutes later. Sennett said the only reason they surrendered was because of the plane overhead. They feared it was the FBI. But the plane carried Dieckmann and a newspaper photographer, although the FBI had gotten involved in the case because a stolen car crossed state lines. Sennett also said he thought the man with the bullhorn was his father and said, "I've always done what my father ordered me to do."

The two men were brought back to Madison and, during eight hours of questioning at the Dane County courthouse, adults and children as young as age five packed the courtroom to get a glimpse of the killers.

The next order of business was to find Carlson's body and C.J. Weller of Sparta recalls when police dragged the Wisconsin River: "I took my own car and drove down to the bridge. I wanted to be able to leave and come back when I wanted to. There was quite a crowd at the bridge already. The sheriff and his men led Sennett back and forth across the bridge several times trying to get him to pinpoint the spot where they dumped the body over. The dragging crew was already in the water. Sennett did not want to cooperate and finally the sheriff grabbed him by the coat collar and said words something like, 'You son of a bitch, you had better start talking or you are going over the rail, too.' Very soon and very accurately, Sennett pointed out where the body was and in less than ten minutes the hooks had hold of the body and were pulling it to shore.

"A sand bar ran out into the river where they were trying to bring the body in and they needed a rope to drag it to shore along with the large rock that was still attached to the body. I had a length of old heavy hay rope that I always carried in the car and went and got it for them to use, along with a good wool Pendleton blanket that I always carried in the car. I got the rope back and it still hangs in my shed. The blanket I never did see again."

The two men confessed to the rape and murder and were sentenced the following day to life imprisonment. They also confessed to a random shooting a year earlier in Neillsville in which two girls, ages fourteen and sixteen, were severely wounded. Detectives said Sennett and Winslow remained "indifferent" about their crimes.

"I do not believe that ever in the history of Dane County has there ever been a more cold-blooded, cruel and revolting crime than this one which has been perpetrated by you two ruffians," Judge Roy H. Proctor said at the sentencing hearing. "I don't believe that I would have any qualms whatever (if Wisconsin had the death penalty) to sentence you to the gas chamber, the electric chair or to be hanged by the neck until dead."

Several hundred university students blocked the jail driveway and police sped Sennett and Winslow to Waupun State Prison directly from court because of fear that a mob demonstration by the students could end in a lynching.

Although they were eligible for parole in eleven years, authorities planned to file additional charges on the rape and kidnapping to prevent the two from ever being paroled.

But both Sennett and Winslow were paroled in the mid-1970s. Winslow settled in the Racine area while Sennett, who had learned the barber trade in prison, moved to Appleton.

He worked about two years as a service station attendant and was a volunteer driver for the Outagamie County Department of Social Services, providing transportation for welfare clients.

"He had his own little apartment that he kept neat as a pin," said John Feabec, a state probation and parole supervisor. "He had one or two friends, I guess. He wasn't out and about in the community much."

Sennett told Outagamie County authorities he earned almost $30,000 by running a betting operation in prison.

After thirteen years of freedom, Sennett, then age sixty-two, returned to prison in January 1987, after he was convicted of repeated sexual assaults of a nine-year-old girl. The assaults occurred during the summer of 1985 while Sennett lived with the girl's mother. The girl said Sennett told her she would be forced to live in a foster home if she told her mother what was happening.

Five sexual assault charges were filed against Sennett, including one involving a thirteen-year-old girl, but several were later dropped. His parole was revoked and he was given a twenty-year sentence on top of the original murder, rape and kidnapping sentences.

The Carlson murder was the first big case handled by the fledgling Wisconsin Crime Laboratory, which less than a decade later would process the grisly scene at the Edward Gein farm near Plainfield.

Sennett was among the drug offenders, robbers and rapists recommended for early release in 1995 when Wisconsin's prison population soared to eleven thousand, about three thousand inmates over capacity. The sixty-nine-year-old convict wasn't set free, but the possibility brought a vehement protest from Jerry Harris of Prairie du Sac, son of William Harris, who had rescued Carlson's sister-in-law from the two outlaws nearly a half century earlier.

"At the time of his sentencing, Sennett swore he would get my father," Harris wrote in an August 31, 1995, letter published in the *Wisconsin State Journal*. "I don't think they should even consider releasing him. My father is seventy-six and lives alone. A person who has spent forty-eight years in jail will never forget or forgive who was responsible for putting him there."

Former Jefferson County Sheriff Roger Reinel said Sennett also once confessed to the murder of Georgia Jean Weckler, age eight, of rural Fort Atkinson, who disappeared May 7, 1947, on her way home from school. But Reinel said Sennett refused to put the confession in writing.

"I visited him several times in prison and he told me the story about how he and his accomplice, Robert Winslow, picked up the girl along the road and were going to hold her for ransom. They later decided against the ransom and were going to return her when they were spotted by a telephone lineman and had to flee with her in the car," Reinel said in 1980.

In 1996, Ed J. Lindloff of Delavan told police that Georgia's body might be buried beneath a greenhouse. Lindloff, in his seventies, said he saw two men pull a package the size of a child from a car trunk, throw it into an excavated area and cover it with dirt. Jefferson County Chief Deputy Michael Sullivan said it would be too costly to try to dig up the area now because of concrete and heat pipes "based on such flimsy evidence."

Lindloff had contacted authorities forty-nine years earlier about the possible connection to the Weckler case and investigators reportedly checked it out.

Immediately after Sennett and Winslow were convicted and sentenced, William T. Evjue, editor of the Madison *Capital Times,* was charged with violating state law by publishing the name of the rape victim, Carlson's sister-in-law. Action also was considered but never taken against out-of-state papers and wire services that picked up the name.

Evjue argued that a Wisconsin law prohibiting publication of a rape victim's name was unconstitutional. Judge Proctor agreed with Evjue but his decision was overturned by the state Supreme Court.

In October 1948, nearly a year after the Carlson murder, the Evjue case was set for trial but Proctor dismissed the case on the grounds that insufficient evidence had been presented to prove him guilty. The Supreme Court declined to hear another appeal of Proctor's decision.

After the ruling, Evjue confronted District Attorney Edwin Wilkie in the court clerk's office. He accused Wilkie of consorting with the *State Journal* publisher in pressing the case and said the *Capital Times* was no more guilty in printing the name than any other paper.

"You didn't have guts enough to prosecute the *State Journal*," Evjue said.

"I've guts enough to prosecute any violator of the law," Wilkie retorted. "But you didn't have guts enough to stand up there before the court and take your medicine like a man. I'm not a water boy for any newspaper, including the *Capital Times*."

Crimes Involving Children

31

The Blood-Stained Nightgown
Madison, 1911

With her long, light-brown hair tied back in a pretty white bow, little Annie Lemberger skipped merrily home from school on September 5, 1911. It was her first day in the second grade and she couldn't wait to show her mother the prize she'd been given for her good work.

The family lived in a small frame house at 2 South Frances Street in the old Madison Italian neighborhood of Greenbush. Annie's father, Martin, worked as a laborer and Annie, age seven, slept with her sister and two brothers in a tiny, eight-foot-square bedroom. Her brothers, Martin and Alois, shared a double bed while Annie shared a single bed wedged beneath a ground-floor window with her sister, Marie, age three. The baby, George Sebastian, slept in an adjacent bedroom with their parents. Despite its small size, the twenty-foot by twenty-foot house was well-kept, freshly painted with neatly trimmed vines and trees outside in the small yard. The family kept a gray cat and a small fox terrier that barked at anyone who came near the house, especially after dark.

On that first day of school, Annie's mother put the children to bed about 7:00 p.m. But they were allowed to get up for awhile when Lemberger's brother-in-law dropped by so they could play with their four-year-old cousin. The company left about 9:00 p.m. and Lemberger went to bed about a half hour later. Then, Mrs. Lemberger said she locked the doors and windows, including the one above Annie's bed, before going to bed herself. Nothing eventful seemed to happen that night. The family slept soundly and the fox terrier was silent. In the morning, Mrs.

A crowd gathers at the Lemberger home to aid in the search.

Lemberger went to check on the children.

"I went in there and I felt cold air and I see the window was open and Annie was not in her bed," she said. "I looked under the boys' bed to see if she walked there in her sleep and under the other bed, too, and in the closet but could not find her."

Mrs. Lemberger woke her husband, then continued the search for the little girl outside. When Annie couldn't be found, he called the police.

As word of the girl's disappearance began to spread, a crowd gathered at the Lemberger house. Annie's father showed police officers how someone must have torn the mosquito netting on the outside, then removed a piece of cracked glass from the window above Annie's bed and reached inside to open it. Then, the culprit must have propped up the window with a piece of lath and quietly grabbed Annie from her bed and through the window. Police found footprints under the window but they were ruined as evidence by the crowd stomping around outside. A band of gypsies was in town and police searched their camp south of the city. Searchers combed vacant buildings, boxcars and storm sewers but found no sign of the missing girl.

Newspapers raised questions about the case. What was the motive? Annie's parents were too poor to pay a ransom. Was she snatched by a child molester? If that was the case, then why would he risk breaking into the house when he could more easily grab Annie or another girl on the street? How could Annie be awakened by a stranger without screaming, especially when police found no evidence that an anesthetic had been used to subdue her? Why did Lemberger and his wife report hearing nothing when the door to the room where they slept was ajar that night? And why was the noisy dog silent, keeping the intruder's secret?

"The curious part of the disappearance is that absolutely no clue to the supposed kidnapping can be found, or any motive for a kidnapping or secretion of the child," wrote Grant Brightman of the baffling case in the *Wisconsin State Journal.*

Although the Lembergers were poor, Mrs. Lemberger's uncle, George

Pregler, had made some money in Madison real estate. But Annie's mother said he wasn't interested enough in her family to pay a ransom. Brightman wrote that sexual assault probably wasn't the motive because such crimes are committed on impulse, not with the forethought and planning needed to open the window and snatch Annie.

But the impatient, outraged crowd that kept growing larger outside the Lemberger home didn't need to know the motive. Spurred by a two hundred dollar reward offered by the mayor for recovery of the girl, bystanders talked of a house-to-house search of the Italian neighborhood. The Black Hand, or Mafia, was suspected of playing a role in the abduction. Newspapers reported that Lemberger had given evidence against Italians in a "blind pig" case — illegal liquor sales — so revenge was a possibility.

Thousands of callers kept phone lines tied up at newspaper offices and police headquarters, seeking the latest word on whether the girl had been found. Rumors abounded that the girl's body was in a boxcar in Chicago, Racine or Elgin, Illinois. The rumors only heightened the fever of outrage that gripped the city over the abduction of an innocent young girl.

"Public sentiment about the city is at white heat," the *State Journal* reported. "It is probable that should the guilty man be found that a lynching would be attempted."

Lemberger paid thirty dollars for the service of a bloodhound. Two days of rain stymied the dog and it failed to follow a scent. But finally, the dog provided by Joseph Barto of Richland Center sniffed Annie's bed and window, then led Sheriff Andrew Brown to the banks of Lake Monona at Brittingham Park. No blood was found along the trail and Brown speculated that Annie's body had been weighted and dumped in the bay. Dragging the bay was nearly an impossible task because of sink holes and gullies in the lake bed created when the lake was dredged to provide fill for Brittingham Park land. Instead, police scheduled a house-to-house search of the Greenbush neighborhood for 8:00 a.m. that Saturday and invited the public to participate.

George Younger, a cement worker, normally left for work about dawn and that Saturday was no exception. On his way to a job at the University of Wisconsin campus, Younger passed by Brittingham Park. As he approached the park that morning, he noticed something floating in the bay near the foot of Erin Street and stopped at Bruno Kleinheinz's saloon for help to bring it to shore. It was the nude body of the missing girl.

An autopsy by Drs. H.E. Purcell and Joseph Dean found no water in the girl's lungs, indicating she had been strangled or suffocated before she was dumped in the water. Bruises were found behind her left ear and over her left eye. Smaller bruises were found on other parts of her head.

Coroner Matthew Lynch described the injuries: "The membrane back of the ear was bruised. There was a small clot on the brain at this point, which undoubtedly either made the girl unconscious or dead before she was put into the lake. Had she been conscious, she would have breathed after striking the water. As it was, she did not, for there was not a drop of water in her lungs."

Lynch also ruled out sexual assault: "The body was not marked in any other way. She was not assaulted."

Determined to get a leg up on its competition, the *State Journal* raised ten thousand dollars to hire crack investigator Edward L. Boyer of the William Burns Detective Agency in Chicago to assist police on the case. The Burns agency often was called to assist local police officers in solving important cases and Boyer was the agency's chief of criminal intelligence.

"Boyer has faced some of the smoothest crooks and swindlers in the country. And he knows how to sweat them," wrote William Evjue in the *State Journal.* Evjue, who reported on the case as managing editor of the *State Journal,* later became founder and publisher of the rival *Capital Times.*

On Sunday, more than four thousand people, nearly a fifth of Madison's entire population of about twenty-one thousand, showed up for a wake at the Lemberger home to get a look at the dead girl. Police had to limit the crowd to ten people in the tiny house at a time. While the mourners filed past, Annie's little sister, Marie, apparently got jealous of the attention her dead sister was getting. Marie jumped up and down on the sofa, screaming, "Look at me! Look at me!" The following day, Annie's funeral was held at St. James Catholic Church and she was buried in Calvary Cemetery.

Early in the investigation, police began to suspect that John A. "Dogskin" Johnson could be the killer. Johnson, who lived down the block from the Lembergers, helped the family search for Annie on the day of her disappearance. But Johnson also had a criminal record. He had once damaged a train and assaulted three young girls. He was questioned about Annie's disappearance, then released. But on the day Annie's body was found, Johnson was taken into custody again and grilled intensively by Boyer and other detectives.

Johnson had an alibi provided by his wife, Bertha, and their two daughters, Selma, age fourteen, and Bertha, age sixteen. The girls worked as strippers at the American Cigar Co. and said they'd been home that night when their father came home about 9:00 p.m. Mrs. Johnson said she sat with her husband in the parlor for an hour, then he went to bed while she stayed up to sew. An open door between the two upstairs bedrooms occupied by the girls and the one Johnson slept in made it unlikely he could sneak outside without waking the family.

Mrs. Johnson told investigators that her husband slept that morning until 6:00 a.m. Some people figured that her support of Johnson's alibi made it more credible because she had filed suit against him for non-support. Others said, however, that she didn't want him to go to prison because then she had no hope of getting support.

By Tuesday, Boyer said he was at work on a new lead and Johnson seemed an unlikely suspect, although he still was held in jail. The Chicago newspapers had begun pointing the finger at the Lembergers themselves, which enraged the Burns detective.

"The charges and stories against the Lemberger family are an outrage," Boyer said.

Questioning of Johnson resumed. At one point, a detective asked the suspect: "Where is the nightgown?" "I can't tell," Johnson replied, referring to the nightgown Annie wore when she disappeared.

The detectives noted that Johnson hadn't said he didn't know where the nightgown was and they thought he could have added: "But I could tell if I wanted to." With that semantic subtlety, detectives thought they

Wisconsin State Journal archives

Mr. and Mrs. Martin Lemberger at the time of Annie's disappearance.

had a break in the case. According to an account by Evjue in the *State Journal,* Boyer grilled the suspect in a dramatic style. But Evjue's account was dismissed as fabrication by the rival newspaper, the *Madison Democrat.*

"Johnson," Boyer said. "I want to play square with you. I want you to tell me the truth. The easiest way out of this is the best way."

"Mr. Boyer, I didn't do it," Johnson replied. "When I done a trick in the past I have always confessed."

"All right, Johnson," the impatient Boyer continued. "You won't play square with me. Now, I am going to tell you what happened."

He moved his chair closer to Johnson's and pulled out a knife. He opened the knife and Johnson looked worried.

"On the night you murdered Annie," Boyer began, "you left your house after your wife and daughters had gone to bed. You came downstairs in your stocking feet and you put your shoes on outside. Then you started for the Lemberger house. You knew the Lembergers. You knew little Annie. She would say, 'Hello, Mr. Johnson' when you went by. You knew where her bedroom was. Then, Johnson, you sneaked to the window in the room where Annie was sleeping. You took out your knife and this is what you did."

Boyer stood up suddenly and went to the window of the witness room with Johnson following him.

"Sit down and get away from the window!" Boyer commanded. "The mob will see you." Johnson rushed back to his chair.

"Then, as I was saying, Johnson, you pried at the sash. You finally got it open. Then you picked up that lath to hold the window up. Then you reached through the window and you pulled Annie out.

"When you got her out, Annie woke up. She looked up at you, recognized you and screamed 'Johnson!' Then you became afraid. When she cried 'Johnson,' you were afraid you would get caught. Then you decided to slug her. Then here is what you did."

Johnson winced at the loud smack when Boyer clenched his fist and slammed it into his open left hand. Johnson instinctively clenched his own fist.

"After you struck Annie, she became unconscious. Then you did become frightened and decided to throw her body in the lake. Johnson, that's the story."

Despite Boyer's dramatic efforts, Johnson still would not confess. He was taken back to his cell, where he later said jail guards rattled the bars and told him it was the mob coming to get him. But the bloodthirsty mob of the week before now wasn't so sure about Johnson's guilt.

"Scores of people have telephoned to the *State Journal* demanding that the investigation be carried on further," the newspaper reported.

"They point out that there are many points that ought to be settled.

"It is said Johnson was intoxicated on the night of the girl's disappearance. And yet he was able to raise the window, drag the girl through it and render the girl unconscious without being heard. Even the dog in the house failed to hear any noise and yet it is an especially active young canine as some of the neighbors have testified."

Twenty years earlier, Johnson had witnessed the brutal lynching of a man at Darlington. He had watched in horror as an enraged mob caught the man, cut him into pieces and then strung him up from a telegraph pole. Now, Johnson was terrified the same thing could happen to him. And despite the change in public sentiment, jailers continued to use Johnson's fear to scare him.

On September 13, he finally had enough. He summoned turnkey John Foye and confessed to the murder of Annie Lemberger. The same day, Johnson pleaded guilty and Judge Anthony Donovan sentenced him to life in prison. Johnson also was sentenced to spend every September 5 in solitary confinement to reflect on his crime. Wisconsin was one of a few states at the time where a confession could be accepted without a jury trial.

On his way to Waupun state prison, Johnson still didn't feel safe from mob violence. He pointed to a dark clump of trees.

"Is that the mob?" he asked Sheriff Brown. "Are they going to get me?"

When they arrived at the prison, Brown said: "Well, Johnson, here is where you are going to spend the rest of your life."

Johnson breathed a sigh of relief. "Well, the mob didn't get me. And I didn't murder Annie Lemberger."

Johnson told the sheriff that someday the real killer would be found. "I will be freed then. It is better to go to prison for a short time than to be hung by a mob."

The ruddy-complexioned Johnson earned the nickname "Dogskin" when someone had skinned a dog and hung the pelt up to dry. Johnson was accused of stealing it. Although he later was absolved of the theft, the name stuck.

"He is weak-minded and he has been used as a fool many times," his wife said. "He is generous and thinks as much of you if you give him five cents as if you give him five dollars. He has been arrested many times, sometimes for things he didn't do, and can be easily scared."

Johnson had twice been admitted to Mendota Mental Health Institute, once for assaulting a young girl and the other time for attempted sexual assault of two girls, ages seven and ten. He served a prison term at Waupun for damaging a train by placing a rail on the track and also spent another stint in prison for trying to knock out his wife with chloroform.

He had been released from prison six weeks before Annie disappeared.

After he arrived at Waupun, Johnson immediately wrote to his attorney, Emerson Ela, to profess his innocence. As the years passed, he continued to insist that he didn't kill little Annie. He applied for a governor's pardon in 1915 but it was denied after a strong letter from the district attorney, who defended the actions of detectives and called it ridiculous that Johnson was scared into confessing by the threat of a lynch mob.

Wisconsin State Journal archives

John "Dogskin" Johnson

Finally, in the fall of 1921, Gov. John J. Blaine agreed to hear Johnson's case. Johnson had served ten years. The hearing, which began in late September, whipped up nearly as much public fascination as the murder. More than 1,000 people jammed the Senate chamber in the Capitol to watch the proceedings.

The hearing had to be moved twice to accommodate the overflow of spectators. When he arrived in Madison by train from Waupun, Johnson carried several bundles of books under his arms. He had turned fifty. He was tall and gaunt; his once-black hair was streaked with gray. He wore a new suit, cordovan shoes and a derby. He had been a model prisoner, earning trusty status.

The pardon hearing was strongly opposed by Annie's father, who was quoted as saying "I'll fix him" if Johnson were freed. During four-and-a-half days of testimony, Lemberger repeated the story of his daughter's disappearance and Johnson said his fear of the mob caused him to confess to a murder he didn't commit. But Johnson's testimony was refuted by several former law enforcement officials, who denied that anyone coerced him into confessing to the crime. Even Johnson's former attorney, Ela, was no help to his cause. Ela gave damaging testimony that Johnson's wife often made him sleep on the porch because she was afraid of him.

Finally, the hearing — which was not going well for Johnson — was recessed for the weekend.

When the hearing was reconvened on October 5 for closing arguments, Johnson's new attorney, Ole A. Stolen, had received permission to introduce new evidence. Stolen recalled Annie's brother, Alois, then nineteen, to the stand.

"I think I have proved that it was impossible for anybody to take

Annie out of that window that night and I think I proved that it was not Johnson," Stolen said. "Now, I am prepared to prove who killed Annie Lemberger."

A hush fell over the packed senate chamber as Stolen paused to deliver his punch line in a performance worthy of Perry Mason.

"Annie Lemberger came to her death by blows struck by her own father!"

The crowd let out a collective gasp, then broke into applause. When order was restored, Stolen motioned to Sheriff William McCormick.

"Sheriff, serve your warrants," he said in his quiet, tight-lipped style.

Lemberger was arrested on the spot for second-degree murder. His wife and Alois were arrested for perjury. Then Stolen called to the stand a slight, sallow cleaning woman who worked at the Orpheum Theater.

May Sorenson had written an anonymous letter to Stolen telling him her story and saying she was afraid to testify. If he made a plea for evidence in the newspaper and promised to protect her, she said she would come forward. Speaking in a whisper that had to be repeated so all could hear, the woman testified that she was a schoolmate of Martin Lemberger and had been a friend of the family for fifteen years.

When little Annie vanished, Mrs. Sorenson said she went to the Lemberger home to comfort the family. Later, she held nine-year-old Alois

Wisconsin State Journal archives

May Sorenson

on her lap. The boy said he wasn't supposed to talk about what really happened to Annie and his father had threatened to kill him if he told. But after a little coaxing, Alois finally gave in and told the story. The boy said there had been a beer party at the house. Annie had gotten up and gone into the living room. Her father, who had been drinking heavily, asked Annie to hand him the stove poker. Annie struggled to lift the poker but it was too heavy for her. Lemberger grew angry and hit the girl on the head with a beer bottle.

"She fell on the stove and he took her in his arms and carried her to bed," Mrs. Sorenson said. "After she got in bed a few minutes, she died. Then he carried her to the cellar. He put her under a big tub there."

The woman told the stunned crowd of spectators that Lemberger paid thirty-five dollars to a man named Davis to throw the body in the lake. She also testified that she found the blood-stained nightgown and tried to put it in the tub with the sheets from the girl's bed but Mrs. Lemberger snatched it from her and threw it into the stove.

"Why have you kept still ten long years?" Stolen asked.

"Because I feared him (Lemberger) and because Mr. Johnson never had a court trial so I could go to reveal," she said, adding that Lemberger had threatened to kill her a few years earlier if she told authorities of the murder.

Shocked by the dramatic turn of events, District Attorney Ted Lewis questioned Mrs. Sorenson. His usual grilling style reserved for defense witnesses was subdued by sheer curiosity. Because of a close relationship with the Lembergers, he declined to prosecute Martin Lemberger.

Some suggested that Stolen be appointed special prosecutor but it was found to be illegal. Instead, attorney Ralph Jackman was hired at a fee of fifteen dollars per day.

Bail of ten thousand dollars for Lemberger and one thousand each for his wife and son was paid by Lemberger's father, George. The day after Christmas, Jackman began a hearing to determine whether Johnson should be freed and Lemberger charged with Annie's murder.

A parade of witnesses testified, including Lemberger's brother-in-law and those who had supplied bloodhounds to search for Annie. Johnson's arm began to bleed after he was forced to put it repeatedly through several panes of glass to determine whether he could have opened the window and snatched the girl.

Jackman delivered his opinion on January 5, 1922. He said Annie probably was killed in her home and was not taken through the window. Although she was killed by Lemberger's blow, Jackman said the action was not premeditated.

Lemberger was charged with fourth-degree manslaughter. But the statute of limitations had expired four years earlier for a manslaughter charge so Annie's father never was brought to trial. Johnson was freed from prison by Gov. Blaine on February 17, 1922, but failed in several attempts to collect compensation from the state for his unjust prison term. Johnson's efforts, however, aroused an active group of supporters in Madison during the 1920s.

After Johnson's pardon, Lemberger said he had nothing against Dogskin but was upset that the blame had shifted to himself.

"I've got no grudge against Johnson," he said. "I don't know whether he killed Annie or not. All I know is that the authorities were barking up the wrong tree when they tried to put the crime on me. They haven't got to the bottom of the thing yet. If Johnson didn't do it, the man who did it will confess before he dies."

Wisconsin State Journal archives

The Lembergers in 1933.

No one ever confessed but, in 1933, the *Chicago Daily Times* resurrected the case. The paper, a predecessor to the *Sun-Times,* hired Professor Leonarde Keeler of Northwestern University to administer lie detector tests to the Lembergers, Johnson and Mrs. Sorenson.

The accuracy of the tests is debatable. The Lembergers passed when they denied that Lemberger killed his daughter. Johnson was nervous throughout the tests but his nervousness may have been just a personality trait. But when Mrs. Sorenson failed the test, she admitted that she was offered five hundred dollars to lie in her testimony against Lemberger. It wasn't clear who paid her but a Mrs. John Cooper helped arrange the meeting between Sorenson and the man who offered her the money. She apparently never collected but, after the he test, she signed a deposition recanting her testimony.

"All of my testimony implicating the Lembergers in the death of Annie was false," the deposition said. "I was at the Lemberger house following Annie's disappearance but I did not see blood spots on Annie's bed as I testified. Nor did I see Mrs. Martin Lemberger burn Annie's blood-stained nightgown. Alois Lemberger did not tell me his father hit Annie over the head with a beer bottle."

The recantation, which destroyed the key evidence against Lemberger but failed to shed any light on the mystery of Annie's death, was played down in the Madison papers, probably because a rival Chicago paper sponsored the tests. It also apparently was overlooked by Wisconsin author August Derleth, who wrote an account of the case in his book *Wisconsin Murders*.

In a 1933 series on the Lemberger case, the Chicago newspaper also said evidence indicated Annie was sexually assaulted before she died, despite the coroner's statement that there were no marks on the body to indicate an assault. Evidence of sexual assault would point to Johnson, not Annie's father, as the killer. Although there was nothing in the official record to indicate that Annie was molested, the newspaper said doctors who conducted the autopsy never were asked directly about sexual assault.

"Why?" the newspaper asked. "It is more probable that the question was asked and answered but it was not included in the record because someone did not wish to embarrass a young stenographer who was taking shorthand notes and who was excused from the hearing for a moment."

The stenographer tale was flimsy but the Sorenson recantation provided comfort to the Lembergers who, the newspaper reported, still were bothered by "wagging tongues."

Anne McCann, formerly Anne Lemberger before her marriage, is the granddaughter of Martin Lemberger and was named after the slain girl. In her home on Madison's South Side, she kept yellowed newspaper clippings about the sensational case in two scrapbooks. She said the Lemberger family has coped for decades with the assumption that her grandfather probably was the killer. Accounts of the case that appeared in a national magazine and other publications during the 1940s ignored the lie test and Mrs. Sorenson's recanted testimony.

The politically charged case boosted the career of Stolen, who served a brief, undistinguished tenure as a judge. A scandal removed him from the bench but Stolen practiced law in Madison until 1957, when he was eighty-six years old and retired to California. Several years after the murder, Evjue quit the *State Journal* and founded the *Capital Times*. Robert S. Allen, the *Wisconsin State Journal* reporter who covered the pardon hearing, went on to found the column "Washington Merry-Go-Round," which later was written by Drew Pearson and Jack Anderson.

Another grandchild of Martin Lemberger, Mark Lemberger, spent several years researching the case for a book. He interviewed descendants of many principal figures and dug through mounds of old records.

Lemberger's book, *Crime of Magnitude,* was published by Prairie Oak Press in 1993. The book makes a strong case that Johnson was the killer. Although the author's research is sound, the book's conclusion is slightly tainted by the fact that Lemberger was out to prove his grandfather's innocence.

32
A Child Killer Confesses
Waupaca, 1994

As she bicycled near her grandmother's Waupaca home on Labor Day in 1994, Cora Jones may have been thinking about
the new year at school. Perhaps she thought about spending time with
girlfriends or about a boy she had a crush on.

But the twelve-year-old Weyauwega girl didn't have much time to
ponder her thoughts. She was brutally attacked and became another sta-
tistic in one of Wisconsin's most vicious crime sprees.

Young Cora's parents had only a few days to wonder about the fate
of their missing daughter. Her decomposed body was found on September 10, 1994, in a Langlade County ditch about fifteen miles north of
Antigo and seventy-five miles from where she had been abducted. She
had been forced into the assailant's car, sexually molested and then stabbed
and strangled to protect the molester's identity.

Cora's abduction and murder was reminiscent of a similar case two
years earlier. Ronelle Eichstedt disappeared while bicycling near her Ripon
home on August 23, 1992. Her decomposed body was found six weeks
later in an Iowa County cornfield. She had been strangled with a cord.

Despite their similarities, the Jones and Eichstedt cases left few clues
for investigators that would lead to a suspect. And the two girls wouldn't
be the only victims before the killer was found.

Two months before he abducted Cora Jones, the killer zeroed in on
Trudi Jeschke's Appleton neighborhood after becoming aroused when he
spotted a woman undressing through a window. On July 9, the man used
a picnic table to climb up to a window, where he cut out the screen and

slipped inside.

The man later told detectives he thought no one was home. But he found Trudi, age twenty-one, in the bedroom, talking on the phone with her boyfriend. Trudi screamed when she saw the middle-aged man enter the bedroom and he immediately shot her in the chest. Then he fled out the front door, which he had unlocked earlier. Trudi had moved to Appleton five weeks earlier from Sault Ste. Marie, Michigan to take a job at a bank.

Investigators in the Cora Jones case compiled a list of known sex offenders and began the arduous task of working down the list in hopes of finding the killer.

On the Fourth of July — five days before Trudi Jeschke was murdered — Miriam Stariha was riding her bike on the same rural Waupaca road where Cora Jones would later be abducted. A car rammed her bicycle, knocking down the twenty-four-year-old woman. A man jumped from the car, brandishing a handgun.

Miriam surely would have been another victim in the brutal crime spree if another car hadn't passed by. The other car apparently scared away the attacker.

By the time Cora Jones disappeared, it was clear that a vicious rapist and murderer was on the loose in the Fox River Valley. But it wasn't clear that the cases all were connected. And it was difficult to identify the killer, especially since authorities concluded he likely was a stranger to the victims.

But this insatiable rapist and killer wasn't satisfied with murdering Cora Jones. He wasn't satisfied by the murders of Trudi Jeschke or Ronelle Eichstedt. He was driven to new thrills and new victims.

"I'm not afraid to kill you," the murderer told a terrified fifteen-year-old girl after breaking into her home on October 20. "Shut up or I'll slit your throat." After subduing the teenager, the man raped her.

On November 2, investigators finally believed they had the killer of Cora Jones. A man jailed in Minnesota earlier had confessed to the murder but his story was discounted. Now, they took blood, hair, fingerprint samples from a rural Richland County man and confiscated his van. The suspect had served a prison term for the 1977 slaying of a Bayfield County girl.

Three days later, which the Richland County suspect remained in custody, a man armed with a knife stormed into a bathroom on November 5, where a thirty-one-year-old woman was taking a bath. The intruder sexually assaulted the woman while her daughter slept in another room.

The Fox Valley killer was getting more brazen and his luck was about to run out. On November 14, a man was tackled by a homeowner as the man tried to break into a Combined Locks home near Appleton. The man's car contained burglary tools similar to those used in the Appleton sexual assaults on October 20 and November 5. The suspect was identified as David Spanbauer, age fifty-three, of Oshkosh.

Spanbauer was sentenced to seven years in prison on February 29, 1960, after a violent spree through four counties that included a January 12, 1960, rape and shooting incident in a Green Bay home. Then nineteen, Spanbauer forced his way into the home, raped a sixteen-year-old baby-sitter and shot the homeowner in the face.

Spanbauer was released from parole on May 12, 1972, but three months later, he was arrested in Dane County for rape and abduction. He was sentenced a year later to twelve years in prison.

Before receiving his 1973 sentence, Spanbauer asked Judge Richard Bardwell to send him somewhere for treatment. He said he had asked for treatment in 1960 but was sentenced to prison instead.

When Spanbauer again was released from prison in 1991, he got a job at an Oshkosh bottling plant.

After he was taken into custody, Spanbauer's resistance collapsed and he confessed to all of his crimes. Instead of evoking sympathy, the confessions merely steeled the community's outage. An analysis by the State Crime Lab fund that a carpet fiber recovered from Spanbauer's 1991 Pontiac Bonneville matched a fiber found on Cora's body.

Four days before Christmas, Spanbauer was sentenced by Judge James Bayorgeon to maximum consecutive life sentences for the rapes, murders and kidnapping of at least six women and girls. Bayorgeon set Spanbauer's earliest parole date on December 20, 2191, when the convicted killer would be over two hundred years old. The sentence was calculated by adding together the life expectancies of the victims.

Bayorgeon said Spanbauer's evil acts had destroyed some people's faith in God.

"They cannot believe that the God they loved would let a piece of offal like you walk this Earth," the judge said.

Spanbauer was unemotional as he was called evil and a coward. He ignored District Attorney Vince Biskupic, who challenged Spanbauer to turn around in his chair and face the family members of his victims in the courtroom.

Despite the harsh rhetoric and stiff sentence meted out to Spanbauer, many weren't satisfied. Rick and Vicki Jones, Cora's parents, campaigned for enacting a Wisconsin death penalty for certain kinds of crimes. Two state legislators called for castration for sex criminals.

"An astonishing number of violent sexual crimes are being committed statewide by repeat sexual offenders," said Rep. Dean Kaufert, a Republican from Neenah.

Wisconsin State Journal file photo

David Spanbauer

Political efforts, however, failed to assuage the grief of the victims' families.

"It will never be over," said Debbie Jones of Waupaca, Cora's aunt. "We need to change the laws now because we know that there's more than just him out there."

Despite his confession, not everyone believed that Spanbauer killed the two girls. Richard Jaeger, a veteran crime reporter at the *Wisconsin State Journal* and co-author of *Massacre in Milwaukee,* a book about the Jeffrey Dahmer case, said Spanbauer may have confessed because he was headed back to prison anyway and sought notoriety and special treatment. A prison inmate who wrote to Jaeger suggested that a fellow inmate with a history of violent sex crimes could have been responsible.

But Jaeger's opinion is a minority view and most people believe that Spanbauer was the brutal killer of Cora Jones and Ronelle Eichstedt.

33

A Newsboy's Final Delivery
Superior, 1966

Valerie Fisher, age fifteen, couldn't figure it out. She knew her brother just wasn't that irresponsible. Sure, he was just fourteen. Sure, they fought sometimes like many brothers and sisters do, especially those close in age. And sure, she had to admit, sometimes she thought he was a jerk.

But if there was one thing that meant a lot to Michael, it was his paper route. She had heard him early that morning, before the sun came up, bringing up his wagon from the basement just like every Sunday morning to deliver his newspapers. The family had returned early that morning from a camping trip and Michael wanted to go out right away to finish his route but his father made him wait until just before dawn.

Their dad, who ran the Lakeview Standard Station, had been called out himself about 5:00 a.m. to remove cars involved in an accident. When he got back home, Michael already had left on his route.

For the past four months, Michael had been delivering the *Duluth News-Tribune*. For a year before that, he delivered the *Superior Evening Telegram*.

Now, Valerie still couldn't believe it as she found Michael's wagon with two newspaper bundles, apparently abandoned along Ogden Avenue. It looked like he'd delivered just one paper! She knew where the papers were supposed to go because most of Michael's customers had called that morning wanting to know when they'd get their papers.

With a growing mix of dread and fear gripping her stomach, she pulled the wagon down the sidewalk, finishing her brother's route. When she got home, there was still no sign of her brother. The family called the police to report him missing.

About 9:00 p.m. that night — twelve hours after Valerie discovered her brother's wagon — Richard Vendela and Richard Orlowski were walking along Hill Avenue, about two miles away, when they spotted something in the ditch. Hill Avenue was a rural highway with brush and trees along the roadside. They had discovered Michael's body.

His head was wrapped in a red sweatshirt. He was lying on his back, fully clothed. There was no sign he had been molested and no bruises on his body to indicate there had been a struggle. Dr. Edward G. Stock, the Douglas County coroner, said the boy had been struck in the head by a single, crushing blow to the head. He had died about fourteen to sixteen hours before the body was discovered and apparently was dead before the body was dumped in the ditch along Hill Avenue.

Small puncture wounds found in Michael's head and neck led to early speculation that he might have been shot but this later proved untrue. No blood stains were discovered where his wagon had been found.

"Was it an accident or was it done on purpose?" wondered Police Chief Charles Barnard. He said perhaps Michael was hit by a car and the panicked driver dumped his body. Or perhaps someone murdered him. But why?

Earlier that month, Michael had finished eighth grade at the Cathedral School and was looking forward to starting high school that fall. Besides his sister, he also had two younger brothers, Carl and Timothy. He was born December 23, 1951, at Fort Riley, Kansas. He was an altar boy at the Cathedral of Christ the King Church.

Within a day or two after the body was found, police began to rule out an accident as a probable cause of Michael's death. A car accident, especially one that killed a pedestrian, would have left some evidence — shattered glass, tire marks. But no sign of an accident was found on Ogden Avenue anywhere near where the wagon had been discovered. Even more ominous was the fact that a single item was missing — the wire cutters used by Michael to cut the steel tape around his newspaper bundles. Could the pair of wire cutters been used as a the murder weapon?

Two days after Michael's death, the Superior Jaycees put up two hundred fifty dollars as the first contribution to a reward fund for information leading to the arrest and conviction of the boy's killer.

"We hope that the establishing of the reward will lead to definite clues and the solution of the heinous crime committed involving the Fisher youth," the Jaycess announced.

Along with the reward, Chief Barnard issued a plea to the public to come forward with information. He urged anyone who saw Michael that morning to contact the police.

On Wednesday, the *Evening Telegram* upped the ante, pledging another $250 for the reward fund. The City Council chipped in $100.

"I feel the city is obligated to do all it can to capture the warped mind responsible for the crime committed," said Alderman Lloyd Frier.

Now that the police had ruled out an accident, catching Michael's killer had become a community crusade. To nearly everyone in the lakeside city, it was a shocking crime, largely because an innocent victim was killed apparently without cause. It could have been anyone.

The State Crime Lab was called in to examine Michael's clothing. A hundred members of the local Civil Defense unit planned a shoulder-to-shoulder search of an area 150 feet on each side of Hill Avenue. They hoped to find the wire cutters, now believed to be the murder weapon. If they could find the wire cutters, perhaps a fingerprint or another clue would lead to Michael's killer, they hoped.

More than 100 people responded to Barnard's plea for information. Many brought in sticks the said could be the murder weapon or rags with what could be blood stain. A paper bag full of blood-stained rags was found on a girder of the Nemadji River bridge at Second Street, just three miles from where the body was discovered. On the rags were fragments of human or animal hair and tissue.

Police hoped discovery of the paper bag was a real break in the case. But, like many of the other leads, it turned out to be a dead end. The hair and tissue was positively identified as coming from an animal.

By Thursday, the reward fund had swelled to $3,000, including a $1,000 donation by the *Duluth News-Tribune*. Radio stations, civic groups and businesses all contributed money to help find Michael's killer. Police began a door-to-door canvass of the area along Michael's paper route in a search for possible witnesses.

"We are going on the theory that a local person or persons are responsible for the death of Michael Fisher," said Chief Barnard.

On Friday, Greg Austreng discovered a pair of tip snips in a burning trash barrel along First Street. The cutters were examined by the Crime Lab. They were similar to the pair used by Michael but no one could make a positive identification.

Over the weekend, the reward fund surpassed four thousand dollars and it appeared that police finally had a major break in the difficult case. A witness said he saw Michael taken away that Sunday morning in a 1959 Chevrolet Biscayne with two men inside. The man went out on his porch to get his paper when he saw two men take Michael by the shoulder and put him in the front seat of the car. At the time, the witness thought one of the men probably was the boy's dad.

One man was described as about five feet six inches tall with a slender build, dark hair and a tan complexion. He wore blue jeans and a jean jacket. The other man stayed in the car so the witness said he didn't get a good look at him. The car was described as a two-tone, white or cream on top and orange or red on the bottom. It was polished to a bright sheen, the witness told police. He had been out of town, he said, and that's why he didn't come forward earlier.

A three-state alert — Wisconsin, Minnesota and upper Michigan — was issued for the car.

That night, police in Minocqua arrested a middle-aged man on a traffic charge. He was from Superior and was in that city on the day of Michael's murder. Police also found blood on the front seat of his car.

Superior detectives rushed across the state to Minocqua. But the car didn't match the witness' description and the man later was released. In Superior, twenty-one cars that did match the description were examined by police but no evidence was found.

By early July, police had received more than two dozen letters and over a thousand calls from people offering information about the case. The crime lab found only Michael's blood on the sweatshirt wrapped around his head. No unusual particles were found on his clothing. Lab investigators officially ruled out a hit-and-run accident as the cause of his death. The case was at a dead end.

The attention of the *Evening Telegram* turned away from the bizarre murder of a newspaper carrier for there were other stories to cover, such as the city's first woman mail carrier and shipyard labor negotiations. A month after the murder, the paper didn't bother to run an anniversary story. But it did run a story about the capture in Chicago of Richard Speck, charged with the murder of eight nurses.

More than a quarter center after the brutal murder of Michael Fisher, the case remains unsolved. Was it a thrill killing by a pair of low-lifes out on a drunken binge? Did Michael somehow cross someone who decided to get even? Was robbery or sexual molestation a motive that somehow was thwarted? Did the killers strike again and were they ever brought to justice for another crime?

It's likely these questions about Michael's brutal murder will remain unanswered.

34

Private Little Torture Chamber
Madison, 1982

"Hey, girlie," Roger Lange yelled out the doorway of his Cypress Way apartment building on Madison's South Side. "Want to make some money? I need a babysitter."

A week earlier, two girls on their way to nearby Lincoln Elementary School had ignored him. But Lange kept trying until third-grader Paula McCormick, age ten, was intrigued by the offer. He told her she could earn a dollar by babysitting for five minutes.

Perhaps she had less fear than the other girls. Maybe she was more outgoing or entrepreneurial. Whatever the reason she accepted, it was a fatal decision. Lange didn't really want a babysitter, but a victim for his sadistic and perverted sexual fantasies.

He had constructed what Dane County District Attorney James Doyle later described as a "private little torture chamber" in the building's basement stocked with whips, clubs and ropes. When she entered Lange's apartment building that afternoon, he gagged young Paula with a washcloth, then brutalized her. He strangled her, hanged her and then sodomized her after death.

"He stood there and strangled this little girl to death, watching her face get blue," Doyle said.

Paula's mother, Donna, immediately knew something was wrong when she arrived home at 3:45 p.m. March 1, 1982, from her job at a medical products firm and her daughter wasn't there. She and her husband, Paul, contacted the police, who circulated a photo of the missing girl to the news media. Detectives began retracing her route from school.

They soon discovered other attempts to entice young girls by a man they identified as Roger Lange.

Lange worked in a State Street restaurant. Sometimes he would stand in the restaurant's front window in his white apron, staring glassy-eyed at passersby. Next to a large fern, he seemed almost to blend into the decor.

Detectives hauled in Lange for questioning and he began a cat-and-mouse game that ultimately led to a confession. At first, Lange claimed he asked Paula to help him move boxes. But Dane County Detective Marion "Dusty" Rhodes

Wisconsin State Journal file photo

Paula McCormick

didn't buy that theory. He told Lange it would have been foolish to ask a young child to help with that kind of physical labor.

Police searched a storage locker where Lange had moved his belongings on the same day Paula disappeared but found nothing. During eight hours of questioning, Lange munched on a McDonald's hamburger and sipped a strawberry milkshake as the horrible tale of Paula's death slowly unraveled.

"Roger stated that he was getting some real bad vibes and that we would find the body in a box," Detective Rhodes said. With Deputy Coroner Phil Little, detectives went again to the storage locker. This time, Rhodes opened a television box and removed a blanket. He spotted a torn plastic garbage bag that contained what looked like the knee of a small child.

Publicity over Paula's disappearance, the discovery of her body and Lange's disjointed confession raised community anger to a fever pitch. Many people said Lange should be released so community justice could take care of him.

The community was further angered by a story by courts reporter Anita Clark in the *Wisconsin State Journal* that revealed Lange's own horrific childhood. The story seemed to provide a reason for Lange's outrageous crime and the community was in no mood for excuses.

His mother, Caroline Lange, was committed to a mental hospital in

1959 after her two youngest sons died at the ages of twenty months and three years. She confessed to suffocating them and was convicted in 1961 in a Dunn County court of two counts of second-degree murder.

Young Roger, the oldest of the three boys, barely escaped death himself at his mother's hand. She burned the boys with scalding water, put poison in their oatmeal, gave them kerosene to drink and once set fire to a bed where Lange was sleeping.

With that kind of childhood, it wasn't surprising that Lange himself had a long history of mental illness. He was committed as a teenager to Winnebago Mental Health Center and discharged from the Army for psychiatric reasons.

Even more significant was the testimony at Lange's trial of his girlfriend, Tina Johnson, age twenty-five, who worked as a motel maid. She described how she also had been bound, gagged and sodomized by Lange, then suffocated until she lost consciousness.

The jury of nine women and three men was selected in Waukesha County because of extensive pre-trial publicity in Dane County. The jury included a teacher, a nurse, an engineer and several homemakers.

Assistant Public Defender Daryl Jensen said Lange's sexual behavior with young Paula wasn't so unusual and wasn't meant to cause her death.

"It was a tragic replay of what he had done so many times before with Tina Johnson," Jensen argued.

But Johnson also testified that Lange sexually assaulted a three-year-old girl when she babysat the child several years earlier. And two girls, ages seven and ten, testified Lange molested them while they played with him.

"He was throwing us up in the air," the older girl said. "When he caught me, he started wiggling his finger where I go to the bathroom."

The younger girl said he grabbed her breast.

Veteran Madison Detective Frank McCoy burst into tears on the witness stand as he identified Paula's picture as the girl who had been found in the box.

Thomas Jackson told the jury he helped Lange move boxes from his basement to the storage locker where Paula's body was found on the day of her disappearance. He noticed one box was unusually heavy and required several men to carry it. Jackson didn't know it at the time, but the box contained Paula's body.

During her testimony, Lange's girlfriend, Tina Johnson, glared at Lange. Later, she would say that he was silently calling her a liar.

When she came home about 3:00 p.m., Johnson said Lange rushed upstairs. He wore no shirt and she saw scratches on his chest.

"The devil made me do it," she heard him mumble.

The jury deliberated an hour and fifteen minutes before deciding that Lange was guilty of the brutal murder of Paula McCormick. Lange was impassive as Judge Michael Torphy read the verdict. Besides murder, Lange also was found guilty of first-degree sexual assault, kidnapping and enticing a child for immoral purposes.

In a jail interview, Lange told psychiatrist Dr. John Griest he must have snapped when he killed Paula. Lange said he heard a voice that said "destroy" and the girl became the image of his girlfriend, with whom he was fighting at the time. Griest, a professor at University of Wisconsin Medical School, said he did not believe Lange could distinguish between right and wrong when he killed the girl.

Dr. Albert Lorenz, an Eau Claire psychiatrist who examined Lange's mother when she was convicted of killing her other two children, testified that Lange's severe physical and psychological abuse forced him to retreat into his own world and trust no one.

But the prosecution presented testimony from psychiatrists who said Lange was sane at the time of the murder and the jury took just forty-three minutes to agree. Although agreement by ten of twelve jurors was all that was required for the sanity phase, the jury was unanimous and apparently heeded Doyle's advice.

Wisconsin State Journal file photo

Roger Lange

"This is a person who simply has to be incarcerated forever so people will be safe," the district attorney said.

Judge Michael Torphy sentenced Lange to life plus sixty years.

"There are some individuals in society that need to be warehoused, taken off the streets, taken out of society," he said. "I think Mr. Lange is one of those people."

Assistant Public Defender Charles Vetzner requested a new trial for Lange because the insanity law had changed and because a jury instruction conference involving the judge and attorneys was not recorded by the court stenographer.

In 1985, Lange's conviction was upheld by the State Court of Appeals. The court rejected all of Lange's claims about the inadmissibility of evidence and faulty judicial instructions.

In November 1983, the McCormicks filed a six hundred thousand dollar lawsuit against the Madison School District, claiming their daughter's death could have been prevented.

The lawsuit claimed school officials failed to take action when another girl reported to a substitute teacher two weeks before Paula's death that she too was solicited for babysitting by Lange. The lawsuit was settled in 1986 for thirty-two thousand dollars.

"I don't want this to happen again to another kid," Donna McCormick said at the time of the settlement. "It's not just the money."

In September 1986, the McCormicks met with Madison School District officials to help fashion a policy for reporting child enticement incidents. Paula's death also spurred another district policy of instructing students how to avoid strangers and protect themselves.

35

A Babysitter Vanishes
La Crosse 1953

Evelyn Hartley was one of those brainy, bespectacled girls with few boyfriends. She was a shy high school junior with a straight-A average. With long, medium-brown hair and blue eyes, Evie was interested in science and conducted her own experiments at home. She played piano, sang in the church choir and was a member of the high school girls' drama club, the science club and the ski club.

Evie had moved to La Crosse four years earlier from Charleston, Illinois with her parents, older brother Tom, age twenty-two, and younger sister Carolyn, age six. Another brother, Richard, had died of polio seven years earlier while serving in the Navy at Bainbridge, Maryland. Evie's father, Richard, was a biology professor at La Crosse State College.

Viggio Rasmusen, a physics professor, picked up Evie about 6:30 p.m. October 24, 1953, and took her to his single-story frame house on Hoeschler Drive so she could babysit for twenty-month-old Janis while the Rasmusens went to a homecoming football game to watch La Crosse State play River Falls. It was Evie's first babysitting job in three months.

About fifteen minutes after she left, Evie's mother had a premonition. Worry about her daughter's safety flashed through her mind. It didn't make sense but, for some reason, Evie's mother couldn't help wondering whether the girl was all right.

"I think we should call Evelyn," she told her husband. No, maybe not. It was just an irrational fear after all. They decided to wait for Evie to call them instead, as she always did when she was babysitting.

Throughout October, the Hartleys had followed the tragic case of

Robert Greenlease, age six, in the *La Crosse Tribune*. The newspaper reported how Bobby was abducted from a Kansas City school by a woman posing as the boy's aunt. The kidnappers demanded a six hundred thousand dollars ransom, which was paid by Bobby's millionaire father. Part of the ransom was recovered but the boy was found murdered. A man and woman later were executed for the crime.

"It happens when people have money but it doesn't happen to people like us," Mrs. Hartley assured her husband.

That night on Hoeschler Drive, several residents heard screams about 7:15 p.m. but dismissed them as coming from children at play. By 9:30 p.m., Evie hadn't called so Hartley phoned the Rasmusen home. He got no answer.

When he drove to the house, Evie's father found the doors locked, the lights on and the radio playing. Hoeschler Drive had no street lights and the Rasmusen living room was clearly visible from the street through a large picture window. Hartley rang both the front and back doorbells. For about ten minutes, he pounded on the doors and shouted for Evie. There was no response.

Hartley walked around the house and found a basement window that had been opened, possibly by an intruder. He crawled inside. Janis was sleeping peacefully in a basement crib. She still was uncovered although Evie, always a conscientious babysitter, had been instructed to cover her at 7:30 p.m. One of Evie's shoes was at the bottom of the stairs.

Her father felt a overwhelming wave of dread flash through his body as he walked slowly up the stairs. Would he find Evie when he got to the top? Was there some kind of accident? Had she been knocked unconscious? Or murdered?

But Evie had vanished from the Rasmusen house that night. In the living room, Hartley found her glasses and the other shoe. The furniture was in disarray and there clearly had been a struggle. Hartley went back outside and crossed the street to a neighbor's house to call police.

The first officers who arrived that night at the Rasmusen home figured it was just another routine teenage runaway case. Evie probably hadn't been getting along with her parents and took off with her boyfriend. Parents always suspected the worst; usually that's all it was. But the officers found pry marks on a bedroom window where an intruder tried unsuccessfully to break in. Blood stains were on the ground outside and more blood was found smeared on a neighbor's house and across a nearby garage. Tracking dogs were rushed to the scene. Four times they picked up a trail but stopped each time about two blocks from the house, where police deduced Evie probably had been forced into a car.

Mrs. Hartley spent a fretful, sleepless night, closeted in her home and trying to imagine what might have happened to Evie. When she first visited the Rasmusen house the next morning, she still hoped her daughter was alive. Then she saw the blood.

"Oh, my poor Evelyn!" she cried, collapsing to the ground. "We know she isn't alive."

Evie's disappearance stirred the outrage of thousands in the Mississippi River city. Local radio stations put out pleas for volunteers. More than a thousand people showed up and organized groups of thirty to sixty searchers who checked under manhole covers down every city street in La Crosse. Boy Scouts and members of the Civil Air Patrol joined Evie's Central High School class-mates in the massive sweep, combing a wooded, marshy area at the southeastern edge of the city near Hoeschler Drive. Police Chief George Long asked everyone to check their garage or shed. Searchers turned up a knife in a sheath, a woman's slipper, a handkerchief and a flashlight. But there was no trace of the missing girl. Among the searchers was Evie's brother, Tom, who rushed back home from Eau Claire, where he was a student at the teacher's college. Tom and a companion picked their way for three miles through the muck and slime of a storm sewer, quitting only when the passage became too small to continue.

La Crosse Tribune

Evelyn Hartley

"Tom is tireless," his companion, Richard Thompson, told a *La Crosse Tribune* reporter. "He doesn't miss a thing. We've looked in every conceivable place and he still won't quit. When it gets dark and we have to quit looking, he's impatient until we can get started again."

The mysterious disappearance of Evie terrified the city. A curfew was imposed that banned teenagers from the streets after 10:00 p.m. Wives were reluctant to be left alone so many husbands stayed home from work. The demand for babysitters fizzled to an all-time low and what little babysitting was done involved husky boys and adults. Meanwhile, the search for Evie was expanded to the sloughs and bayous near La Crosse.

Thousands of volunteers turned out on cool, fall weekends to look for the missing girl.

Three days after Evie vanished, a blood-stained brassiere and panties were found under a Highway 14 overpass about two miles south of the Rasmusen home. The undergarments were Evie's size.

"It looked like they might have been thrown from a car and blew under the bridge," said District Attorney John Bosshard.

Farther east on Highway 14, police found a black pair of bloody tennis shoes that matched footprints found in a flowerbed outside the Rasmusen home. A ragged blue denim jacket was discovered nearby. A pair of trousers found in the same area had Type A bloodstains, which matched Evie's blood type.

Detectives rushed to the scene when flesh and bones were found wrapped in a newspaper bundle beside Highway 33 about six miles east of La Crosse. They examined the remains carefully to see if they could be pieces of the missing girl's body. But an analysis determined the remains were of a calf or small deer.

A month after the disappearance, police received a report that a girl who looked like Evie was seen at Hugo, Oklahoma checking into a hotel with a man. Detectives collected Evie's handwriting samples for comparison with those of the girl. But like many other leads in the case, this one also was a dead end.

Suspicion turned to Evie's father, one of the last people to see her alive and the first to discover her missing. Hartley, after all, had climbed through the same basement window as the intruder. Could he have killed his daughter and messed up the house to make it look like she was abducted? Bosshard received letters and phone calls urging him to investigate Hartley as a suspect. Hartley asked to take a lie detector test to clear the air. He went to the state crime laboratory in Madison and passed the test, ending the speculation.

"Mr. (Charles) Wilson (head of the crime lab) reports to me that the lie detector test without equivocation clears Mr. Hartley of any suspicion in the event under investigation," Bosshard said.

After six months, police had checked 600 cars for traces of blood and interviewed 1,500 people. Stickers were printed and after each car inspection by service station attendants, a sticker was affixed to the car that read: "My car is O.K."

Attendants were told to report anyone who refused an inspection or any suspicious items they turned up. On weekends, people still searched along the riverbank for clues. Sheriff Ivan Wright died of a heart attack, which was blamed on overwork from the difficult Hartley case.

An elderly seer in Norway was asked by a La Crosse resident to help find the girl. The Norwegian obtained maps of southern Wisconsin and said he could "see" Evie and a man on a section of Highway 14. He said the missing girl probably was in Madison.

The county board hired A.M. Josephson, a retired Army investigator, to supervise the case. Josephson had served ten years with the Army's Criminal Investigation Division in Europe and Japan. He reviewed the case with other detectives and decided a school-age person probably was the culprit. Lie detector tests were scheduled for all 1,700 high school and college students in La Crosse, with students and teachers at Central High School to be tested first. After several hundred tests revealed nothing, police called off the time-consuming project.

Four years later, investigators still had not found Evie or identified her abductor. But an examination of the denim jacket revealed a faded spot under the armpits that led police to believe its owner was a steeple jack who had worn a harness to work on towers and smokestacks. The jacket showed evidence of laundering and sewn repairs, indicating the man was not a transient worker. Examination of blood stains on the jacket revealed they were not from an injury to the person wearing it.

"It will be noted that there is not enough paint on the jacket to indicate this individual actually was a painter," said Josephson, still working full-time on the Hartley case. "The man who wore this jacket undoubtedly was around a paint crew but probably cleaned in advance of painters."

Detectives found a La Crosse businessman who made harnesses for two steeplejacks during the summer of 1952, a year before Evie vanished. He recalled that the customers were young and probably from the area. Thread counts of the jacket and another fabric found at the Rasmusen home indicated the jacket probably was worn by Evie's abductor. But like the faded spots on the denim jacket, the promising steeplejack lead slowly wore away and the years passed without any new clues.

Five years after Evie disappeared, retired farmer Howard George, then eighty-four, chipped in $1,500 of his savings to hire a private investigator to work on the Hartley case. George said he wondered what kind of country we're living in where such a mystery could go unsolved. When the money ran out the following year without any new clues, George said he couldn't afford any more.

"Perhaps if others would help out with contributions we could lick this thing," he said. "But I've done my share and the $1,500 is all I care to put on it."

In June 1959, Police Chief Long said the Hartley case could be linked to the 1958 rape-slaying of a Wauwatosa housewife. Long said John J. Watson, then serving a rape sentence for an attack on a young girl, was the "common denominator" in both cases. But a comparison of Watson's fingerprints and hair samples with those found at the Rasmusen house failed to tie him to Evie's disappearance.

After six years, Long lamented that little progress had been made on the baffling case.

"We still haven't got anything more than we did when it happened. Usually these things die out but not this one. It's still alive. Not a week goes by that we don't get a call or letter from somebody who has heard something about the case."

A half dozen people have confessed over the years to abducting Evie but all of their stories were unraveled by police. A few days after she vanished, a roofing salesman was the first of several suspects to be arrested, then released. The latest confession came in 1981 from a forty-five-year-old Kenosha man who recanted the confession a day later. The man, who committed himself to a mental hospital, said he hid Evie's body under a highway that was being constructed at the time.

The unsolved case sparked criticism of the police investigation. A neighbor of the Rasmusens said she wasn't questioned until two weeks after Evie disappeared. Some valuable evidence at the scene may have been destroyed because police officers failed to protect it from the crowd that gathered that night. A series blaming the police for bungling the case was written by *Chicago Tribune* reporter Norma Lee Browning,

The Hartley family moved out of Wisconsin years ago and many people involved in the case, including Long, have died. The Rasmusens remained in La Crosse but moved to a different address.

Evie's case was reminiscent of the disappearance of Georgia Jean Weckler, who vanished May 7, 1947, after she was dropped off by a school bus at the farm lane of her family's home on Highway 12 between Fort Atkinson and Cambridge. Buford Sennett, later convicted of killing UW-Madison student Carl Carlson and raping his sister-in-law, supposedly confessed to the Weckler abduction and murder but would not admit to it in writing.

In 1985, La Crosse Police Chief William Reynolds said although the Hartley case technically remained open, many people believed notorious Plainfield killer Ed Gein was responsible for Evie's abduction and murder. In a book about Gein by Judge Robert H. Gollmar, the judge wrote that sexual organs of two young girls were found at Gein's farm although no young girls were buried at nearby cemeteries during the killer's grave-robbing forays. Gollmar, who tried the Gein case, also said Gein apparently was in La Crosse the weekend Evie disappeared to visit an aunt who lived two blocks away from the Rasmusens. The judge also wrote that Evie resembled an early picture of Gein's mother.

Maybe it was Ed Gein who whisked Evie away to her death on that fall evening. Or perhaps it was someone else.

36

A Halloween Outrage
Fond du Lac, 1973

No crime enrages a community more than the murder or sexual assault of a child. These crimes against children violate a trust that forms one of the major underpinnings of our society. When a perpetrator is caught and jailed, other prisoners often treat him with contempt. If a modern-day lynching ever occurs, the victim probably will be one of these criminals.

Several of these cases have plagued Wisconsin throughout the century. In 1911, Madison residents were outraged by the abduction and murder of seven-year-old Annie Lemberger. The 1953 disappearance of Evelyn Hartley from her babysitting job in La Crosse has never been solved. In 1982, the brutal sexual assault and murder of Paula McCormick, age nine, prompted some in the Madison community to call for the release of suspect Roger Lange so street justice could deal with him.

A similar case occurred in 1973 in Fond du Lac. Nine-year-old Lisa French put on a black felt hat and green parka. She put tape on her blue jeans before going outside. It was Halloween night and Lisa had decided to go trick-or-treating as a hobo. When she walked out the door of her Amory Street home about 5:45 p.m. that day, it was the last time her mother would ever seen Lisa alive.

About an hour later, the brown-haired fourth-grader stopped at the home of Karen Bauknect, a former teacher. Lisa made her way alone through the neighborhood, going up and down each block and collecting her bag of treats.

Not far from where Lisa was trick-or-treating, a woman, Arlene Penn, stopped home about 7:00 p.m. to pick up her live-in boyfriend,

Gerald Turner. They were supposed to go to her mother's house. Turner met her at the door and told her he wasn't feeling well, that she should catch a ride with friends and go ahead with her daughter.

But when Penn got to her mother's house about fifteen minutes later, she remembered that her mother wouldn't be home until 8:00 p.m. She went back to her own house. Turner, still wearing his work clothes, sat with her on the couch. He mentioned a couple of times that he felt sick and went into the bedroom to lie down.

Penn left again before 8:00 p.m. and didn't get home until after 11:00 p.m. When she arrived, Turner was dressed in a bathrobe. She noticed their green bedspread was on the floor of the laundry room and asked him about it. He said he had thrown up on it.

When Lisa failed to return home that night, her mother called the police. A massive search was mounted the following day. More than 700 block parents throughout the city were mobilized. They were assisted by Girl Scouts and auxiliary police officers summoned to duty. They checked bushes, garages and wooded areas but found no sign of the missing girl. An estimated five thousand people participated.

By November 2, Police Chief Harold Rautenberg had lost hope that Lisa would be found alive: "I am satisfied in my own mind that she is not missing voluntarily," he told reporters. "I had that hope. Now, we have to face reality."

Just before noon on Saturday, three days after Lisa disappeared, farmer Gerald Braun was driving his tractor back to his farm along a country road in the town of Taycheedah when he spotted a brown plastic bag behind a barbed-wire fence at the edge of the woods. After parking the tractor at the farm, he returned to investigate. Inside the bag, he discovered clothing that appeared to belong to a child. In a second bag nearby was the body of Lisa French.

An autopsy determined that Lisa probably had died of suffocation. The coroner also found that she had been sexually molested.

Lisa French was buried on November 6 and, at the funeral, the Rev. Paul Piotter appealed to the killer to confess.

"It is your only hope," he said. "Otherwise, you will be tormented for the rest of your days."

Piotter also blamed the crime on a permissive society that fosters conditions for it to occur.

On Nov. 8, just a week after that fateful Halloween night, the chamber of commerce offered a ten thousand dollar reward for the capture of Lisa's killer.

"We promote Fond du Lac as an ideal place to live and work and we wish to prove what we say is true," said chamber president Louis Lange. "We want to bring this person to justice quickly."

But there would be no quick resolution to this difficult and heart-breaking case. A twenty-five-year-old Fond du Lac man was arrested in Madison for contributing to the delinquency of a boy. He was quizzed about the Lisa French case but no connection was found.

Under community pressure to find the killer, Fond du Lac County Sheriff John Cearns assigned six full-time investigators to the case. The detectives consulted psychiatrists at Waupun state prison to put together a psychological profile of the murderer.

Cearns tried to keep most of his investigation under wraps. "If we don't talk about what we are doing," he said, "maybe we can throw the guy off guard."

Due to the lack of any sign of struggle, the investigators believed Lisa probably knew her assailant and trusted him.

"There were no bruise marks on her," Cearns said. "You'd think that if a stranger tried to accost her, she'd scratch or claw or bite or kick. She'd have struggled.

"You've got to figure that the only person she would not do that to was somebody she had previous contact with, somebody she trusted."

Detectives developed a list of about a dozen suspects. In the spring, the chamber of commerce added more than $2,000 to the reward but still it brought no hard information. As summer came and the investigation wore on, Gerald Turner, who worked as a railroad machinist, rose to the top of the list of suspects. He lived close to where Lisa was last seen alive and he knew her.

Before moving a few blocks away, Turner had lived next door to Lisa on Amory Street. She seemed to like him, often bringing him things to show him. In early August, Turner was arrested and charged with first-degree murder in the death of Lisa French.

While Turner was held on $100,000 bond, he made a full confession. He told investigators how he had become sexually aroused when Lisa came to the door that night. He sexually assaulted her but then something went wrong and the girl died. He described how he had put her body and clothing in separate garbage bags and dumped the bags at Braun's farm. Turner said he didn't tell Penn anything about the girl's death due to "fear of apprehension for the murder and sexual molestation of a young girl."

After intense questioning by Louis Tomaselli of the state Division of Criminal Investigation and Rodney Anderson of the state Crime Lab, Turner signed each page of the typed confessions and carefully initialed corrections.

Turner pleaded innocent to the murder and sexual perversion charges. The week before the trial began in late January 1975, he dropped a plea of innocent by reason of mental disease after receiving a psychiatrist's

Wisconsin State Journal file photo

Gerald Turner

report that found him sane.

Using a combination of witnesses and scientific evidence, prosecutor Alexander Semanas built a case against Turner. Pubic hair found on Lisa's clothing and body matched hair samples taken from Arlene Penn. The hair, which indicated Lisa had been in the Turner-Penn house, also matched in one other respect. Both sets of samples showed evidence of crab lice, a parasite.

Penn was a star witness for the prosecution. She described her activities the night of the murder and also, under questioning by Semanas, talked about how she and Turner would view pornographic movies in Oshkosh and have sex afterward.

In his defense, Turner's mother, Dolores, and his ex-wife, Elizabeth, testified that he wasn't capable of murder. But defense attorney Henry Buslee focused his argument on Turner's confession. Turner himself took the stand and claimed Tomaselli and Anderson had coerced him to sign the document and that the words of the confession were not his.

"When does a man reach a point where he says, `All right, I'll sign it'?" Buslee asked the jury.

Although Buslee was unable to convince the jury that the confession was bogus, testimony by Dr. Robert Carlovsky, a pathologist who conducted the autopsy, provided some reprieve for the defendant.

Carlovsky testified that the girl's death was caused by trauma and heart stoppage induced by anal sex.

Buslee swiftly moved for dismissal of the first-degree murder charges. While Turner's actions remained despicable, it appeared the girl's death was not premeditated.

Judge Milton Meister, however, wasn't about to let Turner off that easily. Denying the dismissal motion, Meister told Buslee he would in-struct the jury on which charges were appropriate.

Turner was convicted of second-degree murder, enticing a child, indecent behavior and sexual perversion. He was sentenced to thirty-six years in prison.

An appeal to the state Supreme Court claimed there wasn't suffi-cient evidence to establish that Turner's conduct with the girl was dan-gerous enough to cause her death. The court refused to grant a new trial, ruling that no miscarriage of justice had occurred.

In the fall of 1992, the Lisa French case again aroused public con-troversy when Turner was granted parole after serving about forty-five percent of his sentence. Many people who recalled the high-profile case petitioned the Parole Board not to grant his release. But the man whom the media had dubbed "the Halloween killer" was released to a halfway house in October, then rented an apartment on Milwaukee's East Side in June 1993.

Turner, who was required to wear an electronic monitoring bracelet as part of the terms of probation, didn't exactly receive a warm welcome from his new neighbors.

"If I lived here and had children, I would move out," one young woman told a reporter. "There's no way I would take that chance."

Turner soon was returned to prison after an Appeals Court ruled that the state Department of Corrections has miscalculated good time for prisoners since the 19th Century. The Wisconsin Supreme Court over-turned that decision and ordered that Turner must be freed.

By then, however, the Legislature had found a new way to keep Turner in prison. It had passed the sexual predator law and the attorney general's office filed a petition to hold Turner until he went to trial as a sexual predator.

The sexual predator law, invented to keep Turner and similar child molesters in prison, was challenged but upheld by the Supreme Court in December 1995.

Multiple
Murders

37

Craftsman of Human Remains
Plainfield, 1957

A half-gallon of antifreeze was the last thing Bernice Worden rang up on the cash register at her country hardware store near Plainfield on November 16, 1957. When she was discovered missing later that day, her son, Frank, found the sales slip. Then he remembered that a small, hollow-eyed bachelor farmer had said he would stop by the store Saturday for antifreeze.

Frank Worden told police about the sales slip and they began a search for Edward Gein, Wisconsin's most bizarre killer of the century. They found him at the home of his neighbors, Mr. and Mrs. Lester Hill, where he'd gone for dinner.

Inside the Hill home, Gein cut a piece of meat from his pork chop and put it in his mouth. The Hills thought their neighbor was a little odd and reclusive but they enjoyed his company anyway.

The dinner table conversation turned to the strange disappearance of Worden and Mrs. Hill teased Gein about the case.

"How come every time somebody gets banged on the head and hauled away, you're always around?" she asked him.

Gein grinned and replied, "That was easy."

Later, nobody was smiling when police came to the Hill farmhouse to arrest Gein for Worden's murder.

He later told authorities he recalled going into the store to buy the antifreeze and watched Mrs. Worden pumping out the liquid for him a quart at a time. At some point, Gein also inspected a gun for sale at the store, then fired a .32-caliber bullet into the back of the woman's head.

He dragged her body and the cash register to the rear of the store, then loaded them into her truck. He drove the truck to a nearby lover's lane, hiding it in some trees and went back to get his own car. After transferring the body and cash register to his car, Gein drove home.

At Gein's farm, police found Mrs. Worden's headless, disemboweled body strung up like a deer in the woodshed. They also found the face and head of Mary Hogan, a heavyset woman who disappeared three years earlier from the Pine Grove tavern she operated six miles from Gein's farm.

These are the only murders ever connected directly to Gein. But there was much more to his hideous story. Gein robbed at least ten graves, taking heads and body parts back home, where the handyman made masks, costumes, lamp shades and chair seats from human skin. Sometimes he would wear the masks or skin of his victims.

Gein was described by his neighbors as "pleasant, quiet but very odd and unusual." He got along well with children and often babysat for them. It was reported he also gave neighbors packages of venison although he later claimed never to have shot a deer. Did the packages actually contain remains of his victims? Neighbors who may have cooked and eaten the meat didn't want to think about it.

Despite the horrible evidence found at the farmhouse, the full details of his crimes never were revealed. Gein either blocked out the killings or played coy with investigators, citing failure of his memory at key points.

He said he dug up graves "when I was in a daze like when I killed Mrs. Worden.... The only thing, I'm not too sure I killed her. I didn't have any weapons on my property."

But a revolver and two rifles were found in Gein's filthy house, which was littered with junk except for his mother's room. He claimed both women he killed reminded him of his invalid mother, who had suffered a series of strokes and died twelve years earlier. His mother, the strongest influence in his life, had taught him all women but her were evil.

The nine-room white farmhouse was such a mess with a stench of embalming fluid and strewn with body parts that police began looking for a second house, finding it impossible to believe that Gein actually lived there. Before Worden's body was found, area children often joked about the house being haunted, where shrunken heads were kept.

Children weren't the only ones to joke uneasily about murder with Gein. Mr. and Mrs. Donald Foster of West Plainfield had visited Gein's farm with their baby daughter after Gein offered to trade his entire 150-acre farm for their small house. While inspecting the house, Mrs. Foster pointed to a closed room and asked, "Is this where you keep your shrunken heads, Ed?" She immediately was sorry she said it because Gein and her husband gave her a funny look.

After Gein's arrest, a Plainfield woman talked about her narrow escape — how she'd almost married the bizarre bachelor.

Gein's farmhouse had no electricity, no gas, no telephone. He read cheap magazines, some with lurid pictures, by the light of old lanterns or kerosene lamps. His diet, rumored to include human flesh, also consisted of cans of pork and beans along with fruit.

On a table, Gein kept a collection of children's books, some thirty years old. He had a violin with broken strings and, stored in another room, were a harp and an accordion. Hanging in a room near the kitchen were handkerchiefs with the initial "G" that remained a shade of black despite repeated washings.

Despite the messy house, Gein kept his mother's room neat. The bed was made and he dusted regularly, almost as if the room was a shrine to the dead woman.

Charles Wilson, director of the Wisconsin Crime Lab, said the farmhouse yielded an "avalanche" of evidence, "the greatest amount of physical evidence I have seen in a single case during my career as a criminologist." He estimated the evidence would take weeks or months to process.

Plainfield Village Board Chairman Ralph Wing was incensed when Gein claimed the head of his wife's sister, Eleanor Adams, in his collection of skulls. Adams was buried in Plainfield cemetery in 1951. Authorities estimate he dug up at least eleven graves of women, removing whole bodies or just body parts. Gein said an obsession with sex led to grave robbing and the two slayings. He said after his mother died, "I wanted to become a woman."

Investigators were so disgusted by Gein's crimes that even they weren't really interested in probing the full extent of them. At first, they decided not to dig up any graves that Gein may have disturbed. Then, after public pressure, they decided to check four or five of them. When District Attorney Earl Kileen was confronted with the fact that Gein had parts of at least ten other bodies in his home, Kileen shrugged: "I guess it's unexplainable."

"We just want to get the case cleaned up," he said. "We have no missing people in Waushara County. Why should we rile up the people by digging up graves to prove Gein's story? It would be expensive, too. If someone else wants to start digging up the graves and riling up the people, that's up to them, not us."

Some people believe Gein was involved in the disappearances of eight-year-old Georgia Jean Weckler from Fort Atkinson in 1947; Evelyn Hartley, a teenage babysitter from La Crosse in 1953; and in the butcher slaying of Judith Anderson, age sixteen, of Chicago.

Others found his grave-robbing tales hard to fathom: How could the slight, spindly-legged, 140-pound farmer dig up a grave, open a vault and remove a body? Portage County Sheriff Herbert Wanerski said he didn't believe the human remains came from grave robberies.

Pat Danna, the elderly sexton of the Plainfield cemetery, said it took him half a day to dig a grave with someone helping. A body snatcher would need a block and tackle to lift a body out of a vault, he said, adding that he'd seen no evidence of grave tampering at the cemetery in thirteen years.

But Gein said forty times during the previous five years he'd set out to rob graves. He also claimed to have dug up his mother's body.

"Thirty times something inside of me, something good, told me to go back home. The other ten times, I took something and left the graves in apple pie order."

Many questions about the case never were fully resolved. Authorities angered Plainfield residents by their reluctance to probe the origin of the bodies found in Gein's home. And the killer himself lacked the clear mental capacity to provide a detailed accounting of his crimes.

Even Gein's lawyer showed no enthusiasm for his client. "Everyone is entitled to a lawyer," said Wautoma attorney William Belter. "It's not the most desirable case to have."

Shortly after his arrest, authorities cleared him of the Hartley and Weckler cases, along with the disappearance of Adams County deer hunter Victor "Buck" Travis in November, 1952. A lie detector test showed no conclusive results when Gein was questioned about the disappearance of thirty-year-old Irene Keating from Fort Atkinson in August 1956.

More than two-hundred fifty of Plainfield's seven hundred residents attended Mrs. Worden's funeral, hearing her pastor assure them that her hideous death wasn't a sign that God had forgotten his flock.

With speculators threatening to turn it into a museum, Gein's house burned mysteriously a week before it was scheduled for auction. Volunteer firefighters somehow couldn't — or wouldn't — find the infamous house in time to save it. Area residents stood by and applauded the blaze, which seemed to cleanse the area of the grave robber's gruesome lifestyle. But the fire wasn't the end of Gein's legacy and he remains Plainfield's most infamous inhabitant. Although the house burned, his white Ford, which he used to haul bodies, became a sideshow for a traveling carnival.

Gein told investigators his unnatural attachment to his mother grew into obsessions with sex and, finally, the opening of graves and the two grisly murders.

His Oedipus-complex attitude toward his mother became the basis for Alfred Hitchcock's thriller movie, "Psycho," based on a novel by Milwaukee author Robert Bloch, and, later, "The Texas Chain Saw Massa-

Wisconsin State Journal file photo

Ed Gein is escorted to a court hearing.

cre." While adapting some of Gein's story to the screen, the main character of "Psycho," Norman Bates, wasn't portrayed as a handyman like
Gein, skilled at fashioning household items from human skin.

In his book, *Deviant: The Shocking True Story of the Original Psycho,*
Harold Schechter, a professor at Queens College in New York City, re-
searched Gein's family background in an attempt to find an explanation
for his madness. Schechter traced back to a Mississippi River flash flood
in 1879, the first tragedy that struck the Gein family. He chronicles the
family's struggles on their first farm near La Crosse and, later, near
Plainfield. He describes Gein's early isolationism that later turned to

grave-robbing and murder. Schechter also provides a compelling portrait of Augusta, Gein's domineering mother, and his henpecked father:

"In charge of her own household and joined to a man of feckless and increasingly unreliable character, Augusta quickly assumed the role of domestic tyrant. Her own deformities of character — her harshness, rigidity and fierce intolerance — became ever more pronounced. Her husband was a worthless, good-for-nothing. She sneered at him openly, calling him a lazy dog and worse. In spite of his broad back and blacksmith's muscles, he was a weakling, afraid of hard work."

Spectators packed the courtroom and anonymous callers threatened to blow up the jail when Gein pleaded innocent to the Worden and Hogan murders by reason of insanity. Circuit Judge Herbert Bunde ruled he was incompetent to stand trial and sent Gein to Central State Hospital. Gein's rough-cut hair stood straight up as he displayed a weak but strange smile. He was dressed in the same blue work clothes he usually wore around the farm. He answered three questions put to him by Bunde with a soft-spoken "yes."

"It doesn't look as though Gein will walk the streets of Plainfield again," Kileen said after Bunde's ruling.

The Rev. Kenneth Engleman, a Methodist minister, stood beside Gein in court and prayed with him in jail, kneeling with the mad butcher next to his bunk.

"It was my impression that the press and its readers have the impression Gein was a person who never showed emotion," Engleman said. "I went to see him because I'm a Christian minister and Mr. Gein is a child of God.

"I walked in and said, 'Mr. Gein, I am here to give you spiritual help.' We talked for a while. He gave me no facts. The relationship was as a minister to a person in need of spiritual help.

"After breaking down, he collected himself and then started to talk about it and then cried again. Gein sought forgiveness. I think he was referring to God.

"He is as near to Him now as anyone else, perhaps nearer because our knowledge of God comes through the ultimate issue of life and death. He shows definite remorse for what he's done, for the terrible situation he has created in Plainfield. His concern was not only for himself but for the pain he inflicted on others."

In 1968, officials at Central State Hospital found that the sixty-one-year-old bachelor now was competent to stand trial. During the intervening decade, he had worked quietly in the mental hospital's lapidary department, polishing and cutting stones. He'd also labored as a hospital carpenter and attendant.

Gein faced several legal options because his case fell under both old and new sanity provisions of the law. He could plead guilty and be given a mandatory life prison sentence. In that case, he would be eligible for parole in eleven years. He could plead innocent and have a trial on whether he committed the crimes. He could admit he killed Worden but say he was insane at the time. Or he could plead innocent and innocent by reason of insanity.

Gein chose the final option. Judge Robert Gollmar ruled Gein's 1957 confession inadmissible because Gein had not been properly advised of his rights. Gollmar also said Gein had been interrogated for an unreasonable length of time of about thirty hours during a period when he was too mentally ill to withstand questioning. But the judge denied a defense motion to suppress evidence obtained in the search of Gein's farmhouse. The defense attorney had claimed police officers didn't have a proper search warrant.

The bench trial began in November, exactly eleven years after the Worden murder. Waushara County residents still showed intense interest in the case, packing the courtroom. Some again threatened to blow up the jail and Gein had to be moved to Oshkosh for his safety.

Gein said he recalled visiting the Worden hardware store but thought the gun had fired accidentally. Dr. Milton Miller, a UW-Madison professor and psychiatrist, testified that Gein suffered from a "chronic schizophrenic disorder" and had improved since the murders but said he still remained psychotic.

At the conclusion of the bench trial, Gollmar found Gein guilty of the Worden murder. Gein, wearing a blue-gray suit with a white shirt and narrow tie, told the judge "I ain't happy" in the hospital and "I doubt if anyone could be happy there."

But Gollmar ruled Gein still was insane and returned him to Central State Hospital. In 1974, Gollmar denied a request by Gein for release because he said Gein couldn't handle life outside the hospital.

"This is a Rip Van Winkle sort of thing," the judge said. "We have a man who has been confined for seventeen years and who would be incapable of coping with the simple problems of crossing the street, getting food and finding a place to stay if he were released."

Unlike Gein's trial in 1968, there was little interest in the court proceedings this time, other than on the part of a dozen eager reporters. In 1981, Gollmar gathered his notes, court records and police reports to compile a book on the Gein case.

"Frankly I know of no person like him in the whole history of the world," the judge told the *Chicago Tribune*. "Here was a man who was a murderer, a cannibal, a grave robber and I don't know the term but he took the skin of his victims and manufactured chairs and other things.

"Not even Jack the Ripper, or that Manson crowd in California that mutilated all the bodies, showed the combination of all these skills, if you want to call them skills.'"

By the early 1980s, Gein was said to be senile. He died in 1984 of natural causes at age seventy-seven and was buried in an unmarked grave at Spiritland Cemetery near Plainfield, where he robbed graves three decades earlier.

Upon Gein's death, Gollmar said the Plainfield farmer was the most unique criminal ever with "the largest collection of women's parts in the world."

During the 1990s, Ed Gein was the focus of a cult revival. His name cropped up in heavy metal rock music lyrics and in several books. His case inspired the novel and award-winning film, "The Silence of the Lambs." The Jeffrey Dahmer case in 1991 dredged up Gein memories as Wisconsin criminologists debated which one was the most notorious. Madison's Broom Street Theater presented a play written by Ron Daley titled "Badger Orpheus: The Story of Ed Gein." The play cast the Gein story of murder and dismemberment in a sympathetic context of the Orpheus myth.

Plainfield residents who lived through the Gein era would have little tolerance for this kind of nonsense. But for those with enough distance, the case continues to provide tantalizing fodder for creative efforts.

38

Little People in an Urban Tragedy
Milwaukee, 1979-80

Black children were being found dead in Atlanta in a case that eventually would lead to Wayne Williams but Roosevelt Harrell couldn't be concerned with that. He had matters closer to home that demanded his attention. Harrell, a Milwaukee police detective, was bothered by a string of murders on the city's North Side. Maybe these slayings couldn't even be called a string for it was difficult to separate them from the ebb and flow of urban violence — the regular diet of robberies and beatings and sexual assaults. These killings in a high-crime area hardly seemed unusual and most merited only a brief mention in the Milwaukee papers. Some of the victims were stabbed; others were bludgeoned to death. Half were white and half were black. Some were men and others were women. Was there a pattern in these statistics?

Harrell wasn't sure. Still, he felt the murders could have been done by a single killer. All occurred in the same neighborhood, bounded by Eighth, Holtan, Garfield and Center streets. All appeared to begin as burglaries and end in murder, perhaps when the victims confronted the intruder. But the overriding factor that made Harrell confident of a single-suspect theory was the sheer brutality of the crimes. Several victims were savagely beaten and one woman was stabbed forty-three times. Could there be more than one vicious killer like this on the loose?

Della Mae Liggins, age sixty-nine, was a popular kindergarten teacher who had retired two years earlier from the Milwaukee public schools. Her husband died about the same time she retired and Liggins thought about moving back to her home state of Oklahoma. But she decided to

Wisconsin State Journal file photo

David Van Dyke

stay when she couldn't sell her Milwaukee home at 2341 N. Eighth Street. Even after she quit teaching, her door was always open to neighborhood children or former students, who often came back years later to visit her. A week before her death, Liggins held a marshmallow roast in her backyard for a group of youngsters., She had been dedicated to her profession, spending a summer in England studying the open classroom concept. Neighbor Melvin Brooks said she had "a rapport with children that was unequaled."

On July 19, 1979, about the same time the first black child was found dead in Atlanta, someone walked into the unlocked Liggins home and stabbed her once in the chest. Her body was found on the kitchen floor. The killer had left a blood-stained, six-inch butcher knife on top of the refrigerator. Her 1972 Pontiac was missing.

Nearly a month later, on August 10, two volunteers from Project Involve, a Milwaukee agency that serves the elderly, stopped by the home of Florence Burkard, age seventy-eight, of 2420 N. Hubbard Street, to bring her a hot meal. They found her body in a pool of blood at the bottom of the basement stairs. She had been dying of cancer and it probably wouldn't have taken much to kill the fragile woman, yet

Burkard was stabbed forty-three times, including the fatal wound to her heart. Her purse containing nineteen dollars was found on the kitchen table. It looked like she'd been attacked in the kitchen and a pair of scissors believed to be the murder weapon was recovered.

Another elderly woman, Helen Wronski, age seventy-nine, was found brutally beaten to death November 9 in her home at 2312 N. Holtan Street. She died of severe head injuries and police found partial fingerprints at the murder scene but were unsuccessful in matching them to any known suspects.

Charles Golston, age sixty-three, of 2276-A N. Buffam Street, lived about four blocks from Florence Burkard. A retired Milwaukee Road employee, Golston was known to neighbors as Uncle Charlie. A young friend found him unconscious and bleeding on January 25, 1980. He had been attacked with a claw hammer and spent several months in a coma before his death in early May. The attack wasn't newsworthy enough to make it into the Milwaukee newspapers until after his death.

A few days before Bernard Fonder's death, Fonder, age forty-nine, gave a note to his downstairs neighbor at 2116 N. Booth Street. The note had the name and address of Fonder's former roommate and instructed the neighbor, Michael Harlen, to give the note to the police if anything happened to Fonder. The twenty-two-year-old roommate had beaten Fonder the previous December and Fonder had ordered the young man to move out. Three weeks before Fonder's body was found on March 3, the former roommate had returned and spent the night, saying his girlfriend had kicked him out. Fonder's body was found on his blood-soaked bed after he suffered multiple blows to the head. Fingerprints were found at the scene and the roommate was arrested at the Antlers Hotel, 616 N. Second Street. But police couldn't make the murder charge stick against the former roommate and he was released.

Liggins, Burkard, Wronski, Golston, Fonder. These weren't wealthy or powerful people. The cases seemed to lead in a myriad of directions or nowhere at all. But Harrell couldn't shake the hunch that they were connected somehow. And the brutality of the crimes was about to take a turn for the worse.

On April 14, 1980, Sandy Ellis confronted an intruder in her apartment. She was battered with an ashtray and wine bottle, then slashed with broken pieces of both weapons. The attacker escaped with $128 in cash. Unlike the other victims, Ellis survived. Before the attacker left, she feigned unconsciousness while her assailant ran his fingers along the cuts he had made on her face, feeling them, playing with them in a sadistic way that went far beyond a routine inner-city crime.

A week later, on April 25, the brutal killer struck again. This time the victim was Helen Bellamy, age thirty, the mother of four children who lived at 2471 N. First Street. Her body was discovered partially covered by a sheet on the dining room floor by her son, Sylvester, age thirteen. She had been beaten with a tire jack, which was found in a bedroom. Two men were seen carrying a TV set out of the apartment. An examination of the body revealed that Bellamy had been sexually assaulted.

Harrell pleaded with his superiors to establish a special investigative unit to try to solve the string of increasingly vicious crimes and they agreed. Harrell and his partner, Lt. Carl Ruscitti, compared the fingerprints of known burglary suspects with the prints found at the Fonder and Wronski murder scenes. They put out a request throughout the department that fingerprints of any new suspects be compared with the murder scene prints. They noticed that the killer always took a souvenir from the bloody scene — a money clip, a clock radio, TV set or jewelry.

"The killer had a pattern," Ruscitti said. "He used the same M.O. He used whatever was handy to kill and left it at the scene — a tire jack, an ice pick, a claw hammer or knives. We believe him to be the same man."

Harrell and Ruscitti worked long hours contrasting the disparate circumstances and evidence of each murder. But fingerprint comparisons of burglary suspects old and new failed to identify the killer. Finally, on May 23, they got a break. A man was arrested after an attempted burglary in the 2500 block of North First Street. His prints matched those found at the two murder scenes. His name was David Van Dyke.

Ruscitti and Harrell took Van Dyke to a police interrogation room, where they grilled him for several hours over coffee and cigarettes. The detectives began their questioning in general terms, slowly zeroing in on the killings. As details of the brutal slayings were revealed, Van Dyke sobbed and looked remorseful.

He'd had an unhappy childhood, and was often the target of taunts by other children because of his obesity. Born in early 1959, Van Dyke was raised by his grandmother until 1965, when he moved in with his mother until she died in 1974. He had four older brothers and sisters. After his mother's death, he lived in a series of foster homes. The Rev. Calvin Valentine, one of the boy's foster parents, said he couldn't believe Van Dyke was the killer. Edna Kelly, another foster parent for two years, said he always seemed like a nice boy.

But there was a troubling streak to the young heavyset boy. In 1971, while still living with his mother, he refused to go to school, broke windows and beat up smaller children. A hospital social worker said his relationship with his mother was ambivalent. He wanted more affection than she was willing to give and was angry at her for not giving it.

After seventh grade at Lincoln Junior High School, Van Dyke quit school for good. He repeatedly threatened to hurt his mother and police were called to the Van Dyke home every weekend for six weeks. He once threatened a niece with a knife. He also hit a neighbor woman who called him a "fat boy" and a "big, fat pig."

At age twelve, Van Dyke was awkward and obese. He would steal from his mother's purse to pay off stronger kids so they wouldn't beat him up. One time, he bought a canary and stood over it, laughing uproariously, as he strangled it. A psychiatrist who examined him said: "David talks of murder just like he talks of the weather."

Van Dyke spent some time at a juvenile treatment center at Lad Lake, where teachers said he suffered considerable ridicule because of his weight, which by this time had ballooned to 250 pounds. But they said he enjoyed canoeing, horses and books. He later lost forty pounds in a weight reduction program at St. Luke's Hospital in Milwaukee. When he was arrested, Van Dyke weighed a svelte 175 pounds.

He never married, had no children and said he never held a job. Besides the burglaries, he supported himself as a pool shark, earning about six hundred dollars a month. He often lived in vacant buildings or slept in abandoned cars.

"I think he has a mental problem," his sister said at the time of his arrest. "You never know what he is going to do. He wanted to take over the home, so we wouldn't let him stay here."

Van Dyke received probation in April, 1979, for a burglary conviction. Three months later, the killings began.

On the basis of their extensive interviews with Van Dyke, the detectives prepared fifteen pages of confessions to the murders but Van Dyke never signed them. Besides the fingerprint evidence, Sandy Ellis identified him in a lineup as the man who attacked her. Van Dyke was arrested on six charges of murder and one charge of attempted murder.

The trial began in February 1981, before Milwaukee County Circuit Judge Michael Guolet. District Attorney E. Michael McCann prosecuted the case while Stephen Glynn defended Van Dyke. On the first day of the trial, Sandy Ellis told about how Van Dyke had cut her with a broken bottle, then ran his fingers over her wounds. Later, jurors listened intently as Harrell described his lengthy investigation that ultimately led to Van Dyke. On March 3, Van Dyke took the witness stand in his own defense, apparently against the advice of his attorney.

"Sometimes there is a conflict between a lawyer's advice and client's desire and, in this particular case, it's client's desire that governed," Glynn told the court.

Van Dyke accused the detectives of fabricating the confessions. He admitted to at least two hundred daytime burglaries but said if he were confronted by a victim, he would "just leave." But he said a victim never caught him in the act. Van Dyke said he went to Sandy Ellis' home about 3:00 p.m. on the day of the incident. He had come to buy a car, he said, and she asked him where he got the money, He told her he shot pool. She said she doubted that very much.

"We got to arguing," Van Dyke testified. "We were swearing. She told me to get out. She picked up a vase and slashed me across the elbow. She was screaming, hollering and holding my hand. I was trying to break free. The first time I hit her, the ashtray fell and broke. I hit her with the pieces.

"She said, 'Get the hell out!' I didn't know what to do. I ran out the back door. There was a hammer on the table. I used it to knock the boards (cross bars on the back door) to get out."

Van Dyke said his hand required seventeen stitches after his encounter with Ellis. He denied taking the money, cutting her face or running his fingers along her wounds.

In his closing arguments, McCann used quotes from Shakespeare and Joseph Conrad to enliven his review of the state's evidence. He talked about the "heinous, horrible burden of guilt" that Van Dyke must have felt. He asked jurors to "smell the toast and smell the coffee" in the kitchen of Helen Bellamy, whose body was found by one of her own children. McCann picked up pieces of the broken bottle, the car jack and a hammer, swinging them vigorously to dramatize the violence of the attacks.

"I don't want you to judge him in rage or sorrow," he told the jury, referring to Van Dyke as an "urban nomad" who killed six vulnerable "little people in an urban tragedy." McCann said the deaths of these "little people" went virtually unnoticed until Harrell began putting the pieces together.

That bit of rhetoric aroused the ire of Milwaukee police, later eliciting an angry response from Rudolph Hill, a deputy inspector. He also blasted McCann for saying these slayings couldn't have happened in suburbs such as West Allis or Wauwatosa.

"McCann does not know police procedure," he said. "Crime does not have any boundary lines. From the first homicide report, an intense and thorough investigation was conducted."

Of nineteen homicides at that point in 1981, he said only one remained unsolved and "even that one is not gathering dust." When the second in the string of killings occurred, he said police tried to connect the two cases and come up with the same suspect.

In contrast to McCann's dramatic closing arguments, Glynn tried to keep his remarks low key.

"I'm not here trying to evoke your passions," he told the jury. "I'm not going to ask you any favors. I'm not even going to thank you."

And the jury didn't do any favors for Glynn or his client. After deliberating for four-and-a-half hours, jurors found Van Dyke guilty on all counts. Even in the face of the verdict, the killer continued to maintain his innocence.

"It's a very freaked-out theory the police have," Van Dyke said. "No motive, just a strange theory. The theory is I did these things and have no knowledge of what happened. That this individual goes in with the intent to kill and does not remember that he took anything or what he used to kill.

"There is nothing wrong with me. I have plenty of knowledge about what is happening in the outside world. I remember everything.

"I have to knock everything out of my mind as to what I did on the streets and convince myself I can do the time they gave me. I'm not saying I'll live that long and the first chance of parole is slim. But if it

Wisconsin State Journal file photo

E. Michael McCann

comes down to my getting out, I can say I won't do burglaries again. Maybe I'll be too old or whatever."

Maybe so. Van Dyke will be age 103 when he's eligible for parole. The judge gave him six consecutive life terms, at the time the longest prison sentence in state history. He also received consecutive twenty-year sentences for attempted murder and armed robbery in the Ellis case.

"The court has no illusions at this time this man can be rehabilitated given present realities," the judge said. "There must be no more victims at the hands of Mr. Van Dyke. This sentence is a message to the parole board."

The judge also read from psychiatric reports, including one from Madison psychiatrist Frederick A. Fosdal, who said:

"During the interview there clearly was no evidence of mental impairment present. My tentative diagnosis at this time is that of no mental disorder."

More than twenty children had been killed by this time in Atlanta and police would soon close in on suspect Wayne Williams. But in Milwaukee, detective Harrell had other concerns.

"A lot of people were wondering if he was coming back out in the community," Harrell said of Van Dyke. "This will be a great relief to them."

39

Candy from a Stranger
Sheboygan, 1971

"How are you?" Father Eugene Winkler asked, but the boy didn't respond.

"Are you sick? Do you need help?"

The boy looked like he was trying to nod but didn't have enough control over his body. The priest judged him to be about nineteen, tall and slim and just sitting there on the church steps, holding his head in his hands.

Winkler, pastor of St. George's Catholic Church, had gone outside to call his father, who was working in the church garden, for lunch. When he found the boy, the priest went back into the rectory and called the sheriff's department.

He went back outside to assure the troubled boy that help was on the way. As he spoke, Winkler leaned close to the young man, still sitting immobile on the steps. The priest knew that whatever was wrong, it wasn't alcohol because the boy didn't smell of booze. Winkler tried to talk to him again but the boy just sat there as his glazed eyes looked away.

"Hospital," he whispered, almost inaudibly.

When Deputy Eugene Kohlhagen arrived, he checked the boy's wallet and found out his name was Douglas Dean.

"At least he isn't broke," Kohlhagen said, pulling a piece of paper from the wallet. "He has a fifty dollar check from Ann Rammer."

At the mention of the name, the boy turned and looked at the deputy, the first sign of recognition he had shown. Then his head drooped again, nodding slowly from side to side.

Kohlhagen noticed he was clutching a piece of paper in his right hand. The deputy asked for the paper but the boy kept his fist clenched tight. The deputy slowly pried the boy's fingers apart and uncrumpled the piece of note paper. It said Rammer Sausage Co. across the top and had Ann Rammer's Madison address and telephone number scrawled on it. Dean was taken by ambulance to St. Nicholas Hospital in Sheboygan.

Dean's troubles may have begun one-and-a-half years earlier, in March 1969, when he was dating sixteen-year-old Debra Westenberger, who lived in the town of Wilson. Debra got pregnant and, Dean later told his friends, he entered a suicide pact with her. One day, she entered the Dean home when no one was there. She grabbed a .22-caliber rifle and sat down on Dean's bed, then fired a fatal shot into her head. She left a note saying she was depressed. But if there was a suicide pact, Dean failed to keep his end of the bargain.

The boy's mother, Hildegard Dean, was furious about the suicide. It embarrassed the family, she said, and the incident may have been the beginning of what would grow into a deep resentment between Dean and his mother. The boy's father, Warren, worked as a supervisor at Wisconsin Power & Light's Edgewater generating plant. In May 1970, Warren Dean died of leukemia.

The deaths of Debra and his father began to haunt Dean after his graduation a month later from Sheboygan's South High School. In the fall, he enrolled in an electronics study program at Lakeshore Technical Institute. For a while, he did well in the program but, by December, his interest began to wane. Things weren't going well with his mother. He began to sell drugs and appeared to use LSD, although he later claimed the acid trips were faked. He bought a .22-caliber rifle about the time of his father's death and told friends he was thinking about setting up a target range in the basement so, when his mother came down the stairs, he could shoot her and make it look like an accident.

Mrs. Dean didn't like her son's girlfriend, Ann Rammer. Dean got along with Ann's mother better than his own but often took Ann's side in arguments with Mrs. Rammer, especially over money. Dean told another LTI student, Mary Ann Stier, that he had a plan to kill his mom, then Mrs. Rammer and her three sons so he and Ann could get a lot of money. From his mother, Dean hoped to get the Social Security money from his father's death. Stier didn't know whether to take Dean seriously about the murder threats because she knew he often said things just to shock her. One time, he told her he wanted to become a Mafia hit man and talked about how easy it was to shoot someone from a car.

Stier said: "He told me how much the death of his father and his former girlfriend had meant to him. I was sympathetic to him. The more I knew him, the more he seemed to be taking drugs, and I saw him take a small pink pill one day. Later, he didn't seem to care about anything and was laughing a lot. It was getting so bad that he dropped acid every day. I didn't want to associate with him anymore."

As 1971 dawned, Dean's drug use seemed to pick up. He lost interest in school and soon dropped out. He played an occasional gig as a drummer with a polka band but, other than that, just moped around the house. He told his mother he expected her to support him until he turned twenty-one if she wouldn't give him the Social Security money. He told her not to buy anything so he would have more money when she was gone. She often came into his bedroom to watch the only working television set in the house and wouldn't leave when he asked, refusing to give him privacy. They fought over buying a color television set. He'd get angry because she often picked through his personal belongings.

Dean made occasional trips to Madison, especially after Ann moved there following her graduation from South High School in June. He made friends with Brigid Kuck, a UW-Madison student, and once followed her into the kitchen of her apartment with a switchblade knife. He told Kuck about the suicide pact with Debbie and another time told a man not to sit in the chair Debbie supposedly was sitting in or he'd kill him.

"He said he had no feeling about Debbie's death or about death one way or the other," Kuck said.

In early July, Dean's mother went on a three-day vacation with a friend to northern Wisconsin. She told her friend she was upset about her son becoming a vegetable, having no positive interests in life. She said, if she died, Doug would get the car, a 1970 Dodge Charger, and the rest of the property would be divided with his sister. Her friend asked why she was preoccupied with dying.

"I just have a feeling I'm not going to live very long," she said. Meanwhile, Dean visited Ann in Madison for a couple of weeks. In a parking lot, he had a long talk with student Leslie Dramer, age nineteen. Mostly they discussed the Vietnam War and people in general. Dean told her he would kill anyone who jeopardized his life, "especially my mother." He enjoyed his visit to Madison and bought a five-hundred-dollar stereo, using a postdated check signed by Ann Rammer. He planned to go back to Sheboygan and ask his mother for the Social Security money once more to cover the cost of the stereo before returning to Madison to live. The day before he left for Sheboygan, Dean sat at a table in the UW-Madison Memorial Union, reading a newspaper. A man came and sat at the same table and Dean let him share the paper. In return, the stranger gave Dean a box of Dots candy.

To Ralph Fenn, a widower who dated Mrs. Dean, her son seemed friendlier than usual that Sunday night, July 18. The boy played some new records he'd bought. Mrs. Dean and Fenn went for a ride, then spent some time at the North Star Bar before returning to the Dean home at 1149 Cherry Lane about 9:30 p.m. Dean went over to the Rammer house at 3219 S. Eleventh Street, a few blocks away. He watched a television movie with his friend, John Rammer, age sixteen, the two other Rammer boys and Michael Dagen, also sixteen. Dagen said Dean ran into the house during a light rainstorm, saying he was afraid of lightning. Dagen and John Rammer went for a ride about 9:00 p.m. and Dean said he didn't want to go along so he walked home. He watched TV for a while and read a book on chess. Then he got hungry and remembered the candy he'd gotten at the Memorial Union, which still was in his pocket. He munched four or five pieces and a half hour later imagined he was playing chess with someone and that he was a chess piece, the king or queen. He felt a tingling sensation; his vision was blurred. Things began to vibrate.

Wisconsin State Journal file photo
Douglas Dean

"I have a recollection of lying somewhere warm, like an oven," he said later. "Then I seemed to be walking between two white lines that seemed to stretch into infinity. I recall seeing something, a tall object like a steeple, then a man talking to me friendly and a little monster right next to him that was grinning at me. I tried to ignore the monster."

About two hours after Father Winkler found Dean sitting on the church steps, Constance Schneider, Dean's sister, went to her mother's home. The house was a single-story with white siding and batten trim. Each day about 6:30 a.m., before Mrs. Dean left for work at Wigwam Mills, she pulled open the drapes. But Constance found the drapes still drawn, even though by this time it was mid-afternoon. Constance found her mother's body in bed, shot in the side of the head at the right ear lobe. Two spent .22-caliber cartridges were found on the floor of a hallway outside the bedroom.

Police canvassed the neighborhood for information about the slaying of Mrs. Dean. Six hours later, about 8:10 p.m., they reached the Rammer home and found more bodies. Police Chief Oakley O. Frank described the scene as the "most macabre" sight he'd come across in twenty-five years of detective work. It was the first multiple slaying in Sheboygan history. Spent .22-caliber shell casings were found throughout the two-story house. The body of Mrs. Rammer was in a pool of blood just inside the front entrance. Her son, Paul, had been shot in the bedroom, then struggled into a hallway where he died. Tom's body was found on the staircase. A gunshot split John's brain in half and he also was wounded in the neck, left arm, eye and near his mouth.

At the Dean home, police found an empty gun box and cartridges in Dean's bedroom. They also found seven boxes of ammunition and two empty shell casings. The serial number on the gun box matched the serial number of the murder weapon found at the Rammer house. While police searched the house for evidence and removed the bodies, Dean lay in St. Nicholas Hospital, still feeling the effects of the drug he had taken.

Dean's attorney, Robert Halvorsen, refused to let the police interview his client. Murder charges were filed July 22 on the basis of crime lab evidence. Dean, who appeared at the hearing in jail coveralls, was declared indigent by the judge. Bail was set at $150,000. A private attorney, Paul Axel, was hired by the county to assist District Attorney Lance Jones in prosecuting the grisly case.

Brown butcher paper covered courtroom windows at Dean's preliminary hearing and the public was barred. Judge Joseph W. Wilkus ordered a media blackout on the case and sealed the transcript. A dozen teenagers were among the fifty witnesses allowed in the courtroom during the three-hour hearing. In ordering the secrecy, Wilkus said the preliminary hearing is one-sided, presenting mostly evidence against the defendant, and opening it to the public and reporters could make it difficult to select a jury:

"From this case, there is a danger to the essentially fair-mindedness and impartiality of the public from where many prospective jurors will be drawn. The news stories ignore the fundamental guarantee to all citizens: One charged is presumed innocent of any crime until a valid plea of guilty is entered or he is convicted in a fair trial on evidence establishing guilt beyond a reasonable doubt."

Wilkus said he received two anonymous letters urging that Dean be hanged without a trial. Others threatened to break him out of jail. In closing the hearing, Wilkus cited the Cleveland case of Sam Sheppard, whose conviction for killing his wife was overturned largely due to adverse pretrial publicity.

When jury selection began November 1, fourteen potential jurors were excused and a jury of eight men and four women ultimately was selected. Judge James Buchen ruled that color photos of the victims were too inflammatory and gruesome to show to the jury. Dean appeared cool and confident, wearing a tan corduroy sport coat and with his long hair and sideburns neatly trimmed. Prosecutor Jones presented the crime lab evidence and testimony that placed Dean at the Rammer home the night before the murders.

The final prosecution witness was Kenneth Kregel, an alcoholic jail inmate who testified that Dean described the killings while both men were in jail. Kregel, a work release prisoner, had fled to Duluth, Minnesota, rather than testify in the Dean case, but authorities brought him back. Kregel said Dean exercised in jail by walking up and down the hallway outside the jail kitchen, where Kregel worked. During one of those walks, Kregel said, Dean described the murders. Dean told Kregel someone was crying — a child — and he shot him.

"I asked why he did it and he said the kid kept hollering," Kregel told the court. At that revelation, Dean's confident demeanor broke down and he hunched over the defense table, whispering and gesturing to his attorney.

Dean was the first witness in his own defense. He denied ever talking to Kregel. He described himself as a nonviolent person who enjoyed shocking people like Mary Ann Stier with outrageous stories. He said he never took drugs. He described how he ate the candy tainted with LSD the night before the slaying and hallucinated. When he heard the news about the Rammer deaths, Dean told the court he was "very upset but at the same time I was cheerful because I was told they were murdered and that I was the suspect."

Crime lab investigator Michael Koss said he found LSD tablets embedded in two of six remaining pieces of candy in Dean's pocket. A parade of witnesses testified about Dean's condition when he was found on the church steps. An emergency room nurse at St. Nicholas Hospital said Dean's pulse was weak and that he looked stuporous, chilly, dazed and confused. Doctors who examined Dean that day said they found him disoriented due to drug intoxication. Ann Rammer testified she'd been confronted by an intruder a few nights earlier at her mother's house, raising the possibility that someone other than Dean committed the murders.

Prosecution rebuttal witness Dr. Rodrigo Muñoz, a psychiatrist, testified that Dean would have had to take LSD in the late morning to still be feeling the effects when doctors examined him at 7:30 p.m. on the day of the murders. Muñoz also said he doubted that LSD could produce the amnesia effect that Dean said had blotted out his memory of the crimes.

The jury deliberated about eighty minutes on November 9 before finding Dean guilty of the five murders. When the first guilty verdict was read, Dean slumped forward in his chair and put his elbow on the defense table. With each subsequent guilty verdict, his head sank lower, finally coming to rest on his chest.

"Murder was only half of Douglas Dean's plan," Jones said in his closing arguments. "The other part was protection so he could enjoy the money he expected to inherit. He needed a defense a jury could

Wisconsin State Journal file photo

Dean sits in chains at an unsuccessful 1985 clemency hearing.

believe." Jones called the murders the most sadistic, hideous crimes ever committed in Sheboygan County.

Three days later, Buchen sentenced Dean to five consecutive life terms in prison, the longest prison sentence, at the time, in state history. Dean would have to serve fifty-eight years and four months before he was eligible for parole. A psychiatric exam had found Dean sane at the time of the murders. When the sentence was passed, Ann Rammer sobbed loudly, pressing her hands to her mouth. Dean whispered to his lawyer, then left the courtroom with tears staining his cheeks.

As Dean continued to profess his innocence, anonymous callers to local radio stations and newspapers threatened to kill him. Cost of the Dean trial to Sheboygan County was $29,841. Mrs. Dean's estate was valued at $40,000 while Naomi Rammer left $123,000. In appealing the murder convictions, Dean's attorneys argued that he didn't receive a fair trial because of news coverage, lack of adequate legal counsel and introduction of evidence they said was obtained by police without a search warrant. The Wisconsin Supreme Court sustained the murder convictions on April 10, 1975. The U.S. Supreme Court later declined to hear the case. Dean appealed to Gov. Patrick Lucey that his life terms should be served concurrently rather than consecutively. After a hearing, that request also was denied.

When Dean entered Waupun State Prison in 1971, he found he wasn't eligible to take correspondence courses through the UW-Extension because of his long sentence so he searched for educational alternatives, spending nearly all of his twenty-six dollar monthly salary on postage stamps for sending queries to college admission officers. He gave up smoking, pop and candy bars to mail the letters.

During his prison recreation time, he completed five correspondence courses in law, music, psychology, history and mathematics through the Madison Reference and Loan Library. In one year, he wrote 1,462 letters but most of them were ignored.

After four years in prison, Dean had identified nineteen schools that were interested in considering him as a correspondence student. Most ultimately rejected his application because of the obstacles caused by his imprisonment.

He finally was accepted by the University of Minnesota after he submitted a detailed, thirty-page plan for research projects along with a strong résumé. Dean found two Madison professors willing to travel to Waupun to meet with him one day a week for ten weeks so he could take a statistics course.

In October 1985, Dean asked Governor Anthony Earl for a transfer from Waupun to a minimum security prison so he could finish working on his doctor's degree in clinical psychology. In seeking support for his clemency plea, Dean wrote to a friend:

"What I would like to do is have the governor see that rewarding my example will speak well for the lifer system in Wisconsin, send a positive signal to other inmates and, if nothing else, make the Division of Corrections look good as it tries to justify all these new prisons."

But Earl denied the request, citing public outrage over the plan. He said he had received about a thousand letters opposing clemency for the convicted mass killer.

Dean has earned advanced degrees in psychology. He's been active in counseling inmate groups and in a program for troubled teenagers. Yet, his extensive education hasn't won his freedom and he remains haunted by hideous crimes of nearly three decades ago.

40

A Teenager's Rampage
Madison, 1988

Clyde Chamberlain, the popular Dane County coroner whom everyone called "Bud" was holding court as usual in his basement office. Down the hallway, Eleanor Townsend, a part-time secretary in the corporation counsel's office, had dropped by the Sheriff's Department to deliver some papers. Next to her stood Erik Erickson, personnel director for the state Justice Department. He had stopped by the department to pay a parking ticket.

It was about 12:45 p.m. and on that day, January 15, 1988, Chamberlain, Townsend and Erickson had no idea their routines were about to make them victims of a teenage gunman in one of the worst crimes in Dane County history.

At the Madison Police Department's Detective Bureau, a short distance from the Sheriff's Department, nineteen-year-old Aaron Lindh had stopped in to speak with detectives about a burglary at his apartment the night before. It was the latest of several burglaries he had reported, but his anger over the incidents was just one of several things going wrong in his life.

Lindh had gotten an eviction notice for his downtown Madison apartment that he had shared with University of Wisconsin-Madison students. Three of his roommates left a month earlier because he had fired a gun in the apartment several times. Lindh had stopped by the rental office about 10:00 a.m. and employees said he appeared calm and normal.

The young man also worked his regular Thursday night shift at

Webcrafters, a Madison printing firm, and got off at 7:00 a.m. Friday. He was described by supervisors as a conscientious employee.

Firefighters had been called twice to Lindh's apartment building to extinguish Dumpster fires. Years earlier, Lindh had set a neighbor's shed ablaze near his East Side home and later spent time at the Ethan Allen School for Boys near Wales because of his uncontrollable behavior.

After visiting the Detective Bureau, Lindh walked up and down the stairs of the City-County Building, trying to vent his anger and frustration. But his rage only grew and he left the building. He moved his car to another lot and returned a few minutes later with a sawed-off shotgun concealed under a long coat.

Instead of going back to the Detective Bureau, Lindh walked down the hall to the Sheriff's Department, where Townsend and Erickson were standing at the counter. He fired at them, wounding Erickson behind the left ear and shooting Townsend twice in the back of the head. Townsend, a forty-

Wisconsin State Journal file photo
Clyde "Bud" Chamberlain

year-old mother of three, died on the way to the hospital; Erickson recovered from his wounds.

Lindh went back into the hallway and headed for the coroner's of-fice and coffee shop, where a dozen people were perched on stools eating lunch. He passed the Sheriff's Department's evidence lab, where Deputy John Cavanaugh fired at the gunman from a doorway and missed. Depu-ties Louis Molnar and John Van Dinter also had heard the shots from inside their office.

The coroner's office was a frequent gathering place for police offic-ers, judges and reporters. Chamberlain, coroner for two decades, always had an opinion or a joke to share. Chamberlain was a Democrat who had campaigned with John F. Kennedy. The owner of an East Side tavern and restaurant, he once planned to make a six-hundred-pound, sixty-foot-long sandwich that he hoped would go into the *Guinness Book of World Records*.

On this day, Dr. Billy Bauman, a pathologist who often conducted autopsies, was eating lunch with Chamberlain and his staff.

"Frankly it didn't strike me that this was a dangerous situation until I looked at his face," Bauman later told the *Wisconsin State Journal*. "And I saw his eyes and how they looked, a look of tremendous anger, hostility."

Chamberlain watched as Lindh came in, pointing the gun at him. He told the young man to put the gun down, that it wouldn't solve anything. As he rose out of his chair, Lindh fired again, fatally wounding

Wisconsin State Journal file photo

Over a thousand people gathered at Clyde "Bud" Chamberlain's funeral.

Chamberlain in the neck.

Secretary Evelyn Jones dived under her desk while, outside the door, Molnar and Van Dinter waited with their guns drawn. Molnar crept over to a wall adjacent to the coroner's office. When Lindh emerged, Molnar pointed his gun at Lindh and ordered him to surrender.

"Drop the gun, stay where you are," Molnar said. "I am a police officer."

At that time, Molnar later said he didn't know that Chamberlain was dying on the floor of the coroner's office.

"I'm going to kill you," Lindh said defiantly. "I'm going to kill everybody and I don't care if you kill me."

Molnar ran down the hallway, where a few remaining members of the stunned lunch crowd were watching the scene. He ordered them to hit the floor, then ducked into the coffee shop.

"Stop where you are," Molnar told the gunman. But Lindh kept coming, aiming his weapon at Molnar and the coffee shop patrons.

"If you don't stop, I'm going to shoot you," Molnar warned again. Lindh wouldn't stop or drop the gun.

Molnar's gun was aimed at Lindh's chest and a flick of the trigger would end the young man's life. But Molnar lowered his gun and

Wisconsin State Journal file photo
Aaron Lindh

fired, wounding Lindh in the stomach. Lindh crumpled to the floor and dropped the shotgun.

"I've always hoped I could get through my career without shooting anybody," Molnar said. "It happened so fast, it was the longest three minutes of my life."

More than a thousand people gathered for Chamberlain's funeral at St. Bernard's Catholic Church in the East Side neighborhood where he lived and ran his tavern. The funeral was attended by state, city and county officials, a police honor guard and judges.

"Who can forget this man who wore the coroner's hat and always dealt with death but ministered to the living?" asked the Rev. John Hebl, who gave the eulogy.

At Lindh's trial in September, defense attorneys Robert Burke and Ann Davey presented no witnesses during the guilt phase of the trial. The jury deliberated for about one-and-a-half hours before finding Lindh guilty of two counts of first-degree murder.

During the second phase, several psychiatrists who had examined Lindh testified. Among them was Dr. Leigh Roberts, a veteran forensic psychiatrist who had testified in many criminal cases. Burke and Davey presented a history of Lindh's troubled childhood with his adoptive family. They argued that he was driven insane by internal rage that had been building for years.

Molnar, a deputy for seventeen years, retired after the department fought his disability claim. He suffered alcohol problems and recurring nightmares after the incident. He also was second-guessed by people who thought he should have killed Lindh.

A few months after the trial, Roberts was stripped of his medical license after it was discovered he had sex with a patient. That provided a basis for an appeal of Lindh's conviction — that Roberts never should have been permitted to testify in the case because of the pending charges against him.

In 1996, the Wisconsin Supreme Court refused to grant Lindh a new trial. But in June 1997, the U.S. Supreme Court ruled that Lindh could pursue his appeal in federal court and that the Anti-terrorism and Death Penalty Act of 1996 did not retroactively end his rights.

Now, close to age 30, he is serving his life sentence at the Green Bay Correctional Institution. In 1993, he was among the inmates participating in an open records scheme to collect penalties from public officials. He asked sheriffs to provide home addresses and phone numbers of all deputies, traffic reports and listings of all illegal drugs seized during a particular time period. If the documents weren't provided, the inmates sought to collect penalties.

The murders of Townsend and Chamberlain prompted security improvements at Madison's City-County Building. Clerks now meet the public behind protective glass shields. Circuit judges and others also cite the case as a reason to build a new courthouse with improved security such as separate hallways for jurors and jail inmates.

Two granite benches memorialized Townsend and Chamberlain were placed at the east entrance to the City-County Building and a watercolor painting titled "Sunlit Lilies" by Mount Horeb artist Peggy Zulucha was displayed in the building's basement a few feet from the coffee shop where Molnar stopped Aaron Lindh's rampage.

41

Their Last Dance

Concord, 1980

It's likely that Timothy Hack and Kelly Drew, both nineteen, thought about getting married themselves someday as they attended another couple's wedding dance on August 9, 1980, at the Concord Recreation Center in the Jefferson County hamlet of Concord, just off Interstate 94.

The groom had competed against Hack in tractor-pulling contests and the attractive Fort Atkinson couple had been dating several years, starting in high school. Kelly graduated from the Janesville Academy of Beauty Culture two months earlier and was working at Brothers II styling salon in Fort Atkinson. She also worked part-time at a Dairy Queen restaurant. Tim, a champion in tractor-pulling contests, worked on the family farm near Hebron. Both were religious and Drew had taught Sunday school as a child to younger children on her block.

There was a slim possibility that they'd eloped when Hack failed to show up for Mass the following day at St. Joseph's Catholic Church. If that hope ever existed, however, it soon was dashed when Hack's car with his wallet containing sixty-five dollars in cash and his checkbook locked inside were found outside the dance hall, where they were last seen leaving the reception about 11:00 p.m. to head for a party.

"Kelly didn't have but maybe fifteen dollars with her," said her mother, Mrs. Gerald Walker. "They just didn't have enough money with them to buy a ticket or run away, and, besides that, they wouldn't."

The families of the missing couple recruited about a hundred volunteers to comb the rural area near Concord. The Jefferson County

Sheriff's Department also launched an intense search. They checked campsites and waded through marshland but found no sign of the missing couple. They questioned about seven hundred people who had attended two wedding dances that night at the recreation center. A reward fund of two thousand dollars was established for information regarding the whereabouts of the popular couple and, two weeks later, the reward had climbed to ten thousand dollars.

"We have suspected foul play since this started," said David Hack, Timothy's dad. He was right.

Wisconsin Gov. Lee Dreyfus called Hack and offered the assistance of state investigators in the search. When the couple had been missing for eleven days, the FBI got involved. Wisconsin National Guard planes using infrared tracking equipment failed to locate the bodies of the missing couple.

The case turned more ominous when investigators found Kelly Drew's purse and clothing scattered along a rural road between Concord and Farmington. "I guess we are starting to think the worst," said Jefferson County Sheriff Keith Mueller.

Young people in Fort Atkinson were terrified by the disappearance of Hack and Drew. They began dating in groups so they would feel more secure. They were reminded of the mysterious disappearance of seventeen-year-old Catherine Sjoberg of Oconomowoc, six years earlier during a prom party at the same dance hall. She has never been found.

Wisconsin State Journal file photo

The parents of Timothy Hack, David Hack, from left, and his wife, Pat, join the parents of Kelly Drew, Norma and Gerald Walker, in presenting a poster they hoped would locate their teenagers.

"Every time the phone rings I just about jump out of my skin," said David Hack. "I'd hope they were safe, of course. But the next choice would be to find their bodies rather than not finding them at all."

On October 19, Harmon Banks and Willie McClendon, both of Milwaukee, were hunting squirrels along Hutisford Road near Ixonia when they went into the woods on the Donald Schmidt farm. They spotted the nude, decomposing body of a young woman. The body was identified through dental records as Kelly Drew. The following morning, state agents searching the area found Hack's body in a cornfield about a hundred feet north of where Drew was found.

Schmidt had harvested corn a week earlier and apparently ran over Hack's body without spotting it. Jefferson County Coroner Ewald Reichert said both bodies were so badly decomposed that it would be difficult to determine how they died. Authorities theorized that Kelly Drew was sexually assaulted but an autopsy failed to confirm it.

Investigators focused on similar cases, hoping to find a connection to the Jefferson County murders. They questioned Michael Crabtree of Marengo, Illinois, who was convicted of the murder of Mary Kathleen Thomas, a University of Wisconsin-Whitewater student. They quizzed Daniel Lenz, who was arrested for the murder of Connie Scott, age twenty-eight, of McFarland. They checked Jon Simonis, the "ski-mask rapist" from Louisiana, who admitted raping over a hundred women in ten states including Wisconsin.

Two years passed but investigators seemed no closer to finding the killer. In August 1983, the former wife of a convicted child molester showed investigators maps with a small red devil drawn in the margin. The devil's tail supposedly pointed to the location where the bodies of Hack and Drew were found.

The woman said her former husband participated in black masses and witchcraft. Besides Hack and Drew, she said the cult was responsible for the drowning death of two-year-old Michelle Manders of Watertown, in 1981, as well as the 1979 murder of Jay Kelly Flom of Milwaukee, and the 1974 disappearance of Catherine Sjoberg.

The satanic cult theory, publicized by Milwaukee private detective Norbert Kurczewski, quickly was unraveled by investigators. The map had no devil drawing but had penciled circles which they believed were the locations of jobs where the woman's ex-husband had worked as a painter. The death of Michelle Manders had been ruled an accident.

On the theory that strangers abducted the couple, detectives continued to question killers and rapist arrested in other cases. When Henry Lee Lucas confessed to 360 murders, Jefferson County investigators went to question him but the serial killer was ruled out. They also questioned Norman Freitag, a Viroqua truck driver who confessed to two murders, one in Pennsylvania and one in Alabama; Alvin Taylor, a nightclub singer who admitted killings in central Wisconsin; Roger Lange, convicted of killing Paula McCormick in Madison; Ralph Armstrong, convicted of killing University of Wisconsin student Charise Kamps in Madison; and Hector Reuben Sanchez and Warren Peters of Zion, Illinois, convicted of the 1984 murder of a Waukegan, Illinois woman.

The Sanchez-Peters case was strikingly similar to the Hack and Drew murders. Sanchez and Peters shot the Waukegan woman's male companion, dragged her from a parking lot, raped and murdered her and later dumped her body in Wisconsin. But detectives couldn't prove the two men had been in Jefferson County.

When he retired in 1990, Sheriff Keith Mueller said he believed that more than one person had murdered Drew and Hack.

"The only way this thing will be solved now is for someone who participated in the killings, or who knows who did them, to break down and confess," he said. "After all this time, we need that kind of break to solve it."

Although the killer's trail has grown cold, Drew and Hack haven't been forgotten in Jefferson County. Scholarships were established the year after their disappearance — the Kelly Drew Beauty Culture Scholarship and the Tim Hack Agricultural Award.

In 1995, Hack's relatives and friends restored the Lonesome Loser, a Case 1070 tractor than won him trophies before he was murdered. Hack had named his tractor after a hit song from the late 1970s by the Little River Band. It survived a 1992 barn fire because it had been moved out a week earlier to make room for something else.

The Lonesome Loser took two first place finishes and one second place in its return to the tractor-pulling circuit.

"Every time I get on that tractor, I think of Tim," said Patrick Hack, who was sixteen when his older brother was killed. "I think he'd be proud of us."

42

Breaking the Family Circle
Green Bay, 1963

Jack Hebard would talk about growing up in Hollywood, California, telling stories about his early fascination with movie stunts that later evolved into his own antics.

In 1942, at age seventeen, he said he drove racing cars for wealthy sportsmen and lived near a movie stunt lot in Santa Monica. He joined a traveling show, performing a dangerous act with dynamite. He'd imprison himself in a breakway box. Clad in protective clothes and a helmet, Hebard would set off dynamite in the box, smashing it to bits and knocking himself into near-unconsciousness.

"When I was a kid," Hebard later told *Green Bay Press-Gazette* reporter Charles House, "I kind of hooked up with a daredevil outfit and I changed my name to Lucky O'Hara because I didn't want my mother to read that her son was in that kind of dangerous business. I always told her I worked as a mechanic. I always loved the feeling of seeming to be reckless and I liked the excitement and the travel and I liked the crowds, too."

It was ironic, then, that Hebard didn't meet his end by packing too much dynamite in the breakway box or in a fiery stunt-car crash. He was sleeping peacefully on the couch in his Green Bay home when he was shot to death by his son, Harry, who on February 18, 1963, also killed his stepmother and her three children in the worst crime in the city's history.

Whether Jack Hebard's wild exploits in California were true is questionable because court records tell a different tale. They portray Hebard

The Hebard family with Butch at top left.

as a chronic womanizer who married four times and had a series of minor scrapes with the law. When Hebard claimed he was driving stunt cars in California, the records show he was sentenced to prison in Wisconsin by a Dane County court on an auto theft conviction. He was paroled twenty-one months later and married his first wife, Blanche, in December 1945, at La Crosse.

Their son, Harry, was born the following year. But three months after the marriage, Hebard's parole was revoked when it was learned he had lied about his age on the marriage license application. He later was released from prison and divorced by Blanche in November 1947. She charged him with cruel and inhumane treatment, claiming he refused to work and squandered seven thousand dollars on liquor consumed entertaining his friends and other women. A month after the divorce, Hebard was back in jail on a charge of cohabitation with another woman but the charge later was dropped. In August 1948, he was ordered to spend two months in jail for failure to pay the twenty dollars divorce court costs. He later paid the bill and that charge also was dropped.

Perhaps it was Hebard's Wisconsin woes that prompted him to move across the Mississippi River to Minnesota, where he married his second wife in September 1948. Young Harry was left in the custody of Blanche, who later married a television repairman, Frederick Voss. But Hebard's luck was no better in Minnesota. He spent ten days in jail on a license plate violation. He was ordered to leave Princeton, Minnesota, in April, 1949, on a vagrancy charge and, three months later, he was arrested again in Princeton for reckless driving.

He served sixty days in the county workhouse and, just fifteen months after his second marriage, Hebard was divorced again.

On Nov. 3, 1950, Hebard was sentenced to five years in the Minnesota state prison for knocking down a St. Paul woman and kicking her in the head. He was paroled in December 1953, after serving two years, and took his third wife, a Wisconsin Rapids woman, a year later. This time, Hebard thought the marriage would last and in 1955, when Harry was nine, he petitioned for custody of his son and the action wasn't challenged by the boy's mother. Hebard claimed that Butch, which had become the boy's nickname, was neglected and mistreated by his mother and stepfather. In a letter to his attorney on March 29, 1955, Hebard wrote that the boy was adjusting well to his new home:

"Butch is content, very much at home and fond of his new friends and school already. He has remarked that he'd like to stay with us for good and just visit his mother once in a while. He mentioned that his stepdad was often mean to him and he was hungry often. I spent two hours each night the first two nights scrubbing him. Hands, knees and feet were black and practically grown in with caked dirt. Feet were also raw from the condition of his shoes."

Hebard said he planned to buy a house and was making his son feel that he had a big part in the decision. But the seemingly happy home life didn't last and, in less than a year, Hebard was divorced a third time. He and his son lived alone until 1957, when he married his fourth wife, Joyce Rudell, and moved to Green Bay. Rudell's first husband, Norman, had died when the family lived in Wausau, leaving twin daughters and a son. And so, Hebard and his latest wife settled with their four children into a white, remodeled farmhouse on two acres at 2636 Hazelwood Lane on Green Bay's southwest side. Hebard managed to conceal his criminal record and got a job with North Central Airlines as a ground serviceman. He was promoted to senior agent in November 1960.

Teachers considered Butch Hebard an average student at West High School. He played on the junior varsity football team and was a member of the church club and choir. He had organized and captained a neighborhood pickup football team but his main sport was track. Coach Mike Power said Butch mixed well with his track teammates and that an ankle injury one season seemed only to spur him on to run harder. Algebra teacher Nina McCandless said Butch was "kind of dreamy. He always appeared to be off somewhere. I said had a lot of trouble getting next to Harry but then a lot of people had the same trouble." He carried a C

average and planned to become an architect someday. Principal George
Dauplaise said Butch never had been to his office for any discipline problems.

During the early weeks of 1963, when Butch was a junior, his family life began to sour. His work fell off at school and he seemed to have
trouble getting along with his stepmother. His parents took him to a
psychiatrist for an initial interview in early February and a followup appointment was scheduled for February 20. Butch told his friend, Norbert
Hanson, that he wanted to run away from home. On Monday morning,
February 18, Butch called Hanson at the Carver Boat Co. in Pulaski
where Hanson worked. Butch asked his friend to pick him up at home
about 5:30 p.m. that day and Hanson agreed. Butch's drafting teacher
said the boy seemed distracted and preoccupied in class before he skipped
out of school at noon.

Later that afternoon, Jack Hebard dozed on the couch while, in the
kitchen, dinner cooked on the stove. One of the twins, Judy, age eleven,
was watching television from a chair in the corner while Janice tended a
boiling pan of potatoes and the pot roast in the oven. Fifteen-year-old
John Rudell had kicked off his shoes and also lounged in the kitchen
waiting for dinner. A loaf of bread had been opened on the kitchen
counter. And Butch, as usual, was in trouble with his stepmother.

He wouldn't be allowed to eat with the family that night for although six chairs surrounded the table, only five places had been set.
Butch was frustrated with his family and somehow running away wasn't
enough. He decided to kill them all. He took a .22-caliber pistol and a
rifle from his father's gun collection in the basement. He went into the
living room and placed the pistol close to Jack Hebard's forehead, firing
once. Then he went to the kitchen, firing wildly at the twins and his
stepbrother. Judy fell from the chair while Janice collapsed under the
table. John's knees buckled as a bullet slammed into his body and he also
fell to the floor. All had been fatally wounded. Unaware of the bloody
scene inside, Butch's stepmother came through the back door a few minutes later, carrying a bag of groceries. In horror, she saw the bodies of her
children lying on the floor in pools of blood.

She set the groceries down on a kitchen stool and then Butch shot
and killed her, too.

After the shootings, Butch changed his clothes. He wrapped the
old clothes with the pistol into a bundle and hid the rifle in the basement.
Then he walked up the street to the corner where he'd arranged for Hanson
to pick him up. The two boys drove to Pulaski, cruising the streets until
about 11:00 p.m. Hanson drove to the John Pienta farm and talked Pienta,
the father of a friend of his, into putting up Butch for the night. Pienta
gave Butch a blanket and said he could sleep on the couch.

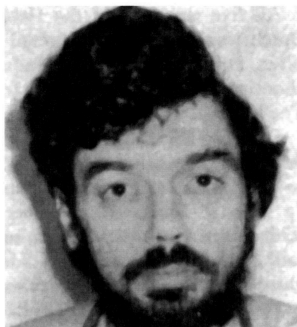

Harry "Butch" Hebard

In the morning, Darold Aebescher was on the way to work about 5:30 a.m. when he glanced at the Hebard home as he drove by. Aebescher, a ground serviceman for North Central Airlines, often looked at the Hebard house in the morning to see if his friend, Jack, was up. On this morning, Aebescher noticed that quite a few lights were on. When Hebard hadn't shown up for work at Austin Straubel Field about twenty minutes later, Aebescher got a little worried and called his wife. Mrs. Aebescher called the Hebard home but got no answer, so Aebescher phoned the police.

When detectives Dale Herfort and Robert Basche arrived at the Hebard home about 7:00 a.m., they noticed two cars were parked in the driveway. They knocked several times on the front door, painted blood-red, but got no answer, so they walked around to the back. Through a window, the detectives spotted the bodies on the kitchen floor. Mrs. Hebard's body lay on the floor next to her son, both in pools of blood. Empty .22-caliber shell casings were scattered around the kitchen among the four bodies. Powder burns on Jack Hebard's face indicated he had been shot at close range. The food that was to provide dinner for the family had cooked all night so that the potatoes were black lumps and the roast was charred. The detectives searched upstairs and found a list of preparations for running away from home hidden in an old pair of pants in Butch's room. A similar list was found in the boy's school locker. On the list in his room, police found the name of Norbert Hanson.

When Hanson was questioned by police, he was evasive at first about Butch's whereabouts. He said he hadn't seen his friend since Valentine's Day. But when the detectives told him about the murders, Hanson suddenly decided to cooperate.

"I thought I was just helping my buddy run away from home," he said. "I didn't know about any killings."

When Butch woke up that Tuesday morning, John Pienta asked if he wanted a cup of coffee. Butch said no so Pienta left for his job at a wood lot and his son also went to work, leaving their guest alone in the house. Butch lounged around the farmhouse until noon, until his friend Hanson knocked at the door. Hanson told Butch he wanted to talk to him about something so they walked out to Hanson's car. Butch got in the passenger side.

Suddenly, Green Bay Police Sgt. Richard Schrickel popped up from the back seat and told Butch he was under arrest.

"Don't worry, I'll explain later," Hanson said apologetically as Butch was taken away. The boy offered no resistance. Eight Brown County squad cars had been dispatched to stand by at the farmhouse along with the Pulaski village marshal and city police officers. Tear gas also was taken to the scene in case it was necessary to smoke out the killer.

Juvenile jurisdiction was waived in the case and Butch was taken to the Brown County Jail. The *Green Bay Press-Gazette* called the murders the worst crime in the city's history. Green Bay's only triple slaying had occurred three years earlier, on September 21, 1960, when Lawrence Ferry shot three people in a tavern and then died when his gun went off accidentally. Never had five people been murdered all at once.

The murders shocked neighbors who knew the family. One said Butch was a moody boy, kind of quiet and sometimes in trouble with the police. He didn't get along with his stepbrother but he liked the twins.

"The Hebards were nice folks, real nice, and I never heard any quarrels in the house except maybe between John and Harry, but it didn't ever seem as serious as this."

On February 20, the day he was supposed to have his second session with the psychiatrist, Butch was charged with four counts of first-degree murder. District Attorney Robert Warren held one charge in abeyance so if the killer somehow was found innocent of the first four counts, he could be tried again.

As Judge James Byers read each charge, he asked Butch if he understood them. "Yes," Butch answered each time in a husky voice. For the court appearance, Butch wore a car coat and light-blue coveralls furnished by the county. He wore no socks and the laces had been removed from his pigskin shoes — a protective measure against suicide. Robert J. Parins, a former Brown County district attorney, was appointed as the boy's public defender.

All five members of the Hebard family were buried February 23 at Mosinee. Butch was told he could attend the funeral under guard but he declined the offer. Police Chief Elmer Madsen said the boy "expressed remorse for the shooting of his father but none for the slayings of other members of the family. The boy felt he was left out of the family circle."

Two days later, Judge Byers ordered two psychiatrists to examine Butch to determine his sanity. On March 13, the boy was judged insane and committed to Central State Hospital at Waupun. The psychiatrists said he suffered from "a mental illness of a severe degree more particularly diagnosed as schizophrenic reaction." Byers ruled he was incompetent to stand trial. Parins said he was convinced Butch didn't know what he was doing at the time of the murders and still didn't realize what he had done.

Four years later, in 1967, Butch Hebard was declared sane and was convicted of the brutal slayings. He's still serving his prison sentence at Kettle Morraine state prison.

43

Tragedy at Taliesin

Spring Green, 1914

On August 15, 1914, newspaper headlines blared about impending war in Europe. The murder of the Serbian Archduke Ferdinand had solidified the battle lines and, now, Italy and Japan were threatening to join the fray.

In Spring Green, Wisconsin, Julian Carlton had troubles of his own. The night before, he had been fired as a cook at Taliesin, the hillside home of renowned architect Frank Lloyd Wright. The reason for Carlton's dismissal wasn't clear but he apparently had been given notice and he certainly wasn't happy about it. The architect himself was in Chicago supervising construction of the Midway Gardens. But as Carlton prepared what would be his last lunch for members of the Taliesin household, he mulled over a plan of revenge.

The Taliesin household, including Wright's mistress, Mamah Borthwick, and her two children plus architects and groundskeepers, gathered in the dining room that day as usual to sample Carlton's meal. This time, however, he had a surprise in store for them. First, he blocked all entrances but one. Then he grabbed a container of gasoline and poured some on Tom Blunkert as he sat at the table. Carlton may have been jealous that Blunkert, a laborer, was permitted to dine with Mamah and her guests.

Blunkert jumped up and the other diners were startled but, before they could react, Carlton had poured more gasoline on the carpet and struck a match, igniting Blunkert and the carpet in a wall of flames.

As flames and smoke engulfed the dining room, the panicked diners got up to flee. They found the doors blocked and began to flee through an unlocked window.

Outside that window, Carlton awaited with a shingler's hatchet held high. As the diners came out to flee the blaze, he swung the axe, trying to kill them one by one. When the slaughter was finished, Carlton decided to take his own life. He swallowed muriatic acid, burning his throat, then fled to the boiler room, where he hoped to burn up in the fire.

In the fields near the Taliesin estate, farm hands operated their threshing machines. They spotted the blaze and rushed to Wright's home, forming a bucket brigade to douse the fire. Outside the dining room, they discovered eight victims of Carlton's wrath.

Mamah Borthwick crawled several feet before she collapsed and died. Borthwick's nine-year-old daughter, Martha Cheney, was rushed to the home of Andrew Porters a half mile away, where she died a few hours later. Emil Brodelle, a draftsman from Chicago, died instantly from Carlton's blows with the hatchet. Also killed were Borthwick's twelve-year-old son, John, and fifteen-year-old Ernest Weston, son of William Weston, a construction foreman at Taliesin.

William Weston suffered hatchet wounds on his head but survived only because he stumbled while coming out the door and caught only a glancing blow from Carlton's weapon. Carlton split open the head of Blunkert, who died a few days later. Herbert Fritz, a draftsman, suffered burns but survived. David Lindbloom, the gardener, was not so lucky. He would die of severe burns several days later, becoming the seventh victim of Carlton's rage.

Within hours of the attack, Wright received a strange telegram in Chicago. "Come as quickly as you possibly can," the telegram read. "Something terrible has happened." The telegram was signed by Mamah Borthwick. It remains a mystery to this day whether Mamah had a premonition, sending the telegram before she died, or, more likely, whether someone signed her name to it.

When Wright received word that Mamah had been brutally murdered, he collapsed. "I can't believe it!" he said upon regaining consciousness. "It's too horrible! She was a good woman, the best on earth. She stood everything so bravely."

Newspaper headlines trumpeted that Borthwick, Wright's adulterous lover, had been murdered at their "love castle" or "love bungalow," as Taliesin had come to be known.

"The insane act of a negro cook today ended the strange romance of Frank Lloyd Wright, Chicago architect of worldwide fame and staunch advocate of free love," said the *Wisconsin State Journal* in a front-page story.

The romance of Wright and Mamah Borthwick made headlines a few years earlier when the lovers spirited off to Europe, abandoning their respective families. Wright left his wife, Catherine, and six children while Borthwick deserted her husband, Edward Cheney, and two children.

When the couple returned, Wright appeared to patch up the differences with his wife while Mrs. Cheney filed for divorce. Then, Wright and Mrs. Cheney disappeared again. He brought her to Wisconsin and they settled in at Taliesin. He had met Mamah Borthwick Cheney in Oak Park, Illinois, when he was commissioned by her husband to design a house for them.

Now, his beloved Mamah was dead and Wright rushed to catch the next train to Wisconsin. At the station, he met the spurned husband, Edward Cheney, and the two men rode together.

Meanwhile, the killer Carlton remained in hiding. The muriatic acid burned his throat but didn't cause his death as he had hoped. And the fire, which caused extensive damage, was extinguished. Several hours later, a weary Carlton opened the boiler room door and fell out of his hiding place into the hands of Iowa County deputies. Had he been spotted earlier by neighbors fighting the fire, Carlton almost surely would have been lynched. Instead, he was rushed to the Iowa County jail, where he was unable to eat for several days due to the burns to his throat.

"It was self-defense," Carlton claimed. "They were all picking on me and I had to fight for my life. I took the acid and tried to burn myself up in the furnace." His wife, who lived with him at Taliesin, fled when her husband began his murder spree and vowed to divorce him afterward. She told officials he had no history of drug use.

Thunder clapped as a rainstorm blew through Spring Green the next night — a Sunday — when Mamah was buried on the Wright family plot near Taliesin in a simple pine casket.

"The hour was hers," said a story in the *State Journal.* "The sermon was his. It was their last together."

Except for a single, simple pledge, Wright was quiet and contemplative during the funeral. "We will rebuild that which is home to me," he said. Within two days, the debris had been cleared away and construction began on a new Taliesin — a memorial to Mamah.

In the Iowa County jail, Carlton still wasn't eating. He would die a few weeks later from the lingering effects of muriatic acid. He would never go to trial and his crazed attack on Mamah and the others at Taliesin never would be fully explained. Some people would say that Carlton was influenced by an evangelical minister to take action against Wright's immorality but that seems unlikely, since the architect was out of town at the time of the attack.

The following week, Wright wrote a moving and lengthy tribute to

Mamah, defending their adulterous affair in the *Wisconsin State Journal.*

"I would very much like to defend a brave and lovely woman from the pestilential torch of stories made by the press for the man in the street," he wrote.

"We have lived frankly and sincerely as we believed and we have tried to help others to live their lives according to their ideals.

"Only true love is free love — no other kind is or ever can be free. The freedom in which we joined was infinitely more difficult than any conforming with customs would have been. Few will ever venture it.

Wisconsin State Journal archives
Frank Lloyd Wright

"She was struck down by a tragedy that hangs by the slender thread of reason over the lives of all, a thread which may snap at any time in any home with consequences as disastrous."

His essay ended by repeating his pledge to rebuild: "My home will still be there."

Several months after the tragedy, Wright received a condolence letter from Miriam Noel, whom he described as an "understanding stranger." A noted Parisian sculptress, she soon provided more than solace to the famous architect. She moved in with him at Taliesin and they traveled together to the Orient. But Wright remained married to Catherine, who refused to grant him a divorce.

Finally, a decade after the fatal fire that killed Mamah Borthwick, Wright won his divorce from Catherine. He and Miriam were married in a romantic ceremony at midnight on a bridge across the Wisconsin River.

But Miriam proved far less understanding than Wright imagined when the architect wanted to resume his philandering ways. In the mid-1920s, he took up with a Montenegran dancer, Olga Milanoff, and wanted to end the marriage, but Miriam fought back.

Exiled from her former home, Miriam sent deputies and process servers to Taliesin but they were met by Wright's own armed guards. She even tried herself to gain access to the estate but was rebuffed. Later, she had the architect arrested in Minneapolis on a bogus violation of the

Mann Act, an archaic law that prohibited sexual relations between un-married people.

Perhaps the tragedy that summer of 1914 at Taliesin bound Wright ever more strongly to Wisconsin. If the murders and destruction hadn't occurred, he and Mamah may have moved on. Instead, he did rebuild Taliesin as a memorial to his lost lover and rebuilt the original "love bungalow" again after a second fire damaged it in 1925. The Wright home in Spring Green ensured that his designs would have a lasting influence in Wisconsin and throughout the world. In July 1997, the Monona Terrace Community and Convention Center, the latest building based on a Wright design, opened in Madison.

44

Serial Killer on the Loose
Wisconsin Dells, 1987

A serial killer is on the loose. That was the terrifying thought of many people in central Wisconsin during the violent summer of 1987. During less than two months, seven girls and women were brutally murdered throughout the state and their bodies were dumped in rural areas.

• June 15: Angela Hackl, age eighteen, was found shot to death in a wooded area near Sauk City.

• July 4: The nude body of Tara Kassens, age fourteen, of Cedarburg, was found under some bushes in Mequon.

• July 5: Helen Kunz, age seventy, of Athens, was missing after four relatives were found shot to death at the family's farmhouse.

• July 9: Barbara Blackstone, age thirty, a business education teacher, was abducted July 9 while mowing the lawn at her rural Lyndon Station home in Juneau County.

• July 10: Tammy Lynn Maciulis, age eleven, disappeared from her Marinette home.

• July 28: Linda Nachreiner, age twenty-nine, of Dell Prairie, was shot once in the head and her raped and tortured body was found tied to a tree about five miles southwest of her Adams County home.

• Aug. 4: Sandra Lison, age forty-four, a Green Bay bartender, was found dead in an Oconto County forest.

These cases were startling both because of the number and the fact that they shattered the peaceful lifestyles of rural residents. Three of these cases — Hackl, Blackstone and Nachreiner — particularly upset people

in central Wisconsin because they were close together in the tourist-fo-
cused three-county area of Sauk, Juneau and Adams, not far from Wisconsin Dells.

Angela Hackl was a fun-loving young woman with flowing blonde
hair who enjoyed swimming and riding her bicycle up and down the
streets of Lone Rock. She lived with her family in a green, ranch-style
house at the west end of town. Two weeks before her murder, she crossed
the stage at River Valley High School in Spring Green to receive her di-
ploma.

Wisconsin State Journal file photo

Angela Hackl

She went with friends on June
11 to watch a ball game in Spring
Green. Later, they stopped at
Hondo's, a Sauk City tavern, where
she was seen leaving with a man in
his twenties. Her body was found
four days later.

Blackstone was a tall, popular
teacher at New Lisbon High School.
She and her husband, Tom, had
built their isolated home themselves.
Her family said she didn't frequent
taverns, flirt with men or take drugs.

She was mowing the huge ex-
panse of lawn near her rural home
for a family picnic. She went to buy
gasoline from a service station near Interstate 90-94 in Lyndon Station,
then apparently returned home. Her car was found near a metal shed
with her keys and purse still in it and the gas can in the trunk.

"The worst part of the whole thing is just sitting here waiting," said
Herbert Fisher, Blackstone's wheelchair-bound father. "Maybe she's lying out in the woods dead or something."

Fisher's words were prophetic for Barbara Blackstone's decomposed
body was found August 5 near Blanchardville in Lafayette County, not
far from Argyle, where she grew up.

Linda Nachreiner was a young mother of two who, like Blackstone,
enjoyed the seclusion of her family's rural Adams County home not far
from Wisconsin Dells. She grew up not far from the brown split-level
home off a county highway.

On July 29, she took a load of clothes out of the washing machine,
poured a cup of coffee and disappeared. The basket of wet clothes and full
cup of coffee were found in her home. Her body was found a day later in
a wooded area about four miles from her home and ten miles from Wis-

consin Dells. Local residents called the lane Beer Can Alley because it frequently was used by teenagers for drinking parties.

Gun sales escalated in central Wisconsin after the murders of Hackl, Blackstone and Nachnreiner. Residents were sure a lone serial killer was stalking the countryside, preying on isolated and vulnerable women.

Pathologists compared the autopsy results of the three victims and noted similarities in the way they died. Blackstone and Nachreiner were about the same age. Both were abducted while working at home and both bodies were found dumped in wooded areas. Both Hackl and Nachreiner were found tied to trees.

Authorities had difficulty determining a cause of death for Blackstone because her nude, decomposed body was found nearly a month after her disappearance and had deteriorated in the summer heat.

The Milwaukee chapter of the Guardian Angels, a vigilante group that formed in New York City protecting people on subways, offered volunteers to help search for the killer. Curt Silwa, the group's founder and national president, came to Wisconsin Dells, where he held seminars for local residents on how to handle a gun.

As August wound down, however, investigators were finding more differences than similarities in the homicides. They had begun to believe that three killers, not one, were on the loose.

The first break occurred in the Nachreiner case when Kim Brown, a rural Adams County dump truck driver, was questioned in early September about a burglary that occurred near the murdered woman's home several days before her body was found. During that break-in, the family dog was stabbed to death. Women's clothing was piled on the floor and furnishings were set on fire.

When officials searched Brown's car, they found a .357 magnum revolver in the

Wisconsin State Journal file photo
Reward poster made by Blackstone's family after her disappearance.

truck. The gun was identified as the gun that killed Nachreiner. Ballistics tests made a positive identification between the gun and a slug found beneath her body.

Brown, a quiet husky man viewed by local residents as just an ordinary guy, also apparently never took the snow tires off his 1975 Pontiac for the summer and the treads matched tracks found at the murder scene and the Nachreiner home.

Wisconsin State Journal file photo
Linda Nachreiner

The Nachreiner case terrified residents of Adams County. Although the county had several murders over the prior decade, the fact that she was a random victim was a loss of innocence and many people began locking their doors for the first time.

The Hackl case was more difficult but Terry Vollbrecht was charged with killing her in February 1989. Vollbrecht was an early suspect and was identified as the man who left the Sauk City bar with her on the night she disappeared.

"The arrest supports the contention of law enforcement all along that we were not looking for a serial killer," Attorney General Don Hanaway said.

He said the twenty-month delay in making the arrest was due to the difficulty in piecing together the circumstantial case. A pubic hair found in Hackl's car had similarities to a hair taken from Vollbrecht.

Vollbrecht told investigators he had left Hondo's Bar with a woman named Angie and they drove to a wooded area, where they had sex on a sleeping bag. But he denied killing the woman and suggested a satanic cult might be responsible for her death.

While he was getting a haircut about a week after the murder, Vollbrecht kept bringing up the murder to Sauk City barber Holly Setzke. "I didn't do it and if I did, I don't remember doing it," he said.

The specter of a serial killer was raised again in 1993 after two young women died in Sauk County under mysterious circumstances. The body of Irene Musch, a student at the University of Wisconsin-Baraboo, was found April 26 in a wooded area near the campus. In March 1990, the partially nude body of Sue McFadden was found in a pine woods near Mirror Lake.

Musch's death was ruled a suicide and an autopsy discovered drugs in her stomach. McFadden's death was ruled a drug overdose after she apparently plunged from a pine tree she had been climbing.

From his prison cell, Terry Volbrecht, who had exhausted all of his appeals, claimed the deaths of Musch and McFadden proved his innocence and that a serial killer remained on the loose. He said authorities failed to investigate two men in ski masks who were lurking in the area where Hackl dropped him off that night.

"I am presently incarcerated at the Columbia Correctional Institution going on my fifth year of illegal imprisonment because of ignorant jurors, a sheriff's department more interested in closing cases than it is in solving them and a court system that refuses to acknowledge the obvious fact that an innocent man has been sentenced to life in the state prison system," Volbrecht wrote in a letter published in the *Wisconsin State Journal.*

The Blackstone case was the toughest to crack and remains unsolved to this day. Her husband, Tom, was a suspect but had been working at his lawn service job the day she disappeared.

"I will probably be looking for Barbara Blackstone's killer until I retire," Lafayette County Detective Steve McQuaid said in 1993. "We haven't had any new leads in more than nine months and that wasn't a major one, but more of a crank call."

Blackstone's father, Herbert Fisher, said he believed money was the motive. He said his daughter had a certificate of deposit at an Argyle bank and she may have told her abductors about it, hoping to escape during the long drive from Lyndon Station.

"My idea of the whole thing is there's so many dopeheads out there, they saw that girl and thought there was a chance to get some money," he said.

Fisher remained obsessed and saddened about the murder until his death several years later. Tom Blackstone returned to Ohio, where he had grown up.

"I still miss her; I always will," Fisher said a year after that summer of terror. "It always seems like the good people get the dirty end of the stick."

The other cases also belied the serial killer theory. Charles "Scotty" Blasingame was convicted in Georgia and sentenced to life in prison for the murder of Tammy Lynn Maciulis. He claimed he accidentally ran her over with a car, panicked and buried her in Georgia. James Duquette Jr. was convicted of the murder and sexual assault of Tina Kassens. The Sandra Lison case remains Green Bay's only unsolved murder.

45

A Theological Murder
Onalaska, 1985

For Father John Rossiter, February 7, 1985, began as a typical day at St. Patrick's Roman Catholic Church in Onalaska, not far from La Crosse. Just before he celebrated a special Mass commemorating Catholic School Week, however, a man knocked at the sacristy door.

The man asked the priest about his plans to let two sixth-grade girls give the first and second scriptural readings at the Mass.

"On what authority do you do this?" the man wanted to know.

"The pope told me I can do that, and that is good enough for me."

The day before, Father Rossiter had noticed the man sitting strangely in a pew, praying with his head down below the pew in front of him. Doris Hammes, wife of custodian William Hammes, told Father Rossiter the man had serious mental problems.

"Can I help you?" the priest had asked.

"No," the man had replied.

A letter was received a few days earlier at the La Crosse Diocese from a man who called himself the prophet Elijah. The writer claimed he was "called by God to go to Israel to bomb one of the holy temples."

It's doubtful that Father Rossiter attached any special significance to these incidents as he finished the Mass, then hugged a few of the children before they went back to class and knelt near the altar to pray.

From behind, however, the man who called himself the prophet Elijah crept up behind the priest and killed him with a shotgun.

"Oh, my God, someone call 911," yelled lay minister Ferdinand

Roth, who was praying nearby. When Roth started to run, the assailant shot him, too, before going to the church basement and slaying Hammes. Three shotgun blasts, three people dead.

"Father Rossiter was lying in a pool of his own blood," said Sister Rose Frances Phalen, the elementary school principal. "Who would do something like that to three good people?"

That's exactly what many people in the quiet Mississippi River community of Onalaska wondered as they prepared for a triple funeral for three good, God-fearing people who had done no one any harm.

Tim Roth, a son of the slain lay minister, was taken out of class and told of his father's murder. Then Sister Rose went on the public address system: "A maniac came in the church this morning and did some shooting," she told the pupils. The church was desecrated by the murders and Bishop John Paul said a special rite would be conducted before any function could be performed.

Bryan Stanley, age twenty-nine, was captured by police a few blocks away, carrying a shotgun in a black case. He was charged with three counts of first-degree murder.

"I meant to kill them," he told a *La Crosse Tribune* reporter in a telephone interview. "I'm not crazy. The public thinks I'm crazy but I am not. I had a job to do and I did it well."

Stanley said he was a solider of Christ, serving the Lord by objecting to the participation of girls in the Mass. He said he was called by St. Patrick and the Virgin Mary to assassinate the priest, lay minister and custodian because they were "leading children into sin." He was called by the prophet Elijah the day before the shootings to pray for the children.

Stanley said he was shaken when Rossiter interrupted his prayer and later saw a vision on a newspaper while having coffee at a restaurant across the street.

"The Lord told me about this evil these people had, the devils or what they had, I don't know," Stanley said. He said he shouldn't be charged with murder because he was acting as a soldier.

More than two thousand mourners gathered to pay their respects to the three dead men during a two-hour service on February 11. The bishop asked the mourners to forgive Stanley "as Jesus taught us to forgive."

Father Bernard McGarty recalled all three victims as men who loved to laugh.

"Evil is the price we pay for the possibility of freedom," he said.

After Stanley's arrest, several other incidents came to light. A few weeks before the murders, police officers had found him in a parking lot at St. Francis Medical Center, staring at the sky, weaving back and forth and saying he was the prophet Elijah. The night before, police found him confused at a convenience store. The previous summer, he had attacked a

Michigan state trooper after the trooper refused to say he believed in Christ.

He was examined at Tomah Veterans Administration Medical Center and determined to need treatment but he never came back. At a March hearing on the murder charges, Stanley ranted for fifteen minutes in a speech that interspersed obscenities and biblical quotations. He was escorted from the court, shouting, "I curse all of you in the name of the Lord."

By the time of his preliminary hearing in June, however, Stanley had begun to recover with medication from the mental illness he claimed not to have. His attorney, La Crosse County Public Defender Michael Rosborough said Stanley no longer claimed he was the prophet Elijah and was competent to stand trial. Rosborough entered a plea on Stanley's behalf of innocent by reason of insanity.

Stanley pleaded guilty to the murders, waiving the evidentiary phase of the trial, but innocent due to insanity. Dr. Pauline Jackson, a psychiatrist at the Gunderson Clinic, said Stanley knew killing was wrong but thought he was operating under special dispensation from God.

Dr. Frederick Fosdal, a Madison forensic psychiatrist who has examined many murderers including Jeffrey Dahmer, said Stanley told him the Virgin Mary talked to him and that he respected Adolph Hitler for the dictator's attempts to rid the world of communism.

Circuit Judge Peter Pappas ruled that Stanley was legally insane and committed him to Mendota Mental Health Institute.

From the beginning, Stanley's mother, Mary, said

Wisconsin State Journal archives
Bryan Stanley at his first court appearance.

she hoped her son's case would prompt change in Wisconsin's mental commitment laws. If the laws had been written differently, she said, her son might have received treatment before the tragedy.

"People are crying out," she said. "There were just four wasted lives, that I can see."

Mary Stanley became active in the Alliance for the Mentally Ill and testified before the Legislature in support of law changes. A decade later, the Legislature enacted a law that would allow involuntary commitment of people who are deteriorating because of their refusal to take psychiatric medicine. But others argued the law could infringe on civil liberties.

Stanley sought release from Mendota three times. Turning forty in 1995, Stanley requested supervised release into the community that would allow him to live in a group home in Madison or Milwaukee. His attorney, Roger LeGrand, said he had made significant progress with an anti-psychotic drug.

But his release was strongly opposed by La Crosse County District Attorney Scott Horne and relatives of his victims.

Bryan Stanley, who murdered three good men in what he thought was a holy mission, may someday be released into the community. Like many psychotics, he may continue to lead a peaceful life if he continues taking his medication.

But many people in Onalaska will wonder whether his release is appropriate justice for his crime.

46
The Capital City Killings
Madison, 1968-82

The university area of Madison, like the city itself, has seemed safe and secure relative to other cities. Until recent years, both the city and the University of Wisconsin campus often exuded a youthful innocence largely unencumbered by violence, poverty and other pressing urban problems. Students often recall their college days of basking in the sun on the Memorial Union terrace or strolling up and down State Street on a warm spring day.

But over a period of fourteen years, a series of bizarre, brutal murders of young women terrorized the peaceful city. What made the slayings more terrifying was that all appeared to be random victims. From 1968 to 1982, seven women were the victims of one or more vicious killers. The victims had striking physical similarities. All were in their late teens or early twenties. All were reasonably attractive, wearing their hair shoulder-length. None of the murders has ever been solved.

The spree began on a spring day of May 1968, when the body of eighteen-year-old Christine Rothschild was found in a clump of bushes outside Sterling Hall, a physics and mathematics building on North Charter Street. Two years later, Sterling Hall would be bombed by anti-war protesters during the throes of Madison's protest era. But on this cool, cloudy day, Rothschild was viciously stabbed at least a dozen times. The clothed body was found early on a Sunday night, when a male student decided to peek in a window for a friend who worked in the building. Judging from the possible time of death, police theorized the young woman may have been attacked in broad daylight.

Besides the stab wounds, they later discovered she also had been strangled.

Christine Rothschild wore her sandy-colored hair long and straight in the style of the time. Students faced upcoming exams and the weather was rainy and muggy, not conducive to being outside. But Christine, who wanted to study journalism, enjoyed early morning walks. Her parents and three sisters lived on Chicago's North Side, where she graduated with honors from Senn High School, finishing with the fourth highest grade-point average in a class of 500 students. Housemothers and other students who lived with her at Ann Emery Hall described her as modest, studious and very attractive. The previous summer, she had worked as a fashion model in Chicago Loop department stores and looked forward that summer to going home again. Her father was president of a brokerage firm and of a company that sold coin-operated parking lot gates, which he invented during the 1950s.

In an editorial, the *Wisconsin State Journal* said the murder had "severely shaken" the peace of mind of many Madisonians.

"Many are saying it is inconceivable that such a despicable act could occur here," the newspaper said. "But it did."

While the community was shocked and outraged, police were baffled by the case. A five thousand dollar reward failed to unearth any significant new clues. A twenty-nine-year-old mental patient confessed to the killing but police discounted the confession after viewing his hospital records. Another man suspected of attacking three Carthage College students in Kenosha also was ruled out. During her walk early Sunday, Christine had stopped for breakfast with a man. She ordered a spinach salad. An FBI laboratory report absolved her breakfast companion as a suspect.

As the summer wore on, a doctor at University Hospital emerged as a possible suspect. Three local lawmen, Madison Detective Charles Lulling, Dane County Sheriff's Sgt. Richard Josephson and Chief Deputy Reynold Abrahams questioned the doctor in New York but his involvement in the case was inconclusive. Lulling and Josephson also worked with Michigan and Iowa campus police, who reported a total of six women slain in campus attacks.

Two years later, detectives again were dispatched to the East Coast to interrogate a graduate student who had worked in Sterling Hall at the time of the murder. Like the earlier leads in the case, that one also led nowhere. Police never found the knife, believed to be a double-edged surgical-type blade, used to stab Christine to death.

As the years passed without any new leads, the Rothschild case faded in the community's memory. It appeared to be an aberration, a unique case, unlikely to occur again. Until July 21, 1976. That's when the burned and partially decomposed body of Debra J. Bennett, age twenty, was found by farm land surveyors in a ditch along Old Sauk Pass Road. The road is about four miles west of Cross Plains, a village in western Dane County. Dr. Billy Bauman, who conducted the autopsy, said the woman probably had been dead about ten days. The body was identified through dental records and by a fractured collarbone.

Debra Bennett was last seen walking barefoot along Loftsgordon Avenue in Madison, leaving an apartment where she had been evicted. Her toenails were painted and she wore blue jeans, carrying a denim

jacket and a brown, shoulder-strap purse. She had rented a room at the Cardinal Hotel but never had the chance to move in. Three weeks after her body was found, the key to her rented room was mysteriously mailed to the hotel.

She was a native of Ridgeway in Iowa County who had lived in Madison about seven months. She was unemployed and her body was found a few days before her twenty-first birthday. Her death may have contributed to the death of her father, William R. Bennett, who died from

Wisconsin State Journal file photo

Julie Ann Hall

an illness a few days after Debra's body was found. A joint funeral for father and daughter was held in Dodgeville.

Like the Rothschild case, police had few leads to solve the murder of Debra Bennett. Two years later, on another summer day, the nude body of another young woman was found in a shallow grave along Woodland Road, just off Highway 12 west of Waunakee. She apparently had been killed by a blow from a blunt instrument. This time, it took two days to identify the body as Julie Ann Hall.

Eighteen-year-old Julie Ann Hall grew up in Fennimore. On May 1, 1978, she got a job as a library assistant at the Wisconsin History Society on the university campus. She was the daughter of Donne and Betty Hall who three years earlier had won $300,000 in the Illinois state lottery. The couple divorced in late 1977. Julie had seven brothers, one of whom shared an apartment with her in the Park Village Apartments on Madison's South Side. Coroner Clyde Chamberlain said Julie Hall probably was dead about three to five days before her body was found. She was last seen on a Friday night, when she went out drinking with friends. She had been drinking with a male friend at the Main King Tap east of Madison's Capitol Square.

Less than ten months later, another woman named Julie would disappear but the body of Julie Speerschneider, age twenty, wouldn't be discovered for two years. Julie Speerschneider left the 602 Club, a bar at 602 University Avenue, on the night of March 27, 1979, to go to a friend's house. She was wearing blue jeans, boots and a blue-and-gray striped Mexican poncho when she and a male companion hitchhiked along Johnson Street. The driver of a compact, white four-door car had

Wisconsin State Journal file photo
Julie Speerschneider

picked up the pair on State Street and left them off at Johnson and Brearly streets. Julie's hitchhiking companion never was identified.

At the time of her disappearance, she worked at the Red Caboose Day Care Center and Tony's Chop Suey Restaurant, where the owner described her as a good employee. Friends and relatives circulated her photograph, offered a $500 reward and consulted a psychic in efforts to locate the missing woman.

In April 1981, sixteen-year-old Charles Byrd of Stoughton, was hiking along the Yahara River on a Saturday afternoon when he came across a barely visible skeleton in an out-of-the-way clearing. The remains were those of Julie Speerschneider.

Before Julie Speerschneider's body was found, however, yet another woman would be snatched from Madison's peaceful streets and brutally murdered. Susan LeMahieu, a 1974 graduate of Madison's East High School, was mildly retarded and physically handicapped. In 1966, when she was age ten, two of her brothers died accidentally when they suffocated in an abandoned refrigerator in the basement of the family's home.

In April 1980, the body of LeMahieu, age twenty-four, was found in dense brush of a marsh about 150 feet from a parking lot in the Madison Arboretum. She had been reported missing the prior Dec. 15 from her room at Allen Hall, a residential center for the developmentally disabled.

When Susan LeMahieu's body was found, seventeen-year-old Shirley Stewart had been missing for three months. Unlike the other victims, the teenager apparently had no connection with Madison's downtown area. She disappeared January 2, 1980, after finishing her shift at the Dean Clinic, where she worked as a maid.

Shirley Stewart's body was found in July 1981 in a densely wooded area of the town of Westport, north of Madison. By this time, authorities began to see a clear connection between the Bennett, Hall, Speerschneider, LeMahieu and Stewart cases.

"I personally feel there are many similarities," said Deputy Coroner Donald Scullion. "The patterns are wooded areas, off the road a-ways in a concealed area."

Wisconsin State Journal file photo

Donna Mraz

But many of the bodies were severely decomposed by the time they were found, making it difficult even to establish causes of death. The random nature of the killings added to the difficulty in finding what appeared to be a serial killer.

Before the murderous spree ended, however, it was to claim one more victim. On July 2, 1982, nineteen-year-old Donna Mraz was brutally stabbed a few feet from Camp Randall Stadium on the Madison campus as she walked home from her waitress job at a State Street restaurant. Witnesses heard her screams and rushed to the rescue, only to see her assailant slipping quickly into the shadows.

The case was eerily reminiscent of the Christine Rothschild murder and, like that slaying, offered few clues. Two years afterward, the victim's body was exhumed to compare her teeth to bite marks on a possible suspect in prison. Like many other leads in the seven murders of young Madison women, that lead also evaporated.

In 1984, two years after the Mraz murder, detectives believed they finally had a break in at least some of the killings. In a Texas prison, Henry Lee Lucas was telling investigators that he and sidekick Ottis Toole had murdered more than a hundred victims during frequent forays across the country. Detectives David Coachems, Mary Otterson and Herb Hanson were sent to interview Lucas.

The confessed mass killer rocked back and forth in a chair as he told the detectives that, yes, he and Toole had passed through the Madison area on the way to visit relatives. After nine hours of questioning, the detectives were convinced that Lucas and Toole had killed Julie Ann Hall.

After analyzing other evidence presented by Lucas, they also linked him to the murder of Julie Speerschneider.

But then the case against Lucas appeared to unravel as quickly as it had come together. After touring murder sites in several states and describing the brutal crimes to detectives, Lucas suddenly had a change of heart. He had been lying, he said. He and Toole hadn't committed all those murders.

The veteran Madison-area detectives had approached Lucas skeptically and used their best skills trying to find holes in his story. Yet they

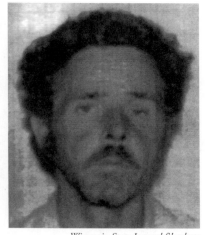

Wisconsin State Journal file photo

Henry Lee Lucas

came away convinced he had committed two of the unsolved crimes. Were they merely the victims of skillful manipulation or was Lucas actually the serial killer stalking young Madison women? The answer likely will never be known.

Was more than one brutal killer responsible for the deaths of Christine Rothschild, Debra Bennett, Julie Ann Hall, Julie Speerschneider, Susan LeMahieu, Shirley Stewart and Donna Mraz? Was Henry Lee Lucas involved somehow? As the trails on each of these crime grow colder, the answers to these questions seem ever more elusive.

47

Living with a Cat
Wautoma, 1967

James "Butch" McBrair had been drinking early on March 5, 1967, when he reached through a plastic window to unlock the back door of a cottage on Fish Lake near Wautoma. Six people were inside. It was a cottage where, until their separation, he had lived with his wife, Carol, and their two daughters.

In high school, Butch had starred in basketball in high school but life seemed to go sour ever since. McBrair would say later that through his foggy brain he seemed to hear voices — talking or yelling in duplicate or triplicate.

As he entered the kitchen, McBrair leaned his .22-caliber semi-automatic rifle against the wall next to the door. Someone said something about calling the sheriff. McBrair went back outside and yanked out the phone wires.

"Does he have a gun?" McBrair recalled hearing someone say through the blur. McBrair picked up the gun and turned around, seeing a figure in a dark jacket coming at him.

He lifted the gun and fired into the house two or three times, lighting up the kitchen with the flash. He ran into the house, then toward the girls' playroom, passing a woman crouched in a doorway. McBrair hurried into a bedroom and nearly toppled into a bed, then turned and went back to the living room. He heard a voice coming from the kitchen and saw someone coming toward him out of the corner of his eye. He turned and fired several times but the shots didn't seem to slow down the man, who went to the phone. Somehow, according to McBrair's account, his estranged wife, Carol, grabbed the gun and the struggle moved back outside. Wading through the deep snow and slipping on ice, McBrair tried to get the gun away from her but she tried to bite his hand. He grabbed a garbage can lid and tried to hit her, then noticed an ax lying at his feet.

"Oh, my God, no!" Carol McBrair cried as her husband picked up the ax. She dropped the gun. McBrair picked up the gun and headed back toward the cottage with his wife following. She shouted that he needed help. She grabbed the gun again and McBrair fired several times, wounding his wife at close range. She dropped to her knees and told him to kill her.

"Something rang through my head about dad always saying never leave anything suffer," McBrair would say later. "It seemed like I was hunting. They didn't seem like people to me."

He reloaded the gun and went back to the cottage to finish off all the victims. While he was shooting, McBrair felt something tugging at his pants leg. It was his youngest daughter, Kathy, age five.

"Please don't shoot anymore, Daddy," she pleaded. "We have blood on us." McBrair put the two girls in bed with their slain babysitter and left the cottage.

About 4:00 a.m., McBrair's father, James Sr., heard a noise downstairs. "Is that you, Butch?" he asked, but there was no answer. The elder McBrair found his soon in the living room, looking disoriented.

"I shot Marge, Marve, Carol and someone else," McBrair told his dad. "You better call the sheriff."

Besides his wife, McBrair had brutally murdered Marve Behr, his father-in-law; Barbara Behr, his 15-year-old sister-in-law; and Sheryl Oleson, the babysitter. He mistakenly thought one of the victims was Marge Behr, his mother-in-law.

About 5:30 a.m., Waushara County Sheriff Virgil "Buck" Batterman picked up Deputy Edward Oligney at home.

"We have a bad one," the tight-lipped sheriff told him.

About fifteen minutes later, the lawmen approached the cottage. The lights were on and two cars were parked in the driveway. The outside light was on, a door was ajar and, as Oligney later described it, "there was a striking silence about the place." In the kitchen, he noticed a Samurai-type sword lying on the floor.

"Hey!" Batterman shouted.

"Anybody home?" Oligney yelled.

Batterman reached the bedroom and the light from his flashlight swept across the floor. "Oh, my God!" he said. Two bodies were on the floor and three more were in the bed. Both of the people on the floor were dead. Oligney noticed the two children in bed were still breathing, lying with their faces to the wall. Batterman left to recruit a local newspaper photographer to take pictures of the scene and Oligney found the body of Marve Behr in the living room. Oligney took the two girls home. The next morning, Mrs. Oligney fixed breakfast for the girls.

"My mommy won't mind if we stay here," Kristie said. "My daddy shot my mommy and she's never coming back." Later, Kristie observed that "grandpa was the worst because he had more blood on him."

For James McBrair, the murders marked the lowest point of his life. Now twenty-seven, he had been a handsome lad, growing up on a 400-acre farm near Plainfield, made famous by the grave-robbing, murders and crafting of human remains of Ed Gein a few years earlier. At Tri-County High School, the tall, blond, young McBrair was a star athlete in basketball and football. He was prom king, class vice president and a B student. In his junior year, he played a lead role in the school play. To those who knew him, it seemed incredible that a young man held in such high esteem could commit such a gruesome crime.

Many small-town athletes seem to reach their peak in high school. Some leave for college and find they can't handle the lack of recognition in a larger city. They often return home in an effort to recapture those years of glory. For McBrair, his world began to crumble before he graduated. During his senior year, he married Barbara Cummings in a shotgun marriage. The couple had three children before they separated. Then, McBrair met the beautiful Carol Behr.

Carol, who also had three children by a previous marriage, moved in with McBrair at the family farm near Plainfield. But McBrair's father finally asked them to leave after he became upset that Carol seemed to be coming and going at all hours of the night. The couple married and moved to Milwaukee, later moving back to Waushara County and renting the cottage on Fish Lake.

As McBrair's trial loomed, he worked with a court-appointed attorney, Jon Wilcox, to prepare his defense. A crucial part of the defense was building a case against the victim, his wife, Carol. McBrair and his lawyer hoped to plant the idea in the jury's mind that she got what she deserved.

"Living with Carol was like living with a cat," McBrair said. "She could change from one mood to another faster than anyone I ever knew. She could change from a purr to a snarling fighter at the drop of a hat."

McBrair recalled the night he met Carol. Both had been drinking at a local watering hole. When Carol went to the bathroom, a male friend with them elbowed McBrair and winked.

"You've got it made tonight, Butch," he said. "Get one of the Behr girls drunk and you've got a sure sack job."

During the first part of the trial, the state had no trouble proving that McBrair committed the murders. Then the trial went into a second phase as the jury was asked to decide whether McBrair suffered from a mental disease at the time of the killings. Before the trial, he had been examined by several psychiatrists.

In the first blow to the state's case, Dr. E.F. Schubert, superintendent at Central State Hospital, testified that McBrair was insane and that testimony was corroborated by a defense psychiatrist.

Then McBrair himself took the stand. His straightforward testimony of his early life, two failed marriages and the killings clearly impressed the judge, Robert Gollmar.

"My own impression of the defendant was a sincere, remorseful young man who was caught in an emotional trap from which he could escape no other way," Gollmar later wrote of the case in his book, *Tales of a Country Judge*. "His crimes horrified me, but I felt an instinctive liking for this confused and unhappy man."

Jurors also showed sympathy for the young man, apparently agreeing somewhat with the defense's contention that McBrair was wronged and driven to murder by his promiscuous wife. In the end, however, they found him sane and guilty of murder.

It's significant that the case reflected social attitudes of the time. McBrair's defense of claiming his wife's promiscuity had caused his insanity wouldn't fly today, in an era where women are judged more equally and divorce is more common. Clearly, jurors today would question why McBrair just didn't divorce his wife if he was upset about her conduct.

In prison, McBrair accepted his punishment and refused to allow his attorneys to appeal to the state Supreme Court. He pursued a college degree and, unlike Douglas Dean, his charm and efforts apparently impressed parole officials. In a case with some similarities to McBrair, Dean murdered his mother and three members of his girlfriend's family in 1970.

But Dean, who earned a doctorate in psychology and argued he had been reformed by the prison system, remains imprisoned while McBrair was paroled after serving fourteen years. Members of a state pardon board called McBrair "the epitome of the rehabilitative process" and McBrair's parole efforts also were supported by University of Wisconsin-Madison Dean Mary Rouse, who came to know McBrair when he was imprisoned at Oak Hill Correctional Institution in Oregon and took courses at the university.

Today, McBrair has remarried and lives quietly in northern Wisconsin near the Upper Michigan border. But the suffering hasn't ended for all of his victims. His daughter, Kathy, who witnessed the brutal crimes a quarter century ago, was working on a book about the case. While she supported her father's clemency efforts, now she feels cheated of her mother's companionship by her father's crime.

48

Unless He's a Soldier

Tomah, 1942

Something bothered Anne Baun about the idea of her daughter driving across Wisconsin from Kenosha to Sparta.

"Why don't you take the train?" she suggested. "I just don't like it, Dorothy."

"Oh, mother, don't worry," Dorothy Baun replied. "I'll be riding with Neil."

"I still don't like it — the two of you girls alone out on the highway. But I guess there's no talking you out of it. Well then, if you must go, just don't you go picking up any hitchhikers."

"We won't," Dorothy promised. "Unless he's a soldier!"

How could Anne Baun argue with that? It was early September 1942, after all, and the nation had been at war with Japan and Germany for less than ten months. Giving a soldier a ride seemed like a patriotic thing to do.

The flash of independence shown by Dorothy Baun toward her mother wasn't out of character for the times. The war seemed to enhance the independence of many women, making it acceptable to stay single and pursue careers. Women were expected to contribute to the war effort by filling the jobs left behind by men who had gone to war. Afterward, most women would go back to their roles as housewives until the late 1960s and early 1970s when the modern feminist movement took hold.

Dorothy Baun and her friend, Neil Pietrangeli, were rather plain-looking women in their early thirties. Both held state jobs as social workers. Dorothy had worked less than a month as a case worker for the State

Parole Board at Eau Claire. Neil had been a case worker for two years at the State School for Dependent Children in Sparta.

Dorothy had graduated six years earlier from Stout Institute (now the UW-Stout) in Menomonie. Her new job involved monitoring women on probation or recently paroled from Tacycheedah State Prison. Neil, a graduate of Lake Forest College who did post-graduate work at the University of Chicago, was responsible for supervising the placement of children in private homes from the school in Sparta.

The two women first met in Kenosha County, where Dorothy had been employed by the county probation department and Neil was a welfare worker. That weekend in early September, the women decided to visit some of their old haunts. Both were scheduled to return to work on Tuesday and Dorothy planned to drive with her friend to Sparta, then take a bus to Eau Claire.

They left Kenosha about 5:00 p.m. in Neil's 1941 light-green Oldsmobile coupe. About 7:00 p.m., they stopped in Sauk City and bought ten gallons of gasoline. They never made it to Sparta. L.H. Schroeder, the gas station attendant, apparently was the last person to see the two women alive.

Alick Chambers was driving his milk truck along Highway C near Tomah about 7:00 a.m. the next morning. It seemed like a routine fall morning as he made his regular milk pickups when he suddenly spotted something lying along the side of the road. At first he thought it might be a dead animal, perhaps a deer. But when he looked closer, Chambers saw it was a badly wounded nude woman. He braked his truck and pulled over, then ran back to where the woman lay to see if he could help.

"My friend is in the bushes there," Dorothy Baun said as Chambers helped the dying woman into his truck. "They hit us and robbed us. There is another girl up there in the woods hurt worse than I am."

She was covered with mud and bleeding severely from multiple bullet wounds. Chambers raced to the nearest doctor for help but it was too late. Dorothy Baun died en route.

Neil Pietrangeli was found minutes later. She had clung to life for about a hour after she was shot before she also succumbed to her gunshot wounds. She had been shot with a large-caliber revolver in the abdomen, side and shoulder. Dorothy Baun had been shot seven times in the back.

Before the shooting, the assailant forced the women to disrobe and raped them, although Neil still wore a brassiere when she was found. Their car, purses and clothes were missing but their watches, jewelry, shoes and stockings were found nearby. Police theorized the assailant carried the women to the thicket where Pietrangeli was found. After raping the women, he shot each of them several times. Dorothy Baun apparently crawled out of the bushes to the roadside seeking help.

Less than an hour after Chambers happened on the murder scene, Pvt. Edward Helgeson, a Chippewa Falls soldier on furlough from a New Jersey Army camp, was hitchhiking near Tomah when a light-green Oldsmobile stopped to pick him up. When the hitchhiker threw his duffel bag into the trunk, he noticed women's clothing inside. The driver, also a soldier in uniform, had been drinking heavily, the hitchhiker later told authorities, and bragged he had "stolen the car from two girls."

The biggest clue, however, was a ten-dollar paycheck from the Kenosha welfare department endorsed by Dorothy Baun and cashed by a soldier at a Tomah gas station on Monday night — minutes after the two women were left for dead.

As gas station attendant Ralph Hilgen filled the tank of the Oldsmobile, the soldier told him he was coming from an Army camp in the South to visit his sweetheart. He guzzled a bottle of pop and those who saw him, including Hilgen, later described the man's demeanor as calm and deliberate.

"We'll have the murderer before night," vowed Monroe County Sheriff Hallet T. Jenkins. But it wouldn't be that easy.

Another twenty-five-dollar check made out to Neil Pietrangeli was cashed later Tuesday at a bank in Le Sueur, Minnesota. Bank cashier J.D. Peterson said the man who presented the check wore an Army uniform and used the name of Robert Bailey.

"When I asked him about signing her name to the check, he told me the signature was authorized in a Sparta, Wisconsin bank," Peterson later told authorities.

He accepted the check without further question, writing the man's Army serial number on the back. The check was forwarded for collection to a bank clearing house in Chicago.

Another report led authorities in the opposite direction. A bundle of women's clothing, including two girdles, lingerie, several pairs of stockings, gloves, a striped pink gown and a polka-dot dress were found near Gary, Indiana. But the clothing turned into a false lead when relatives of the two slain women were unable to identify it as owned by the victims.

As suspicions focused on a military man, Monroe County District Attorney Leo Goodman met with officials at nearby Camp McCoy and Camp Williams. A list of soldiers on leave at the time of the slayings was compiled and photographs were gathered of all soldiers AWOL. A tip prompted authorities to check for suspects at the Madison Air Forces Technical School. These efforts, however, also failed to locate the killer.

In Santa Clara, California, Robert Taylor Bailey arrived a few days later at the home of Cyril Simmeon. Bailey was accompanied by a pair of sixteen-year-old girls he had picked up in Sioux City, Iowa. One of the

Wisconsin State Journal archives

Neil Pietrangeli   **Dorothy Baun**

girls was a niece of Mrs. Simmeon.

Simmeon thought it was mighty suspicious that Bailey was trying to paint the whitewalls on the 1941 Oldsmobile he was driving. Simmeon contacted police, who connected Bailey's name with the person who had endorsed the check in Minnesota. Strangely, he had used his real name. When detectives questioned him, it wasn't difficult for them to persuade Bailey to confess. Not only did investigators find the Oldsmobile, but they also found many belongings of the two women in Bailey's possession. In short, they had him cold.

"I am the man wanted for the Wisconsin murders," he said calmly.

In fact, Bailey offered four separate confessions, each differing significantly in the details. First, he said his accomplice was a man named Joe Cortez, who forced the women off the highway and actually raped them. Then, he claimed the accomplice was Manuel Smith. Bailey said Smith shot the women "when they raised too much hell." Bailey claimed he later shot Smith and dumped his body in the St. Croix River.

Another confession named his accomplice as Jesse Fletcher, with whom Bailey had escaped a year earlier from a Mississippi reformatory. Later, Bailey said he named Fletcher to get even for a grudge he carried against him.

Despite the mystery surrounding Bailey's possible accomplice, some facts were clear: Bailey had deserted his Army post at Fort Bragg, stealing a .45-caliber revolver. He fled to Ohio, then Chicago, hitchhiking to Madison on September 7. About seventy-five miles from Madison along

Highway 12, he hitched a ride with Dorothy Baun and Neil Pietrangeli.

Bailey forced the two women to drive down a rural road. He made them disrobe and go into the woods, where he finally admitted raping "the smaller one" (Pietrangeli).

He fled into Minnesota where, ironically, he was taken into custody on a minor charge by Minneapolis police but released after telling the officers he was on the way to visit his mother in Tacoma, Washington. The officers dropped him off at the train station but Bailey instead drove the Oldsmobile to Sioux City, where he met the two girls.

He waived extradition back to Wisconsin, pleaded guilty to the murder of Neil Pietrangeli and, in late September, Bailey was sentenced to life in prison. He wasn't charged with the murder of Dorothy Baun, possibly so he could be charged with that murder if, despite the confession, he somehow got off the first murder charge.

Bailey was twenty years old at the time of the murders yet already a hardened criminal. At age eleven, he was sent to reform school for burglary. Two years later, he was back in reform school on another felony charge.

When he was arrested for the Baun-Pietrangeli murders, Bailey's father wrote a letter to Monroe County Sheriff Jenkins. The elder Bailey said he was glad his son was arrested so he couldn't cause any more trouble.

49

Execution of a Farm Family

Athens, 1987

Athens, namesake of the ancient Greek city of learning and enlightenment, is a sleepy, rural town of less than a thousand residents in north central Wisconsin. The village lies about six miles north of Highway 29, the main artery between Wausau and Chippewa Falls.

In a dilapidated farmhouse on a dirt road west of Athens, four bodies were found in early July 1987. Each of the victims was shot twice in the head with a small-caliber weapon.

Kenneth Kunz lived in a travel trailer next to the farmhouse. When he came over to the main house after the Fourth of July, Kunz found the bodies of his Uncle Clarence, age seventy-six, his aunts Marie, age seventy-two, and Irene, age eighty-two, and his brother, Randy, age thirty. Missing was Kunz' seventy-year-old mother, Helen. She was last seen attending a Fourth of July fireworks display with Randy.

Discovery of the slain Kunz family not only became one of Wisconsin's most perplexing murder mysteries. It also provided a glimpse into the bizarre relationships of an isolated and unusual farm family.

Believing the missing woman to be the key to the case, Marathon County Sheriff Leroy Schillinger quickly circulated a three-year-old photograph of Helen Kunz. The faded photograph showed an elderly woman in a babushka and winter coat. Her eyes were closed and her head cocked to one side while her mouth curled upward in what could be a half-smile.

Could Helen Kunz have played a role in the murders? Was she the cold-blooded executioner who methodically put her family to death?

Schillinger wasn't sure but the sheriff believed finding Helen would lead to answers to these questions. He began the search by ordering his deputies to comb the swampy woodlands behind the farmhouse.

Helen Kunz stood five feet three inches tall and weighed one-hundred thirteen pounds. At the fireworks display, she wore a white blouse with a large floral print, slacks and sneakers.

The family farmhouse had no indoor plumbing and cooking was done on a woodstove. But the family had a microwave oven, a videotape recorder and a television set covered in plastic. One investigator remarked the plastic covering almost made it appear the family viewed the television set as sacred. Rooms were cluttered with stacks of newspapers, piles of magazines, garbage and other items in paper bags. Investigators used an end-loader to move a four-foot stack of boxes, old newspapers and magazines from the attic. Detectives wearing rubber gloves sorted through the debris.

Hidden in the messy house, however, investigators found something far more valuable than old newspapers and magazines. They found cash, lots of it, all over the house. More than twenty thousand dollars was recovered but authorities refused to rule out robbery as a motive in the killings.

"There was no way of knowing if twice that amount was taken," said District Attorney Rand Krueger.

Early on, investigators also discovered a strange twist to the case that went back several decades. In 1933, when Helen Kunz was fifteen, a

Wisconsin State Journal file photo

The Kunz farm, scene of the family slaughter.

neighbor named Frank Gumz was convicted of raping her in the hayloft. During the trial, Helen had testified that she became pregnant as a result of the rape and had a son named Kenneth. In his defense, Gumz's lawyer tried to prove the boy was fathered by Helen's brother, Clarence, instead.

Gumz was sentenced to eighteen months at Waupun Correctional Institution and later transferred to Central State Hospital for the Insane. He died in a car accident in 1936. Years later, Kenneth Kunz would claim that his real father was Clarence Kunz, his uncle.

After the bodies were found, Schillinger told reporters he was investigating continuing reports of incestuous relationships within the family. He suggested that Kenneth Kunz or his missing mother could be suspects. "It has many, many twists," he said.

By the time of the murders, the Kunz family didn't farm the land themselves anymore. Clarence Kunz had grown oats and hay on the 108-acre tract until his health gave out and he wound up renting the land to neighbors. Neighbors saw little of the reclusive family. They watched Irene split wood for the stove and carry it inside. The elderly sisters tended a vegetable garden and Randy routinely drove his mother into town, where she paid bills, shopped for groceries, did her laundry and tended to other family business.

Helen Kunz also complained about the "dirty movies" other family members liked to watch on the videotape machine. Gale Weiler, who ran Weiler's Hardware Hank in Athens, recalled Helen's comments when she once accompanied Kenneth to town to buy some ammunition. The movies, coupled with the allegations of incest, helped create an atmosphere of sexual intrigue surrounding the family and the killings. Did Helen kill her family over the movies and then disappear? Were the family members killed in some kind of lover's quarrel or to settle an old score? Schillinger believed he wouldn't find out until Helen herself was found.

"You find me Helen, and I'll probably tell you what happened," he told reporters.

He hoped, of course, that Helen would be found alive, that she had been taken hostage or escaped after playing a role in the murders. Although Kenneth was cooperative with authorities, he couldn't provide answers about the family's violent demise and the case continued to puzzle investigators. Air and ground searches of the farm failed to turn up a body, a weapon or a single clue.

Through the summer and early fall, the sheriff received numerous reports that Helen had been sighted. None of the reports checked out. Schillinger asked deer hunters to help in the search. Meanwhile, residents of the German-Polish village of Athens were terrified by the crime. Before the murders, the 988 residents hadn't been concerned about locking their doors. That changed dramatically after the grisly discovery on the Kunz farm.

By January 1988, investigators had identified several suspects. They began a methodical examination of guns owned by area residents. When .22-caliber shell casings were found in a room during a search of a Medford home, Chris Jacobs III became the strongest suspect. Two rifles, ammunition and a car were among the items seized at the ninety-three-acre Jacobs farm.

Wisconsin State Journal file photo

Chris Jacobs III

An analysis of the shell casings by the Wisconsin Crime Laboratory found they matched casings found at the Kunz farm. But it would be nine months before investigators built a case they felt was strong enough to arrest Jacobs. He was questioned, charged with being party to the crime of murder and released.

Word that people with local ties were among the suspects in the brutal mass murder was unsettling to local residents, who wondered whether the killers would strike again. "It's so quiet," an employee of an Athens store complained. "It's kind of scary they don't give us any information."

The spring thaw allowed investigators to search more thoroughly for the still-missing Helen Kunz. Under the scrutiny of reporters from as far away as Minneapolis and Milwaukee, they dug for three days in a manure pit but came away empty-handed.

Finally, in late March, they found skeletal remains scattered in a marsh on a Christmas tree farm in Taylor County, about ten miles south of Rib Lake. Investigators searched the area about sixteen miles from the Kunz farm after receiving an informant's tip. They believed the remains were those of missing matriarch Helen Kunz.

Instead of clearing up the case, however, the discovery of Helen's remains only raised more questions, deepening the mystery. If Helen was dead, then who killed her family at the farmhouse? Why were her remains found elsewhere? What was the motive for the brutal murders?

As investigators searched the marsh for further clues, the remains and clothing were sent to the Wisconsin Crime Laboratory in Madison for forensic tests. An autopsy showed that, like her four relatives, Helen Kunz had been shot at least once in the head and murdered execution-style.

A year after the slayings, investigators still suspected Jacobs knew a lot about the murders but they continued to move cautiously. He remained charged as a party to the crime but enough evidence could not be found to upgrade the charge to murder.

"We only get one chance in court so we have to be so sure of ourselves before we go to court," Schillinger explained. Residents were concerned the killer, whoever he might be, remained on the loose. Kenneth Kunz, the lone surviving family member who had discovered the bodies, had some regrets.

"Maybe, if I could have been home, they wouldn't have done it," he said. "(But) if I would have been there, I would have been gone, too."

Kenneth and other relatives wanted to tear down the house to help assuage their horrid memories. But Schillinger said the house had to remain standing, even as it grew more dilapidated and overrun with vegetation.

In late August, nearly nine months after the search of his home, Jacobs was taken into custody and charged with participating in the Kunz slayings. Besides the shell casings, tire tracks on Jacobs' car matched those found in the Kunz garden tended by Helen and Irene.

When detectives showed Jacobs a photograph of the tire tracks and told him they were B.F. Goodrich belted tires, he responded that's what he had on his car. Detective Randall Hoenisch told Jacobs there weren't many tires like that around.

"Oh no, oh no, oh no, there's no way I killed somebody," he said. "Oh no. I ain't saying no more till I get a lawyer."

Kenneth Kunz also recalled that Jacobs was among four men who visited him three years earlier to look at two junk cars he had for sale. Five days after he came upon his slain family, Kunz told investigators he remembered that a guy named Jacobs bought a 1969 Oldsmobile and a 1975 Ford. The purchaser was Jacobs' father but the young man had accompanied his father to the Kunz farm. The men came inside to transfer the title. Afterward, Kenneth said he noticed that a calculator, funnel and chain were missing. He called Jacobs and the items were returned the following day.

Jacobs told investigators he couldn't have committed the murders because on that Fourth of July he went to the fireworks show in Medford with a seventeen-year-old girl. But the girl destroyed that alibi. She told detectives she didn't even meet Jacobs until the following December.

Jacobs, of course, had been a suspect since January. Some people raised questions about why he finally was taken into custody just two weeks before Schillinger faced a primary election challenge. Jacobs had been arrested in early February on a charge of being party to the crime of murder but was released after he led investigators to the spot where he had suspiciously buried a car. Did the car contain valuable evidence?

In July, Jacobs was charged again with obstructing the investigation and two tires were confiscated from him. His mother later told authorities that after he became a suspect, her son had talked about "blowing his brains out."

Despite the multiple charges, which stopped short of actually accusing him of the crime, the case against Chris Jacobs III remained nothing more than circumstantial and, following a three-week trial in 1989, the Medford dairy farmer was found innocent of five counts of being the party to a crime of first-degree murder. Perhaps authorities hoped the legal pressure on Jacobs would cause him to confess but it never happened, possibly because he wasn't guilty.

"I was shocked," Detective Wendell Roddy, the chief investigator on the case, later said of the verdict. "I still feel there was enough evidence. I am satisfied I did my best. Maybe it wasn't good enough."

The pivotal testimony at the trial was a startling revelation by a Wausau man that he bought cocaine four times from Randy Kunz in late 1986 and early 1987. Jacobs' lawyers seized on the testimony by Tracy Bartlett, saying it was evidence that drug deals were the motive for the murders and that their client was innocent. Bartlett, however, later was convicted of perjury after confessing that he lied about the cocaine deals.

Five years after the murders, Detective Roddy retired but said the Kunz case still haunted him.

"I don't consider it unsolved," he said. "A man was charged. He was acquitted. I have to accept that. It doesn't change the investigation. It doesn't change the evidence."

But Chris Jacobs Jr., the prime suspect's father, maintained all along that his son was framed. He blasted Roddy as an incompetent detective.

"He was an ex-grease monkey that walked out of a garage," he said. "Maybe he read Dick Tracy magazine."

The elder Jacobs said any further investigation should focus on why his son was framed and on the involvement of police officers in drug dealing.

Although he was exonerated, Chris Jacobs, III said he still felt that people blamed him for the brutal murders.

"I don't trust a lot of people," he said. "I am always looking behind my back."

In July 1993, the on-again, off-again case against Chris Jacobs III was on again. A former girlfriend, Stacy Weis, came forward, claiming

Jacobs confessed the murders to her in 1991 after a night of drinking. According to her story, Jacobs said he drove to Kunz house and, during an argument, he knocked Randy down and shot him. After shooting the other family members, Jacobs allegedly tied the hands of Helen Kunz behind her back, drove her to a wooded area and shot her, too.

Public Defender Weldon Nelson immediately dismissed Weis' story as the claims of "a disgruntled, jilted ex-girlfriend who threatened to get Chris Jacobs when they broke up last fall." Just before the statute of limitations ran out on kidnapping and false imprisonment, Jacobs was charged with

Wisconsin State Journal file photo
Survivor Kenneth Kunz

those crimes. Once again, he wasn't charged with murder, for which there is no statute of limitations.

Weis was sentenced in August 1993 to 90 days in jail for burglary. She agreed to cooperate with investigators as part of a plea bargain in which she would not be charged with a February 1993 bank robbery at White Rock, Minn.

Jacobs appealed the kidnapping and false imprisonment charges at every level until the U.S. Supreme Court in 1996 refused to consider his case. A decade after the murders, in July 1997, Jacobs finally was ready to go to trial for the second time with Stacy Weis as a key witness. Circuit Judge Douglas Fox put a gag order on attorneys to prevent the need to move the trial out of Wausau.

Did Chris Jacobs, III kill five members of the Kunz family on that Fourth of July in 1987? Was it someone else after the family fortune? Were the family members executed over a drug deal gone awry? Or were the murders the result of an intra-family squabble in the bizarre household?

50

Doctor of Death
Milwaukee, 1991

The strange story told by Tracy Edwards when he flagged down a patrol car that hot July night was difficult for the Milwaukee police officers Robert Rauth and Rolf Mueller to believe. With a pair of handcuffs dangling from his wrist, Edwards looked to them like he was drunk or on drugs. He told the officers someone was trying to kill him and that he had been "with the devil."

It probably was nothing, they thought, but they might as well check out the guy Edwards was raving about. A six-foot, sandy-haired, pale young man met them at the door of the Oxford Apartments. Despite a faint odor of beer on his breath, the man appeared sober and certainly more credible than Edwards.

Mueller headed for the bedroom to look for a knife Edwards said was used to threaten him. The officer found the knife and a Polaroid camera on the bed. He glanced up at some photographs on a dresser. At first glance, they seemed to depict men engaged in sexual acts. It was beginning to look like this whole thing was a domestic squabble between two gay guys. But when Mueller examined the photos more closely, he was shocked. Some of them showed the mutilated and dismembered bodies in excruciating detail.

That wasn't all there was to the grisly scene, however. In the freezer were packages of some kind of fleshy material. On the bottom shelf of the refrigerator in a cardboard box, the officers found a human head.

Five skulls, some painted, were removed that day from Jeffrey Dahmer's apartment as Mueller and Rauth uncovered the worst series of

crimes ever committed in Wisconsin and certainly one of the most nause-
ating crime scenes in human history. When the body parts were identified, catalogued and added up, Jeffrey Dahmer admitted killing seventeen men and boys. But he didn't stop there. He had sex with some of the
victims after death, ate some of their body parts and, in the worst living
nightmare out of a horror movie, tried to lobotomize some of his victims
by drilling holes in their heads and freezing parts of their brains so he
could keep them alive for his own sexual pleasure.

In a literal sense, Dahmer was a doctor of death and his murders
went far beyond the daily diet of urban violence. They were crimes against
humanity itself.

Through it all, Dahmer's appearance and composure belied the sav-
agery of his acts. Far from a raging madman, he appeared to comprehend
his situation. He made no claim of mind control by aliens or the devil.
During hours of interrogation by police, he was calm, polite and generally cooperative. Most of the details about his crimes came from his own
recollections and admissions.

Dahmer's dissections, cannibalism and necrophilia rivaled the murders and grave-robbing of Ed Gein more than three decades earlier. Unlike Gein, however, Dahmer had no readily apparent mental illness. But
how could a man commit such atrocities if he were sane? The answer
didn't come easily.

His interest in dissection apparently began in childhood, when he
enjoyed collecting bugs and saving them in a woodshed behind the Dahmer
family home in a suburb of Akron, Ohio. As he reached puberty, the
hobby advanced to small animals. Occasionally a dog or cat would disappear around the neighborhood but it didn't occur often enough to raise
suspicions.

Young Jeffrey was always sort of an oddball. In high school, other
students would pay to watch him perform at a suburban mall. Downing
a six-pack of beer in preparation for his act, he would feign seizures,
scream and knock over drinks at the Woolworth's lunch counter. The
performance became known as "doing a Dahmer" but he never was stopped
by police or security guards.

At school, he gained a reputation as the class clown but young Jeffrey clearly was a clown with an underlying mean streak. He would do
cruel imitations of people with cerebral palsy or draw chalk outlines of
dead bodies in hallways.

When he graduated from high school, young Jeffrey was abandoned
by his family. His father, Lionel, had moved out of the house as the
marriage to the former Joyce Flint of Chippewa Falls disintegrated.
Dahmer's mother and younger brother soon moved to Wisconsin, leaving him alone in the house in Ohio.

About the same time, Dahmer committed his first murder. The victim was Stephen Hicks, a hitchhiker on his way to an outdoor rock concert at Chippewa Lake Park west of Akron. Hicks accompanied Jeffrey back to his home on Bath Road. When Hicks said he wanted to leave, Dahmer picked up a barbell and smashed his skull. Then he held the barbell over Hicks' throat, strangling him. Fearful of being discovered, Dahmer cut up the body, put the pieces in plastic bags and hid them under the crawl space. Later, after an unsuccessful attempt to bury the pieces, he cleaned off the flesh and smashed each bone with a hammer, scattered the tiny fragments in a rocky area behind the house.

Dahmer didn't kill again for several years, a period he spent serving in the U.S. Army in Germany and working at a fast food restaurant in Florida. His drinking problem, however, continued unabated and his Army roommates sensed there was a secret the young man carried.

"Someday you're going to hear from me again," Dahmer predicted to his platoon leader. He was right.

After a short time in Florida, Dahmer's father, Lionel, and his new wife, Shari, persuaded Jeffrey to come back to Ohio. Soon afterward, however, the young man was in trouble again. In a final effort to help his son, Lionel Dahmer sent him to live with his grandmother, Catherine, in West Allis. Young Jeffrey always seemed fond of his grandmother and perhaps she could straighten him out.

On the surface, moving into his grandmother's suburban home seemed to have a positive effect on Dahmer. He got a job as a phlebotomist at Milwaukee Blood Plasma Inc., an ironic but perhaps not coincidental occupation in light of his later activities. But he was laid off by the following summer and soon was getting into trouble again. He was arrested August 8, 1982, at the Wisconsin State Fair for exposing himself in front of a crowd. In 1986, two twelve-year-old boys came upon Dahmer standing along the banks of the Kinnickinnic River. His pants were pulled down to his thighs and he was masturbating. One boy asked if he was enjoying himself.

A conviction of disorderly conduct for the incident forced Dahmer into psychological therapy but his antisocial activities would only grow far worse. By 1987, he began frequenting the Club 219, a gay bar on Second Street in Milwaukee. To other bar patrons, he seemed like a non-threatening loner but that was far from the truth. It was at Club 219 that Dahmer may have met Steve Tuomi, a white twenty-eight-year-old man who grew up in Michigan's upper peninsula. Dahmer apparently went with Tuomi to the Ambassador Hotel, where he later told authorities he woke up lying on top of Tuomi's dead body. As he had in the Hicks killing, Dahmer started to panic as he tried to devise a way to dispose of the body. He rushed to a nearby shopping mall and bought a suitcase. He stuffed the body into the suitcase and brought it to his grandmother's house, where he dismembered the corpse and disposed of the remains.

Four months later, in January 1988, Dahmer struck up a conversation with James Doxtator outside the Club 219. He offered money if the fourteen-year-old boy would come with him back to his grandmother's house to pose for photos. James agreed. At the West Allis house, Dahmer gave Doxtator a drink with a sleeping potion mixed into it. When James passed out, Dahmer strangled him. As he had done with Hicks, Dahmer used a sledgehammer to smash the bones into small fragments.

Less than three months later, Dahmer met Richard Guerrero, age twenty-three, in front of the Phoenix, a bar down the block from Club 219. Following what was becoming a pattern, Dahmer invited Guerrero to his grandmother's house where they could watch videos, take some nude photos or have sex. Dahmer drugged Guerrero and strangled him, then disposed of the remains.

Dahmer's activities didn't entirely escape the notice of his grandmother. During the summer of 1988, she noticed a disturbing odor in her garage and sent Dahmer's father to check it out. All Lionel Dahmer could find was a small amount of slimy, black residue he couldn't identify. That fall, however, Catherine Dahmer finally forced her grandson to move out when she came downstairs and found him with a black man. Both men were drunk. By this time, Dahmer had found another job at the Ambrosia Chocolate Co. in Milwaukee, and could afford to get his own apartment.

Dahmer rented a place and didn't waste any time taking advantage of his new freedom. The day after he moved in, he offered fifty dollars to a thirteen-year-old Laotian boy if he would pose for pictures. Dahmer served his customary knockout drug and began fondling the boy. But unlike the other victims, the boy didn't lose consciousness. Instead, he fled the apartment and reported the incident to police. Dahmer was arrested for second-degree sexual assault and enticing a child for immoral purposes. He was released on bail but convicted of the charges in January 1989.

Dahmer was apologetic before the judge, begging for leniency and calling the incident "the climax of my idiocy." In retrospect, Dahmer's humility was sheer duplicity and an outright lie. During the five months he awaited sentencing, Dahmer lured Anthony Sears to his apartment, served his knockout drink and killed him.

During his ten-month work-release sentence, Dahmer's stepmother, Shari, noticed a marked change in him.

"He had no light in his eyes," she said. "Jeff lost his soul in there."

But Dahmer didn't lose his penchant for killing and, upon his release, he picked up right where he left off. Raymond Lamont Smith, also

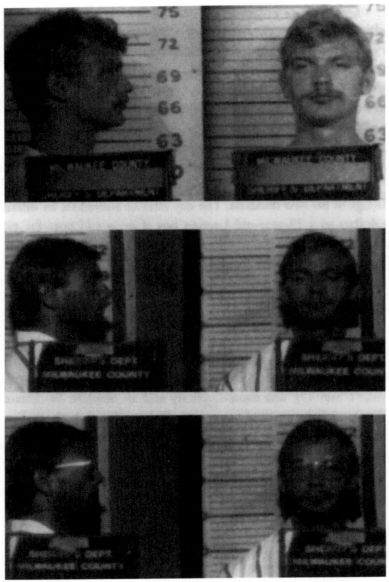

Milwaukee Police Department

Jeffrey Dahmer at the time of his 1982 arrest, top, and in July 1991.

known as Ricky Beeks, became the next victim. He was followed by Edward Smith, who was nicknamed The Sheik because of his habit of wearing a turban-style wrap on his head. He met Ernest Miller at a small business area on North 27th Street, lured him back to the apartment and killed him. A few weeks later, David Thomas became yet another victim of Jeffrey Dahmer.

During the killing spree, Dahmer met frequently with his probation officer, Donna Chester. He told her he was no longer interested in boys and young males and he realized alcohol was the root of his problem. She noticed he appeared depressed, refusing to look at the positive side of anything. While appearing cooperative to Chester, Dahmer was saving the skulls and body parts of his growing list of victims back at his apartment. The following spring of 1991, Curtis Straughter, Errol Lindsay and Tony Hughes would die at the hands of Jeffrey Dahmer.

On Memorial Day weekend, Dahmer's killing spree was nearly exposed when three Milwaukee police officers visited his apartment. Body parts were hidden in various parts of the apartment and Dahmer's dissection pictures were strewn about. The officers were repelled by a pungent smell and noticed the pictures but didn't look closely enough to find out about the murders.

The incident began when Konerak Sinthasomphone, brother of the Laotian boy Dahmer had molested a couple of years earlier, was lured to the killer's den. While fourteen-year-old Konerak was succumbing to the knockout potion, Dahmer went out to buy beer and cigarettes. Konerak woke up and ran naked into the street. Dahmer spotted the boy and tried to get Konerak back to the apartment without arousing suspicion. But two women from the neighborhood intervened and called police.

To the officers, however, Dahmer's story seemed more credible than the suspicions of the women. Dahmer lied about the boy's age and identity, persuading the officers the incident was nothing more than a spat between two gay lovers. Later, the officers would be fired for their failure to intervene and perhaps cut short Dahmer's career of horror.

After his brush with the law, Dahmer resumed killing but decided to seek some of his victims in Chicago. He met Donald Montrell of Flint, Mich. at a Chicago gay pride march and lured the young man back to his den of death. Matt Turner and Jeremiah Weinberger also succumbed to Dahmer's horror, although Weinberger survived an extra day, probably the longest relationship the serial killer ever had in his life.

By this time, Dahmer was running out of space for his growing collection of body parts. The refrigerator and freezer were crammed and parts were stuffed in dresser drawers and on closet shelves. Neighbors were starting to complain about the smell. Dahmer bought a huge vat and filled it with acid. The vat became a liquid grave for two of his victims.

The frequency of killings increased. Dahmer became too busy managing his grisly collection to show up for work and was fired. The landlord served him with an eviction notice. That presented a real problem. How would he be able to dispose of the parts or move them to a new apartment? Oliver Lacy and Joseph Bradehoft became the final victims of Dahmer's terror.

The narrow escape of Tracy Edwards and the discovery of Dahmer's den of horrors brought a media circus to Milwaukee. Edwards sold his exclusive story to several tabloids and TV talk shows. Long before the trial, four books quickly materialized, detailing the gruesome story. Families of the victims filed multi-million dollar lawsuits to ensure that Dahmer couldn't profit from his crimes. The killer himself unraveled his incredible tales for police investigators. His only demand in return for the detailed information was that he be permitted to smoke.

For many Wisconsin residents, Dahmer's case dredged up unpleasant memories of Ed Gein three decades earlier. Gein, who killed two women and robbed graves for body parts, inspired the movies "Psycho" and "Texas Chainsaw Massacre." But moviemakers didn't seem as interested in Dahmer's story.

Actually, Dahmer's case bore more similarities to Dennis Nilsen, a London serial killer credited with fifteen murders over a four-year span beginning in 1978. Loneliness may have been an important factor for both men, who shared conflicts over their unresolved homosexual urges. Like Dahmer, Nilsen cut up the bodies of his male victims and his killing spree was uncovered when a plumber called to clean out a backed-up drain found body parts.

At Dahmer's trial in early February 1992, expert testimony centered on whether the serial killer met the requirements of Wisconsin's insanity law. In order to be judged insane, it had to be proven that he wasn't aware of the wrongfulness of his acts.

Forensic psychiatrists testifying for the prosecution and defense gave their views about whether Dahmer was insane. Focusing on the narrow standards of the law, however, the psychiatrists at the trial failed to deal with the larger question of how a man could commit such inhuman acts and lead a normal appearing life at the same time.

That answer was provided by Dr. Gary Maier, a Madison forensic psychiatrist who provided consultation for *Massacre in Milwaukee*, one of the books about the Dahmer case. Maier compared Dahmer to doctors in Nazi Germany who were able to kill in the name of healing. Both suffered from what Maier called a doubling of personalities, allowing two conflicting sets of ethics to operate simultaneously.

"I think this concept is one that makes a Dahmer more understandable," Maier said. "Because there aren't, by day when he goes to work, many clues that this is anything like a quirky guy or a guy who has unusual values. But something happens to trigger or cause this other part of himself to come out. For serial killers where there doesn't seem to be a major change in them, this process of doubling makes the most sense."

Dahmer was found sane and convicted of fifteen of the murders. At another trial two months later in Ohio, he was convicted of the Hicks killing. He began serving fifteen consecutive life terms at Columbia Correctional Institution at Portage.

The convictions didn't end the legal aspects of the Dahmer case, which moved to civil court whenever anyone connected with the case was suing. In April 1993, Dahmer was shackled and brought back to Milwaukee to testify in a lawsuit brought by the parents of Konerak Sinthasomphone against the Milwaukee Police Department.

On November 28, 1994, Dahmer and another inmate, Jesse Anderson, were in the prison gymnasium working on a cleaning detail when they were brutally attacked by inmate Christopher J. Scarver, who had been working with them. Dahmer and Anderson were bludgeoned to death.

Scarver pleaded insanity, claiming that God told him to kill Dahmer and Anderson. He told authorities he felt like he was in a fog that day. But those claims and the fog seemed to evaporate when Scarver was offered a plea bargain. He pleaded no contest in exchange for a transfer to the federal prison system. He sentenced by Columbia County Circuit Judge Richard Reim to two consecutive life terms plus thirty years on two convictions of first-degree murder.

Dahmer's body was stored at the Dane County Morgue in Madison as evidence in Scarver's case. When Scarver was convicted, the body was released to relatives. But not Dahmer's brain.

Joyce Flint of Fresno, Calif., Dahmer's mother, wanted her son's brain preserved so it could be studied to determine whether biological factors caused his criminal behavior. His father, Lionel, of Akron, Ohio, wanted the brain cremated. In December 1995, Columbia County Circuit Judge Daniel George granted Lionel Dahmer's wishes and ordered the brain cremated.

Burning the serial killer's brain, however, didn't destroy the last vestiges of Dahmer. What remained were the refrigerator where he stored human heads, saws, blades and utensils he used to cannibalize his victims. Families of his victims obtained a court order turning over the items so they could be auctioned. The families hoped to raise $1 million in compensation.

Milwaukee business leaders stepped in, raising $407,225 to buy Dahmer's grisly collection so it could be destroyed. Joseph Zilber, a real estate magnate who organized the Milwaukee Civic Pride Fund, said his intention was that no one "will see this freak show and think he can outdo Dahmer." Zilber donated a hundred thousand dollars himself to start the fundraising.

"It's never going to be over for us," said Dawn Tuomi, the sister of Steven Tuomi. "I still have unopened Christmas gifts from ten years ago. The memories are still there."

Dahmer's death also didn't mean that no more victims would surface. Vickie Hines, a former court clerk who sat through the Dahmer trial, filed a worker's compensation claim in June 1997, claiming that her history of panic attacks and depression were caused by the gruesome testimony.

She sought sixty-five thousand dollars in lost wages after her disability claim forced her to quit the job in 1994. Milwaukee County fought the claim.

"In a way, she's Jeffrey Dahmer's last victim — at least the last victim we know about," said Hines' lawyer, Robert Blondis.

Are there other Jeffrey Dahmers out there, leading normal lives by day but releasing their vicious Mr. Hyde personalities in the shadow of darkness? We can only hope not.

Bibliography

Articles published by *Appleton Post-Crescent, Chicago Daily Times, Chicago Tribune, Green Bay Press Gazette, Hancock News, Milwaukee Journal, Milwaukee Sentinel, Playboy Magazine, Rhinelander Daily News, Superior Evening News, Tomah Journal, True Detective Magazine, Wisconsin State Journal.*

Balousek, Marv *Wisconsin Crimes of the Century,* Madison Newspapers Inc.:1989.

Balousek, Marv *More Wisconsin Crimes of the Century,* Waubesa Press:1993.

Bates, Tom *Rads,* Harper Collins:1992.

Bembenek, Lawrencia *Woman on the Run,* 1992.

Englund, Steven *Man Slaughter,* Doubleday:1983.

Gollmar, Robert *Edward Gein,* St. Martin's:1984.

Harter, Karl *Winter of Frozen Dreams,* Pinnacle Books:1992.

Hollatz, Tom *Gangster Holidays: The Lore and Legends of the Bad Guys,* North Star Press:1989.

Jaeger, Richard and Balousek, M. William *Massacre in Milwaukee,* Waubesa Press:1991.

Kanieski, Colleen Kohler *Please Pass the Roses,* Waubesa Press:1995.

Lemberger, Mark *Crime of Magnitude,* Prairie Oak Press:1993.

Moe, Doug, "Without a Trace: The Homberg Murder Case," Madison Magazine:1990.

Potter, John M. *The Tangled Web,* Waubesa Press:1993.

Radish, Kris *Run, Bambi, Run,* Birch Lane Press:1992.

Rosholt, Malcom *The Battle of Cameron Dam,* self-published:1974.

Samenow, Stanton E., *Inside the Criminal Mind,* Times Books:1984.

Schechter, Harold *Deviant: The Shocking True Story of the Original Psycho,* Pocket Books:1991.

Sifakis, Carl *The Encyclopedia of Crime,* Facts on File:1982.

Twombley, Robert C. *Frank Lloyd Wright: His Life and Architecture,* John Wiley and Sons:1979.

Index

Symbols